THE ARCHBISHOPS OF CANTERBURY

THE ARCHBISHOPS OF CANTERBURY

P. G. MAXWELL-STUART

TEMPUS

First published 2006

Tempus Publishing Limited
The Mill, Brimscombe Port,
Stroud, Gloucestershire, GL5 2QG
www.tempus-publishing.com

British Library Cataloguing in Publication Data.
A catalogue record for this book is available from the British Library.

ISBN 0 7524 3728 3

Typesetting and origination by Tempus Publishing Limited
Printed in Great Britain

Contents

Foreword   7

1 A Mission to the Angles:
St Augustine of Canterbury (596–604/9)   9
2 Labouring for Establishment:
Laurentius to Dunstan (c.604–988)   33
3 Surviving the Millennium and the Conquest:
Aethelgar to Lanfranc (988–1089)   51
4 Who is the Greater Primate?
Anselm to Becket (1093–1170)   67
5 Saints, Scholars and Violence:
Richard of Dover to Pecham (1174–1292)   89
6 Royal Self-Aggrandisement:
Winchelsey to Arundel (1293–1414)   109
7 Spiralling to Disaster:
Chichele to Cranmer (1414–1556)   131
8 Vicars of Bray: Pole to Laud (1558–1645)   155
9 The Long Durance of the Eighteenth Century:
Juxon to Moore (1660–1805)   209
10 Squabbling in the Face of Disbelief:
Manners Sutton to Temple (1805–1902)   231
11 Struggling with Atheism:
Davidson to Williams (1903–)   255

List of Illustrations   279
Notes   285
Select Bibliography   293
Index   305

Foreword

This is not a history of the Church of England, nor does it offer detailed portraits of each of the Archbishops of Canterbury. Walter Hook, who began such an enterprise in the nineteenth century, took eleven volumes to get as far as Juxon (1660–63), so a single book can scarcely do more than glance at the essential traits of the individuals who occupied that office. A series of brief sketches or silhouettes, however, has the advantage of giving the reader a notion of the type of men who have been elevated to Canterbury during the past millennium and a half, and of the pressures – personal, social, political, religious – which have helped to mould their public personae and the way in which the characters and experiences of the archbishops have impinged upon their office. Canterbury is not Rome, however much some of the archbishops would have liked to transform it that way, and so the relationship between the archbishopric and the Crown is crucial to the formation of the primacy. This account therefore concentrates as far as possible upon the personalities of both, in an endeavour to convey to the reader an impression, however slight,

of the extraordinary variety of individuals involved in that relationship, and of their reactions to the press of events which have shaped,
and continue to shape, the institution they represent.

I

A Mission to the Angles
St Augustine of Canterbury
(596–604/9)

When Pope Gregory I commissioned the monk Augustine in 596 to go to the Anglo-Saxons and convert them to Christianity, Augustine's heart may well have sunk at such a depressing prospect. Kent, which is where he was bound, was a faraway country of which he probably knew little or nothing, and this commission to journey into the near-unknown was, in effect, a sentence of perpetual exile, for there was little chance that so enormous a task, which would require years of consolidation even if he were successful in the first place, could be accomplished to the Holy Father's satisfaction in a single lifetime. Nevertheless, obedience to one's ecclesiastical superior was required of all monks, and a command from the Pope himself demanded immediate and unquestioning compliance. So Augustine and (we are told) forty other monks left the familiar surroundings of Pope Gregory's own monastic foundation dedicated to St Andrew, and began the long journey, perilous enough in itself, to a land of mists, mellow fruitfulness, idolatry, and an obsessive concern for the polluting effects of various sexual acts on ritual purity.

The monastery from which they came had a number of attractions. It occupied Pope Gregory's ancestral home on the Caelian, the most south-easterly of Rome's hills, which, in ancient times, had become a favourite place of residence for the rich, whose gardens covered a large part of the hill. Even in late sixth-century Rome, when constant warfare, coupled with neglect, had reduced the city to a shadow of its earlier self, St Andrews Monastery – designated in the sources as the *monasterium ad clivum Scauri* – will have provided a well-endowed haven of peace and a refuge from the ravages of marauding Lombards, an ever-present danger. It is sometimes referred to as a 'Benedictine' institution on the grounds that the Rule of St Benedict probably supplied a model for the governance of such a house. But there is doubt whether this is so. All we can be sure of is that Augustine (whose early life and provenance are a complete mystery: we do not even know his name, because 'Augustine' will have been the name he took on entering religion) had spent many years in Pope Gregory's foundation and that by 596 he was its *praepositus*, a monastic post which involved assisting the abbot in administering the estates and farms which provided the monastery's endowment, having some knowledge of Roman civil law, and being something of an expert in both the Holy Scriptures and the Rule of his own monastery. One can, therefore, see that such experience would have fitted him, in some measure, for the task which the Pope was about to lay on his shoulders. One says 'in some measure' because, of course, his exact fitness for the task would depend on the nature of the task itself.

What did Pope Gregory have in mind? According to an early biography, the *Whitby Life*, written between 704 and 714, before he was actually Pope he saw some Northumbrian boys for sale in a Roman slave-market. They were light-skinned and fair-haired, somewhat striking in appearance, and Gregory asked where they came from. He was told that their people were known as 'Angles'. 'Angels of God', he replied, and then asked the name of their king. 'Aelli', he was informed. 'Alleluia! God's praise must be heard there!' he said. Then he asked the name of their tribe and was told 'Deira', which prompted yet another play on words: 'they will flee to the Faith from the anger of God [*de ira Dei*]'. The story is redolent of those sickly puns which appealed to the Victorians. Why is a certain type of bicycle known as a 'tandem'? Because it is a lengthy bicycle (*tandem* = Latin, 'at length'). In the case of Gregory's anecdote, however, one's misgivings that this story may turn out to be a Victorian *trouvée* or improvement on history are unfounded. The same story is told by another of Pope Gregory's biographers, John the Deacon, living in the ninth century, and these early Christian centuries were just as taken by word-play which teased out significance from the stoniest of ground. A further anecdote, for example, has Gregory setting out to convert these *Angli* himself. While he was resting on the third day, a locust settled on the book he was reading. 'Look', he said to his companions, '*locusta* signifies *loco sta* [stay in this place], which means we shall not be able to continue our journey' – as indeed turned out to be the case, because messengers arrived, recalling him to Rome.

As pretty as the tale of the slave-boys may be, however, it does not explain why, several years after this supposed encounter, Pope Gregory should have decided that the time was ripe for a conversion of tribes living near or, indeed, just beyond the edge of the civilised world. Gregory had been interested in missionary work from the very start of his Papacy. Even before he became Pope, he had a clear notion that the Church had a mission to the whole world – by which, however, he and his predecessors tended to understand 'the Roman Empire' – and a duty to bring not only the Christian message, but also the civilising concepts of law and harmony which were, in theory if not always in practice, key notes of the *imperium Romanum*. Britannia, whatever its present status, had once been a Roman province and so by converting its peoples to Christianity, Gregory would be restoring the country, in some sense, to the Roman fold, to the inheritor of the old Western Empire, the Church. Secondly,

the Anglo-Saxons were thoroughgoing pagans, not heretics, and so
it was important to convert them to the correct version of the Faith
before other missionaries – say, Arians – got there first and mud-
died their minds, thereby creating a more awkward situation for
Roman missionaries to deal with than persuading people with no
preconceived ideas about Christian theology to abandon their gods
in a grove for the God on the Cross. Thirdly, the 'king' of Kent, to
whose territory Augustine and the others were bound in the first
instance, was married to a Christian, and might therefore be expected
to view Christian evangelism with at least some degree of tolerance,
something which would allow Augustine an encouraging start to
his mission.

We should also bear in mind that Gregory had been a monk
and therefore took very seriously a descriptive phrase often used of
Popes, *servus servorum Dei*, 'the slave of the slaves of God', with its
implication of service to everyone; and the world, as he saw it from
Rome, was in a dreadful state, and thus in need of all the service he
and the Church could give it. The Holy City itself was in dire eco-
nomic straits, partly because the Lombards were invading the Papal
States and causing havoc every time they came; and the year before
he became Pope the Tiber had flooded and a devastating plague
followed, so virulent that even at the beginning of his pontificate,
while he was leading the people in litanies of penance, designed to
appease God's anger and beg Him to lift the plague, eighty people
fell dead in the midst of the prayers. War, plague, famine, death. Was
the world actually coming to an end, as was prophesied in the Book
of the Apocalypse? If so, the *servus servorum Dei* surely had a duty to
look after those in immediate need and draw remaining unbelievers
into the Christian fold before the Day of Judgement arrived. Perhaps
this is what Bede meant when he said that 'divine inspiration' had
prompted Gregory to send Augustine and the others to preach the
Word of God to the Anglo-Saxons.

Gregory seems to have been thinking about this, or something like
it, as early as 595 when he wrote to his agent in Gaul, asking him to
purchase Angle boys and place them in monasteries; and in his commentary on the Book of Job, which may have been in circulation at

about the same time, Gregory speaks of the Christianisation of Britain as though it were a present and continuing fact. In 596, it certainly was. Augustine and his forty companions – a remarkably large number to be drawn from a single monastery: it shows how extensive and how wealthy *ad clivum Scauri* must have been – left Rome (with what reluctance will soon be made clear) and, armed with the knowledge that Papal letters of introduction had been sent to the bishops of Marseille, Aix, Arles, Lyon, Vienne, Autun and Tours, they set out along a route which, despite the geographical distribution of those letters, is not altogether clear. A land route would have taken the party along a number of still-functioning Roman roads: the Aurelian Way, which followed the Italian coast until it reached Provence; another from Aix to Arles; and then another running beside the left bank of the Rhône (unless they chose to travel on the river itself), which would see them through to Vienne. But if they had wanted to avoid at least some of the discomforts attendant on travel by land, they could have risked the attendant discomforts of travel by water and sailed from Ostia to Marseille before taking a largely overland journey via Aix, Vienne, Lyon, Autun and Sens to Paris, where they spent the winter, before ending up in Tours preparatory to their final stage, then embarking at Boulogne and making the sea-crossing over the Channel not long after Easter.

Pope Gregory, however, had not written only to bishops, whose co-operation in the missionary venture he could reasonably expect to command. He had also sent polite explanations of what Augustine and his companions were pledged to accomplish to important secular rulers and officials, such as Arigius 'the Patrician' (an Imperial courtesy title), who seems to have been the principal man of influence in the south of France, and was probably stationed at Arles. More importantly, though, the Pope lavished diplomatic praise on Queen Brunhild, a formidable woman who was acting as regent for her two grandsons, Theuderic and Theudebert, the inheritors of a large part of Frankish Gaul from their father, King Childebert. Gaul, as it happened, was enjoying at this time a small period of peace in the midst of a much longer state of turmoil caused by dynastic struggles between the descendants of Clovis 'the Conqueror'. But strangers were always in some need of protection, and Queen Brunhild had a personal interest in the mission to the Angles because her niece, Bertha, was the Christian wife of King Ethelbert of Kent, to whose territory Augustine was about to direct his evangelising efforts. Not that Brunhild's motives were entirely unmixed. A power across the Channel, friendly to her two grandsons, would be very helpful in curbing the ambitions of Chlothar II, a northern Frankish ruler whose intimate ties of hatred with Brunhild made him a possible source of danger for her grandsons and a rival for the friendship of Ethelbert. Were Augustine to owe her a favour, he would speak favourably of her to both Ethelbert and the Pope, and thus she would outflank Chlothar and those controlling him.

But before he had even arrived at the coast of southern Gaul, Augustine's journey suffered a major setback. He and his party seem to have stayed at the island-monastery of Lérins, about three miles south of Cannes and perhaps a hundred miles east of Marseille. Here was a vivid reminder of the attractions of monastery life, and perhaps it was this which caused Augustine's monks to revolt; or perhaps a realisation, now that they were within sight of the barbarities of Frankish Gaul, about which they may well have heard both in Rome and during their outward journey, that permanent exile from everything familiar to them was really to be their lot. Bede tells us that the monks 'were seized by a sudden fear and began to think about going home rather than going forward to a race of unbelievers who were uncultivated and fierce and whose very language they [the monks] knew nothing about'. Whether Augustine shared their apprehensions, we do not know. He was not their abbot and therefore could not command their obedience; so, either because he agreed with them or because he succumbed to their collective pressure, he consented to break off the journey and return to Rome to ask Pope Gregory if he would permit them to abandon the mission and let them all come home.

His interview with the Pope was bound to have been uncomfortable. What Gregory said to him, however, can be gauged from a letter addressed to the recalcitrant monks, which Augustine brought back with him:

Gregory, slave of the slaves of God, to the slaves of Our Lord.

It would have been better not to begin doing something good rather than deliberately turn your backs on what you have begun. Dearly beloved sons, you must, with the greatest eagerness, fulfil the good work which, with the Lord's help, you have started. Therefore, please do not let the distress of your journey or the distress caused by the tongue of abusive individuals discourage you. But, with all earnestness and fervour, carry out, with God's approval, what you have started, knowing that a great labour is followed by the greater glory of an eternal reward. On the return of your *praepositus* Augustine, whom We appoint your abbot, obey him humbly in everything, knowing that whatever you accomplish according to his direction will be in all respects good for your souls.

May Almighty God protect you with His grace and grant that, in the eternal homeland, I see the fruit of your labour. Although I cannot labour with you, I hope I may participate with you in the joy of the reward, because I am willing to labour with you. May God keep you safe, dearly beloved sons.

However this may be glossed, there is no denying it was a Papal reprimand, and therefore when Augustine returned, the monks' disappointment is likely to have been acute. But what, one may ask, did they expect? Gregory's eagerness to convert heathen peoples was well known – it has been referred to as one of the occupations which formed a continuous thread throughout his pontificate – and it is beyond any likelihood that he would have been willing to forego the prospect of converting the Angles merely because his missionaries were suffering from cold feet. This the monks must have known, so one wonders why they thought their request stood a chance of being granted.

Gregory's letter appointed Augustine their abbot. This altered their relationship considerably. The obedience which the monks had sworn to the abbot of their old monastery was now transferred wholly to Augustine, so they could no longer take advantage (if that is indeed what they had done) of his not having ultimate authority over them to press a point of view he could not entirely resist of his own right. Nevertheless, pressure from below is not really a convincing explanation for the expedition's stalling before it had got very far. Augustine had been the man chosen by Gregory to lead the mission, and therefore must have been on good terms with the Pope. He had discharged offices in the Roman monastery for some time – one did not become a *praepositus* until one had done many years of service – and was thus wedded, in a sense, to that particular establishment. Setting out on a long, dangerous journey with the prospect, at very best, of dying years hence in a foreign, unknown land or (who could tell what intervening barbarians they might not meet?) even sooner could hardly have been inviting for a man possibly in his late forties or early fifties and therefore, according to the calculation of the time, a *senex* – an old, or at least an elderly man. So was it actually Augustine himself who wavered during that stay in the monastery of Lérins, found support from some, if not all, of his companions, and returned to Rome, relying on what he conceived was his personal rapport with the Pope to change Gregory's mind and have himself and the others recalled from this perilous and distasteful mission?

Bede, naturally, gives no hint of such a possibility. His account of the conversion of Anglo-Saxon England is biased in favour of the Roman mission, and plays down the missionising activity undertaken by other people – the Irish and Franks, for example. The Church could hardly have been planted among the Angles by someone who had been so faint-hearted at the prospect that he had tried to run away from his duty. Blaming the monks shifted attention away from Augustine and allowed Bede to represent him as merely their spokes-man. But the possible sleight of hand becomes clear the moment one asks why Augustine, who surely had all the coercive authority he needed, even without being their abbot, agreed to disobey the Pope and be their mouthpiece. (Similar caution, incidentally, ought to be exercised over the eleventh-century description of Augustine as a man standing head and shoulders taller than his companions. Leaders, especially successful leaders, *should* have been tall, runs the logic, and therefore Augustine *must* have been tall. He could, of course, have been rather short and compensated for his lack of inches with a charismatic personality, but that is not how ancient rhetoric worked).

Pope Gregory's letter, then, allowed no further delay or question, and so the mission to the Angles packed its bags, loaded its pack-animals, and started the long trek via land and river to whatever uncomfortable barbarities awaited it in the north. But the clergy, whether secular or monastic, were actually used to travel. Since the Imperial letter-service had rarely been open to them, they developed their own, supplementing travelling monks and priests and deacons with professional letter-carriers – Paulinus of Nola (late fourth century AD) notes in one of his letters 'the bearer of this is running for the boat this instant' – and thus established widespread lines of communication which stretched over the western half of the old Empire like a spider's web. So in fact Augustine was hardly venturing into regions devoid of any marks of the civilisation he was leaving behind. He would be making for bishops' palaces and local royal houses, preparation having been made in advance by Papal letters of introduction and commendation. It was possible that, from time to time, he and his party would be obliged to put up at a sizeable hostelry, the *pandocheion* – this is the establishment to which the good Samaritan brought the traveller he rescued, and which provided St John Chrysostom with an image of the temporal world in which humankind was permitted to stay for a brief period – but, generally speaking, a company as large as forty would have needed the resources of a wealthy host to afford them suitable and comfortable lodging.

The final stages of the journey would have been the most wearisome. Between Autun and the coast there was no available transport by water, so they would have been obliged to follow the road, whatever its state, to Boulogne and there wait for a ship to take them across the Channel. The pause was necessary. It is unlikely they had a ship waiting for them already, so passage would have to be negotiated and favourable weather prayed for. They also required interpreters, since none of them, as far as we know, could speak or understand Saxon. These interpreters will have been locals. There was frequent intercourse, mainly by way of trade, between northern

Gaul and southern Britain, so people familiar with the others' tongue would not have been hard to find and would play an essential role in Augustine's mission until he and his companions were able to communicate in some fashion with the natives. At last, when all was ready, they embarked and made for the Isle of Thanet.

Once landed, probably at Richborough, they stayed where they were. Augustine sent messengers to King Ethelbert, announcing his arrival and saying that he had come from Rome, bringing 'the best of messages, namely, the assurance to those who received it of eternal joys in Heaven, and an everlasting kingdom with the true and living God'. Ethelbert was by no means unprepared for this. The Christianity of his wife Bertha will have accustomed him to the outward practices of the religion at least, since part of their marriage-arrangement had said that she must be allowed free practice of her faith and the attendance of a Frankish bishop, Liudhard, as her chaplain. Apparently the Queen heard Mass in the old Roman church of St Martin, on the eastern outskirts of Canterbury. Whether Ethelbert ever came with her, and if he did, how he reacted to the spectacle, we do not know. But he replied to Augustine's message with instructions that the missionaries were to stay where they were for the time being. The king sent them supplies, but remained at a cautious distance, not inviting them to come to him or going to meet them himself for several days.

The reason for his caution became clear when they did meet. He was afraid they were magicians. Bede tells us that Ethelbert believed 'a traditional superstition' that if he met these monks inside a building, if indeed they did practise any magic, they would be able to deceive him and get the better of him the moment he entered it. Here we must be careful not to misunderstand what Ethelbert was doing. It was not a meeting inside a building he feared, but the necessity of stepping over a threshold, which that would entail. One of the commonest magical practices involves burying some object underneath a threshold, which will then have an effect – in this case, presumably dire – on any individual who steps over it. Not only did Ethelbert want to protect himself against such a possibility. The thegns who accompanied him would suffer likewise unless the king prevented it. So he and his companions, and Augustine and his monks, met first in the open air. The monks had with them a silver cross which Bede says they carried as though it were a military standard, and an image of Christ painted on wood, perhaps a picture in the manner of a Byzantine icon. They sang litanies and prayed, both for their own salvation and for that of King Ethelbert and his people. The Latin word *salus* means 'safety' as well as 'salvation'. Were the monks' prayers tinged with ambiguity as they faced the heathen Angles they were supposed to convert?

Ethelbert then invited them to sit. One must presume this was actually an invitation to Augustine, since he alone of the monks was likely to have a chair or stool; the monks and the thegns may have seated themselves on the ground, but it is most unlikely. Sitting illustrated social status, as it was to do for centuries, and Ethelbert and Augustine were the two most important people present. Besides, if trouble flared, squatting thegns would be in no position to react promptly, and squatting monks would find it difficult to flee. Let us grant, therefore, that the thegns and monks probably remained standing. Once the king had sat down, Augustine launched into a sermon, 'preaching the word of life', as Bede says. Which language did he use? Presumably Latin, which would have entailed the participation of at least one interpreter and protracted Augustine's discourse as small groups of sentences were translated into Saxon for Ethelbert's benefit. The sermon may or may not have been a long one. It is easy to underestimate the willingness of earlier peoples to listen for extended periods of time, and one must remember that Ethelbert would have been accustomed to hearing sagas from his court bards. Besides, Augustine was a novelty, and a lengthy discourse would have given Ethelbert time to appraise him and work out what he wanted to do about him. How much did Ethelbert really understand of what Augustine was saying? Even if Augustine kept himself to Christian generalities on this particular occasion, the opportunities for Ethelbert to misconceive or misinterpret Augustine's words were manifold. When Augustine spoke of 'God', for example, what did that convey to the pagan king? Did 'the Word' in its technical Christian sense mean anything at all to

Ethelbert? What did he make of the painted image of Christ? To him, surely, it meant something quite other than it did to Augustine; and if the picture showed Christ crucified, the god nailed to a tree must have had quite remarkable, even disturbing, associations for a worshipper of Tiw, Woden and Thor, and a frequenter of sacred groves.

When Augustine finished speaking, the king replied, and again we must probably envisage Augustine's receiving the speech via an interpreter. According to Bede, Ethelbert was polite and welcoming, but puzzled by Augustine's message – a clear indication that his wife's Christianity had had little effect upon him. Augustine's words, he said, were 'new' and 'doubtful', meaning he did not really understand what Augustine had been talking about. There was to be no instantaneous, miraculous conversion – the East Saxons, in any case, were especially attached to their own religion – but the king granted the monks somewhere to live in Canterbury, an allowance of food and drink, and permission to preach and make converts within his domain. It was all quite satisfactory. Both sides gained, and whatever initial groundwork had been done by Pope Gregory had provided a foundation of polite and wary amicability on which Ethelbert and Augustine could build a fruitful relationship.

Why Canterbury? It was an old Roman settlement, originally called Durovernum until Jute invaders built a new town on top of it and renamed it Canturara-byrig. A Roman road connected it with Richborough on the coast and Rochester and London, while another ran through to Dover. Much of Kent was covered by forest and woodland, and the population must have been very small by modern standards. But while many inhabited places suffered under successive waves of invasion from continental Europe after the withdrawal of Roman troops at the beginning of the fifth century, Canterbury seems to have survived to enjoy a long period of relative prosperity, helped no doubt by the old Roman links with the southern and eastern coasts, and it thus became the principal town – it would be anachronistic, perhaps, to call it 'capital' – of Jutish Kent. Ethelbert was therefore granting Augustine a foothold in the heart of his kingdom.

The foothold was the church used by Queen Bertha, St Martin's. There, says Bede, 'they began to meet to chant the psalms, to pray, say Mass, preach, and baptise'. This sounds quite like a monastic establishment (and we must remember that Augustine and his companions were all monks, and he was their abbot); but the church was just a church and had none of the usual additional buildings pertaining to a monastery, so special arrangements would have to be made, at least initially, to accommodate the new situation. Pope Gregory, however, had not sent Augustine to found a new monastery but to convert the Anglian heathen, and the monks must have realised they were not simply going to replant *ad clivum Scauri* in foreign soil. To achieve Pope Gregory's purpose, Augustine would surely need to train native secular priests as well as future monks, and therefore Canterbury would have to become more a cathedral planted in the temporal world than the recreation of a desert hermitage, which was the inspiration for monastic houses as opposed to the corporation of secular clergy.

Chanting the psalms and saying Mass supposes either that the monks knew all the texts and music by heart, or that they had brought liturgical books with them, not to mention vestments, although Catherine Cubitt has warned us against importing modern ideas of uniformity into an earlier period. 'The task of copying new books was laborious and expensive; the standard to be striven for was not necessarily that everyone should chant the same words, but perhaps rather that the same feasts should be celebrated and in services broadly following the same pattern'.[1] On the other hand, Augustine's mission was specifically Roman in origin, and establishing right from the start liturgical and ecclesiastical practices which would look to Rome as their ultimate authority and justification would give them a powerful legitimacy in the face of competing Frankish or Celtic customs. Bede tells us that the monks, newly installed in the house given to them by Ethelbert, soon impressed quite a number of people (*nonnulli*) by the austerity and fervour of their lives, and that in consequence they were converted and baptised.

Ethelbert, too, was baptised before long – almost certainly within the first year of Augustine's mission – and began to show further indications of his favour towards the monks, although he did not,

according to Bede, compel anyone to follow his example and convert.
His caution was understandable. Kent may have been ready to fall
from the tree into Augustine's hands, but the neighbouring kingdoms
of Essex and Sussex were still heathen strongholds, and Mercia would
not be long in revealing itself as a champion of paganism. What we
are to understand by 'baptism' in this instance is not altogether clear.
The administration of the sacrament was usually confined to Easter
or Pentecost, and in the early Church was preceded by a lengthy
period of teaching and preparation of adult catechumens. Candidates
were then exorcised, anointed with oil, questioned before they were
partially or wholly immersed in water, then dressed (usually in white)
and anointed a second time. A ninth-century Vatican manuscript
containing a baptismal text in Old Saxon tells us that the candidate
was asked if he or she renounced the Devil and all sacrifices to him,
to which he or she replied 'All the works and words of the Devil,
Thunaer and Woden and Saxnot, and all the evil spirits who are their
companions', after which the officiating priest was to blow in the
candidate's face and command the unclean spirit to depart.

A ritual of this kind may have been performed for King Ethelbert
and perhaps a few of his principal thegns who wished to convert,
but not, surely, for the immense number said to have followed their
example on Christmas Day, 597. Pope Gregory, writing to Eulogius
of Alexandria the next summer, rejoiced that more than ten thousand worshippers of trees and stones had been baptised that day, a
number we may safely suggest is somewhat exaggerated. Numbers
in the Biblical and Classical world and late antiquity often tended
to be symbolic rather than literal, and 'ten thousand' has significant
resonances in the Bible. The most obvious example comes from 1
Kings (Samuel) 18.7, 'While the women were taking part in [this]
public rejoicing, they began to sing, saying, "Saul has struck down a
thousand, and David ten thousand"' – a refrain which is repeated in
21.11 and 29.5. 'Ten thousand' converted pagans therefore represents
an unspecific but large number of Satan's unwitting foot-soldiers
struck down in the battle between Good and Evil, to be resurrected
as Catholic Christians, now the spiritual children of Rome. Their
baptism, depending on how many there were on this Christmas

occasion, may have taken place in the Church of St Martin, Queen Bertha's church which Augustine and his monks were permitted to use: or, like that of the crowds which flocked to St Paulinus in the 620s after the baptism of King Edwin of Northumbria, in the nearby river – convenient and Biblically inspired.

Why did Ethelbert and many others convert with such apparent ease and willingness? Bede puts it down to 'the public display of many miracles' which confirmed the particularly pleasant promises made by the missionaries. We have only one specific example of one of Augustine's miracles. At a conference with Celtic bishops, we are told, the Celts were making difficulties over Augustine's efforts to get them to surrender their own traditions over the date of Easter in favour of Roman practice. Since he was making no headway, Augustine resorted to an appeal to a higher court. Let God send a sign, he said, regarding which tradition to adopt. A blind man was then brought into the conference. The Celts tried to cure him and failed, but Augustine knelt down and prayed, and the man received his sight. It is all perfectly possible, of course, and that may indeed be exactly what happened. But one cannot help feeling the incident falls too pat. The Celtic bishops are blind to the truth of what Augustine is saying, and after the miracle realise how wrong they have been. A blind man is cured at Augustine's earnest prayer. Confirmation of his being right is provided by a sign from God, just as he had asked. Could the miracles of which Bede writes in connection with King Ethelbert's conversion have been signs of a similar kind, rhetorically apt rather than historically genuine, or were they real and thus theologically significant? Augustine's miracles were reported to Pope Gregory and it seems the Pope had reservations, not about the miracles themselves, but about the effect they may have been having on Augustine. He wrote to Augustine in 601:

> I am aware, my very dear brother, that almighty God is manifesting great miracles as a result of your love for the nation He has wanted to be chosen. Consequently, you must be pleased at that heavenly gift, and be afraid at the same time; and you must become very afraid even while you are being pleased. What I mean is, be pleased because the

souls of the Anglians are being drawn to inward peace by outward
miracles, but become very afraid lest while these signs are taking place,
[you] put on airs through weakness of character, get above yourself
through public recognition, and head for a fall because of meaningless self-esteem… If at any time you remember having offended our
Creator by something you have said or things you have done, keep
on recalling them so that the memory of your guilt may throttle
the self-regard rising in your heart; and whatever [abilities] to work
miracles you will receive or have received, please assign these gifts
not to yourself, but to those for whose salvation they have been
bestowed on you.[2]

It was a crushing snub, whether Augustine actually deserved it or
not, although we must always be aware that the Pope may have
received the report from an ill-natured source. Two of his companions, Laurentius and Peter, were sent to Rome after the Christmas
Day success in order to report to the Pope on progress so far. Did
either or both slip a stilettoed phrase into the Pope's ear? Perhaps
Augustine entrusted them with a letter whose expressions of pleasure
and triumph struck Gregory as a touch too exuberant for comfort. But whatever the cause of the Pope's elegant acerbity, by the
time Augustine received it, his mission was well under way. By now,
Augustine had been consecrated a bishop and reinforcements had
arrived from Italy, along with sacred vessels, vestments, relics and a
good many books. Pope Gregory also sent him the pallium, in his
day a large rectangular cloak made of lamb's wool, nowadays reduced
to a narrow band worn over the shoulders, with lappets hanging
down in front and behind. It was a mark of delegated authority, but
in Augustine's case he was instructed to wear it only while celebrating Mass – an honour given with one hand and almost taken away
with the other, especially since the Papal letter instructed Augustine
to consecrate twelve bishops and send one of them to York, this
one being promised the pallium too, an honour which would put
him on almost an equal footing with Augustine, save for Augustine's
priority of consecration. Augustine, with King Ethelbert's permission, had embarked on an ambitious programme of building new

churches and restoring old ones. The most important restoration was that of an old Romano-British church now consecrated in the name of the Saviour, which Augustine intended to be the principal church of the kingdom, which he and his successors would occupy. His most significant new building was the Monastery of Saint Peter and Saint Paul, and the relics Pope Gregory had sent – small pieces of cloth which had lain all night next to the tombs of those two Apostles – were destined to be placed under the altar of the monastery church.

Miracles, conversions, building and royal favour must be accounted marks of success for this missionary venture envisaged and set in motion by the Pope. But all was not entirely well. Christianity had already been implanted in Britain and the Celtic Church, structured according to monastic principles, not a hierarchical episcopate, was cut off from the Frankish and Roman worlds by a large mass of hostile pagan tribes who had deprived them of their lands and were pushing them ever westwards. To the representatives of Celtic Christianity, Augustine must have seemed like yet another suspicious interloper seeking in his own way, just like the Anglo-Saxons in theirs, to destroy their mode of life and impose alien customs and practices on them. Consequently, his efforts to invite – Bede uses *convocavit*, 'summoned' or 'mustered', a verb which implies authority – the bishops or learned men of the nearest province to discuss their differences and, in effect, to submit to Rome, were almost doomed to disappointment, in spite of the miracle of the blind man which crowned their deliberations. The Celts admitted that what Augustine had been preaching to them was fair and valid, but refused to abandon their ancient customs without the consent and permission of their own people – an excuse which bears all the hallmarks of a political get-out clause.

A second synod held much further north, near Wales, and attended by seven bishops and a larger number of very learned men, got off to a bad start. Augustine, presuming on his authority as primus of the newly established Roman mission in Kent, was seated *in sella*, on a chair of office, and failed to rise when his visitors approached him. This they took as a sign of arrogance – they may have been right, but it is more likely that Augustine was mindful of the position he occupied by Papal appointment and did not intend to lose face by greeting the others as equals – and so, in the words of Bede, 'they began to make every effort to object to everything he was saying'. Augustine offered a degree of compromise. He would accept many of their distinctive customs and usages, but he wanted conformity with Rome on three points: the date of Easter, the rite of baptism, and co-preaching the Gospel with the Roman missionaries. The Celts retorted they would do nothing of the kind and that they did not consider him to be an archbishop. Augustine's failure in courtesy rankled. Their refusal to co-operate irritated him to the point where he threatened them with a prophecy – if they were unwilling to accept peace with their brethren, they would be accepting war from their enemies – and thus the conference ended. It had been bad-tempered. The result was a withdrawal of both sides to entrenched positions, and thus they remained until after Augustine's death.

If Augustine failed to reach an agreement with his fellow-Christians, he had more of a success in undermining the local heathen religion. Pagan adherence to Tiw, Woden and Thunor varied in its fervour. Place-names, for example, reveal that in Essex it was strong, whereas in East Anglia and in Northumbria a distinct lack of surviving names indicating a heathen religious centre suggests it was pretty feeble. In both latter regions, at any rate, Christianity swept all before it with little resistance. Part of the reason for its attractiveness may have been its simple coherence. The pagan religions missionaries encountered in the north of Europe did not have, and did not need, a structured theology. Their mythological basis consisted of disparate stories about gods and goddesses, their ritual practice of magic and animal sacrifice and their explanation of human existence – *wyrd*, 'ineluctable destiny' or 'an event decreed by Fate'. While *wyrd* could have translated itself into the Will of God, and sacrifice into the Mass, the central story of God's birth, death, and resurrection in the incarnate person of Jesus offered pagans the particular intellectual satisfaction of what Aristotle demanded of any dramatic plot – a beginning, a middle and an end. This coherence, allied to promises of sure rewards for the good and punishment for the bad (promises which, in the case of Augustine and his monks, were verified by many miracles), would have appealed to high and low alike. The high would have been content that their thirst for martial glory was ratified by the Christian God of Battles, while the low would have been reassured that the new religion would bless their crops, cure their diseases, deliver them from hostile magic and protect them from evil spirits. Whatever misunderstandings may have lurked in the translation of theological concepts such as 'sin', 'redemption' or 'charity', the broad sweep of Christian propositions and promises accompanied by signs of divine favour and supernatural sanction stood a very good chance of appealing (or at least not proving intractably alien) to a large number of the heathen English.

As for the pagans' temples and sacred groves, Pope Gregory had certain views on what Augustine should do when confronted by these places of heathen worship, views he transmitted through Mellitus, leader of the Roman reinforcements to the Kentish mission in 601. He had been thinking about the problem (the Pope said), and had come to the conclusion that these places should not be levelled – although the idols they contained should certainly be destroyed – but asperged with holy water and reconstituted as Christian churches with altars and relics. It was sound advice, given that the local tribespeople, the Cantware, were by no means enthusiastic about King Ethelbert's conversion to what they saw as the religion of their serfs and their enemies, the Welsh. As Margaret Deanesly points out, 'the conversion of the Cantware depended almost entirely on [Ethelbert's] personal will... and now, as it seemed to many of the Cantware converts, the king had flouted the old gods and placed himself under the protection of this new god, the Saviour, whose priest was Father Augustine, who had a new temple and many servants'.[3] The fact is, Augustine's mission within the bounds of Cantware territory hung upon Ethelbert's continued health and favour; beyond that region there stretched large areas belonging to hostile pagan rulers at whose conversion Augustine certainly aimed, but who were unlikely to prove as complaisant as a king who had had a Christian wife.

Still, if Augustine could not do everything at once, he had made a good start and, in addition to his programme of building and restoration – nothing fixes an abstract idea in people's minds more effectively than the concrete solidity of a building which embodies the reality of its power – he set about constraining his flock to the disciplines of their new religion. This we can tell from a number of questions he sent to the Pope for authoritative answers. The first was personal. How should he best use the revenues he was receiving, in cash and in kind, to support his own household as archbishop, pay at least some of the clergy wages, and maintain certain aspects of a monastic establishment, such as a school and a guesthouse; and how should he comport himself in church? Gregory answered the first part and virtually ignored the second (such a fussy question), referring Augustine to 1 *Timothy* 2.2-7 as a Scriptural guide to his behaviour. Even if we accept the suggestion that these inquiries were made before Augustine set out for Britain rather than after he was established there, asking the Pope how a bishop should perform his duties in church is taking lack of initiative to a remarkably supine degree.

Secondly, what should he do about variations in the liturgy? The Pope replied that Augustine could adapt as he saw fit. Augustine here was being pernickety, since he knew perfectly well that Rome did not insist on liturgical uniformity outwith her own metropolitan area. Augustine's question on this point suggests a man unwilling or unable to do something of his own volition, even when that thing was perfectly obvious. Thirdly, how should someone be punished if he stole anything from a church? Again, one wonders why Augustine asked this. Local theft, even if it was sacrilege, must have come, for all practical purposes, within the purview of King Ethelbert. Perhaps Augustine had already asked the king what to do and Ethelbert had said 'Ask the Pope'; but that seems unlikely, because Ethelbert passed a law, perhaps as a result of Augustine's inquiry to the Pope, that theft from God or the Church should be compensated twelvefold. This was both more and less than Gregory had suggested. The Pope said that the thief should restore what he had stolen, and that he should also be fined heavily, or flogged, according to what the judge deemed were his motives for stealing in the first place.

Two questions dealt with marriage. Can two brothers marry two sisters (not their own, of course)? Again this is a question which clearly irritated the Pope. Yes, yes, certainly they can, he said. There is nothing in Scripture to prevent it – something Augustine should have known perfectly well.[4] But, nothing daunted, Augustine asks another silly question. If it is too difficult for other bishops to get to a consecration, can a single bishop legitimately consecrate someone to that office? Gregory's answer is scathing. 'Considering you are at present the only bishop to be found in the Anglian Church, you cannot do otherwise than consecrate a bishop without the help of others!' The other bishops Augustine probably had in mind were those from over the Channel, and Gregory acknowledges that, no, they do not stir themselves to leave their own territories. In reply to a specific question from Augustine about what should be his relationship with bishops from Gaul and Britain, however, Gregory points out that Augustine has no authority over those from Gaul, and that mutual co-operation should be their guiding principle. As for the bishops from the rest of Britain (by whom Augustine in his question will have meant the Celtic bishops of the west), the Pope says 'We entrust all the British bishops to membership of your community' – *tuae fraternitati. Fraternitas* had a particular significance to someone who, like Augustine, was a monk and an abbot. It referred to the body of monks in a monastery and therefore implied that the other bishops should render absolute obedience to him, a declaration of Canterbury's primacy which they would neither have welcomed nor felt obliged to regard.

Finally, Augustine addressed to the Pope various questions on ritual pollution connected with sex. Should a woman be baptised while she is pregnant or after she has given birth? In the latter case, how long should one wait before allowing her to enter a church? How long should be it before her husband can start having sex with her again? If she is menstruating, can she enter a church or take communion? If her husband has had sex with her and failed to wash himself afterwards, can he enter a church or receive communion? 'The crude Anglians need authoritative answers to all these points', he explained. Pope Gregory replied at length, beginning with what sounds rather like another snub for an unnecessarily fussy question. 'Why shouldn't a pregnant woman be baptised? The fruitfulness of the flesh is not a fault in the eyes of almighty God'. Then comes the last question. Can a man receive communion or, if he is a priest, celebrate Mass 'after a nocturnal emission which usually happens because of a dream?' Gregory's answer is that of a careful moral theologian who takes into account both the circumstances which produced the dream and the individual's response to the emission.

Through these questions, then, we may catch a glimpse of some of the practicalities which were occupying Augustine's attention during the years following his initial establishment and success in Kent, and also a little of the man himself. Even if the questions and answers were interpolated into Bede's text later, Augustine's finicky determination to ask the Pope's opinion on matters to which his own knowledge of the Bible and, indeed, experience as a *praepositus* in Rome should have supplied the answers argues a temperament which tended to panic under pressure. Perhaps this had been disguised or had not been evoked in the familiar routine of *ad clivum Scauri*. Not everyone who makes a good subordinate can be transformed into a leader. Perhaps he needed a written document from the Pope to persuade King Ethelbert and his thegns that the rules and prescriptions he was issuing were not his own, produced extempore, but were those common to the universal Church and therefore authoritative. (In light of the future history of the Church of England, it seems just a touch ominous, perhaps, that Augustine can appear to have been so reliant in many respects on the favour of the king, a skewed balance of Church-state relationship which would work only if the incumbent archbishop was able to withstand any untoward pressure the temporal ruler might care to exert). Augustine seems to have been a man without much personal charisma. In fact, even though he was credited with working miracles, it is worth remembering that the initial favourable impression made on the Cantware, accompanied as it was by 'many miracles', was made by the whole body of the missionary-monks. Augustine is not singled out or, indeed, even mentioned in the relevant chapter of Bede's *Historia*.

Nevertheless, he was by no means unsuccessful. Pope Gregory's commission had been carried out – perhaps one should say begun – and the conversion of the heathen Cantware propelled by a momentum it would prove impossible for subsequent pagan rulers and sympathisers to bring to a halt. 'Civilising', in the sense of Romanising, them was also bearing fruit. As Edward Carpenter has pointed out, 'It is significant that the laws of Athelberht were the first to be written down',[5] and almost certainly Augustine founded a school in Canterbury, which provided the model for King Sigbert's later foundation in East Anglia in 631. He also consecrated two bishops to significant dioceses, Mellitus to London and Justus to Rochester, thereby consolidating the initial mission in Ethelbert's capital and an important western city. So within a period of only eight or thirteen years (depending on whether he died in 604, 609, or at some point between the two), he had achieved a great deal, and if he had done so in spite of any personal failings as a leader, he deserves this acknowledgement the more generously because of it.

He was buried in the grounds of his new monastery with its church dedicated to St Peter and St Paul, the first Pope and the Church's greatest Apostolic missionary. An epitaph later engraved on his tomb when the church was finished recorded that his success in converting King Ethelbert and the Cantware was verified by the working of miracles – hence, almost certainly, the impetus behind his becoming *Saint* Augustine. In the seventh century, the elaborate canonisation process we know these days had not yet come into existence. People were acclaimed locally as saints by the growth of a cult round their tomb which was the focus for continued signs and miracles, often manifested as cures of the sick, testifying to God's approval both of the individual's sanctity of life and of the cult which sprang up because of it. Augustine's signs and wonders, and those of his original companions, were thus crucial in sealing the vision Pope Gregory had had when he decided to send these forty reluctant monks to extend God's spiritual empire in the north.

2

Labouring for Establishment

Laurentius to Dunstan (c.604–988)

A ugustine's immediate successor, *Laurentius* (c.604–19), may not, strictly speaking, have had any right to the archbishopric at all. Augustine chose him and consecrated him as his successor in c.604, perhaps the year in which he himself died, perhaps as many as five years before that happened. In either case, the consecration was uncanonical. One can see the practicality of the decision, of course. A delay of many months while a name – or even two or three in the event of a disputed succession – was sent to Rome for the Pope's approval, waited there until the Pope gave it (or, Heaven forfend, objected, in which case even more weeks or months of delay could be expected), and while the appropriate letters of appointment made their long way back to Kent, would leave the infant Anglian Church without a figurehead, without someone to make decisions and consecrate local bishops, so necessary for the furtherance of the mission, and without a negotiatior with the king upon whose continued good will the Cantware Church still rested. Nevertheless, however prudent Augustine's action, the idea that an archbishop could behave like an Egyptian Pharaoh or Roman Emperor and appoint someone his co-ruler while he himself still lived was unacceptable. According to Bede, Augustine relied on the precedent of St Peter, who was traditionally believed to have consecrated Clement I as his successor; but if Augustine did indeed do so, he forgot that St Peter was Pope and therefore the font of ecclesiastical authority, not a cog in its machine, and that actually Linus and Anacletus were Supreme Pontiffs before Clement.

We know little or nothing about Laurentius. He had been one of the original forty and thus had known Augustine in Rome while they were both brothers of *ad clivum Scauri*. His name, like that of Augustine, is almost certainly not his own, but one he took upon entry into the religious life. There are two saints called 'Lawrence' who could have provided him with the inspiration to adopt them as his patron. Lawrence of Spoleto came originally from Syria in 514 and settled in Rome where he was ordained by Pope Hormisdas. Later he founded a monastery in Spoleto and was named bishop of the city, where for twenty years he gained good will as a peace-maker and dispenser of charity. The more famous Lawrence, however, was the martyr (died 258), who was slowly burned to death on a red-hot griddle by the Prefect of Rome, his martyrdom leading to the end of paganism in the city and its complete conversion to Christianity. It would obviously be tempting to see this as a reason for Laurentius's choosing his name, but since we do not know how old Laurentius was when Pope Gregory chose him to accompany Augustine to Kent, we cannot say that it was the martyr who furnished the name rather than the more contemporary charitable abbot.

But Laurentius was surely not an untried youth, because in 597 he accompanied Augustine to Arles, where Augustine was consecrated a bishop, and from there was sent with one 'Peter' to Rome to report on the success of the Kentish mission thus far. (Bede distinguishes Laurentius as a priest and Peter as a monk, so clearly Laurentius was the senior, in status if not in age). They arrived in Rome in the early summer of 598 and stayed – or were delayed – for nearly three years. It is not too difficult to guess why the delay should have been so long. When they returned, it was with fresh missionaries and a very large number of books including (if we may believe the *Liber Cantuariensis*) a Bible in two volumes, two psalters, two copies of the Gospels, and two volumes of accounts of the sufferings of the Apostles and other saints. It may have been these books which caused the trouble. Books were entirely manuscript. They took a long time to produce and were very expensive, and neither Laurentius nor Peter could have walked into a shop and bought a supply for the Cantware mission. Each book would have been copied to order – it is how the specialist book-trade worked – and that took time. Each needed illustration, that took more; and each needed to be bound, which took even longer. In any case, the Papal Court was not one in which individuals could expect a rapid response even to their turning up, let alone to their inquiries. The Pope had to deal with much more than a single report from a small mission to a barbarous clump of heathen on the edge of the world. Priority governed access to the Pontiff, and the success or failure of one mission, even if he himself had set it in motion, could scarcely be expected to jump the long diplomatic and ecclesiastical queue.

Laurentius's long episcopate was dominated by two preoccupations: the continued building of the monastery of St Peter and St Paul, begun by Augustine, whose church Laurentius consecrated in *c.*613; and the death of King Ethelbert on 24 February 616 and the succession of his son Eadbald, who lost that overlordship of the neighbouring kingdoms which Ethelbert had enjoyed since 597 – an overlordship which passed to Raedwald of East Anglia, a nominal Christian who continued to reverence the old gods. Eadbald himself had never converted, and so Augustine's legacy was immediately put

in considerable peril. Mellitus, Bishop of London, was expelled from
his see and fled to Gaul where Justus, Bishop of Rochester, decided
to join him; and Laurentius, too, prepared to abandon Kent. But
then came the needed miracle. Laurentius spent what he thought
would be his last night in England asleep in the abbey church he had
consecrated three years before, and while he slept he dreamed that
St Peter appeared and flogged him, asking him why he was about to
abandon his sheep who would be left in the midst of wolves. 'Have
you forgotten my example?' St Peter asked, reminding Laurentius of
his imprisonment and crucifixion. Next morning, Laurentius sought
out King Eadbald, stripped off his clothes, and showed him the
lacerations caused by the flogging he had endured. When the king
learned these were in fact miraculous, caused by a saintly spirit and
not by a human being, he took fright (*extimuit*) and converted to
Christianity at once.

It is fairly easy to detect the various influences which produced
this version of Laurentius's miracle. Incubation had long been known
in the ancient world, a religious practice whereby one spent the night
in a temple, hoping for a dream which would provide the solution
to a particular problem. Laurentius was either a Roman or had spent
long enough in Rome to have inherited the cast of mind which
found incubation a natural way of looking for divine help in a time
of crisis; so when he ordered a bed to made up for him in the abbey
church on this crucial occasion, he was almost certainly hoping to
receive a meaningful dream. The appearance of St Peter was no
accident. There was a long-standing story, derived from the apocry-
phal *Acts of Peter*, that St Peter had been fleeing Nero's persecution
of the Christians in Rome when he met Jesus, who told him He
was making His way to the city to be crucified once again. St Peter
turned back at once, and was arrested and put to death. Laurentius's
identification of himself with St Peter is interesting. Augustine had,
perhaps unwillingly, done the same when he took it upon himself to
consecrate Laurentius his co-bishop, and cited St Peter and Clement
as a precedent. Did these early Archbishops of Canterbury have some
kind of subliminal grandiose, and mistaken, notion of their own
importance? Their behaviour sometimes suggests it. Like Augustine,

Laurentius tried to suggest to the Celtic bishops in Britain, for example, that they should acknowledge Roman authority (that is to say, in practice, his own), a suggestion they repudiated; and at the same time he 'took pains to expend his pastoral solicitude', as Bede expresses it, not only to them but also to the Irish, who refused point-blank even to eat with the Roman bishops. 'Expend' is an interesting verb for Bede to choose. *Impendere* means 'to pay out' or 'devote time and energy', but it may also mean 'to spend to no purpose', 'to waste one's effort', and this undoubtedly both Augustine and Laurentius did when they tried to extend their jurisdiction well beyond the reaches of Kent and the south of England.

The lash-marks on Laurentius's back, however, were an unmistakeable sign not only to him but also to King Eadbald. They told the king (to express the miracle in a way a heathen may have understood it) that Laurentius's magic was greater than that of any of the Cantware pagan priests because it flowed from a god more powerful than Tiw or Woden or Thunor, and so it seemed politic to do as his father had done, and ally himself with this foreign but potent deity. But if the Christian god was powerful, Eadbald was not. He arranged for Mellitus and Justus to return from Gaul, but could not insist that London receive back Mellitus. The influence of the heathen priests in that city proved too strong for him. Laurentius died not long afterwards, on 2 February 619. By staying in Canterbury rather than running away, and by facing the king and standing his ground instead of crumbling before the resurgence of paganism, Laurentius undoubtedly showed personal courage and preserved the work Augustine had begun. But he left his see in a precarious situation, and it would take a brave man and a skilled politician to steer it to safety.

Laurentius became a saint after his death, probably in much the same way as his predecessor, and for similar reasons. He was succeeded by *Mellitus* (619–24), translated thither from London. Bede tells us he was of noble birth and suffered from gout, but that his mind was healthy, and that he used to skip over anything of earthly concern and fly to heavenly things which were the constant object of his desire and striving. It makes him sound like someone deeply fitted for the contemplative monastic life, but less suitable for any position involving political savvy or diplomatic manoeuvring. Perhaps this is why he failed to make a sufficient impact in London to counter the pagan forces ranged against him. His name, too, may point the same way. *Mellitus* is the Latin for 'honeyed', and may have referred to his voice or way of speaking – one thinks of John *Chrysostom*, 'golden-mouthed' – or to the sweetness of his character. In any case, his personal holiness could seem to explain the famous miracle whereby he stopped a fire in Canterbury from spreading further. The fire threatened to destroy the city, but Mellitus had himself carried to the Church of the Four Crowned Martyrs where the flames were at their worst, held up his hands, and began to pray; whereupon the wind, which had been carrying the fire all over the city, died down and its flames were checked. Unfortunately for Mellitus, however, Pope Gregory had recorded exactly the same miracle of the bishop of Ancona, Marcellinus, so it looks as though Bede simply borrowed it for the occasion. Had there been a great fire in Canterbury, a saintly archbishop *ought* to have put it out by means of a miracle. At any rate, miracle or no miracle, Mellitus was later declared a saint.

When he died in 624, his colleague from Rochester, *Justus*, became archbishop (624–27/31). He had been dispatched to Kent along with Mellitus in 601 to help reinforce Augustine's mission, so the relatively small pool of Roman priests and monks in Kent was still being fished for the job of directing the Church in English territory. Pope Boniface V sent him a pallium, perhaps an inducement to set about more vigorous missionary work since Augustine's initial impetus seems to have slowed down; and the gesture may have worked, because it was during this time (625) that a marriage between Edwin, King of Northumbria, and Ethelburga, King Eadbald's Christian sister, paved the way for priests and monks to go north with her and thus establish the Faith in this even more distant region. Indeed, Paulinus, another of those who had come to Kent with Mellitus, went with Ethelburga as her personal chaplain and, when Justus died in 627 or 631, consecrated his successor, *Honorius* (627/32–53), in the newly finished cathedral at Lincoln, a convenient midway location for them both.

Justus enjoyed the honour of canonisation as, in due time, did
Honorius. Honorius had been born in Rome and was yet another
of the monks sent by Pope Gregory to convert the Angles. His episcopate, long as it was, however, can scarcely be called more successful
than 'holding the fort'. He managed to persuade Pope Honorius I to
establish another metropolitan see at York for the vigorous Paulinus,
and in 634 both men received the pallium from the Pontiff, a presen-
tation which implied an equality of status. (A letter attributed to Pope
Honorius, granting Canterbury the primacy over York, is no more
than a forgery). King Eadbald of Kent, now fully and firmly converted, strengthened the hold of Christianity over the area, but was
unable to extend it further, although he did found a novel religious
establishment at Folkestone in 630 – a double monastery. This consisted of two communities, one of monks, the other of nuns, living
separately but worshipping in a single church and being ruled by an
abbess. It was a pattern borrowed from Gaul, and when Eadbald's
sister Ethelburga was forced by the defeat of her husband and son
at the battle of Hatfield Chase (633) to flee south to her brother, he
allowed her to establish another such double monastery at Lyminge
as a refuge for herself and her remaining son.

When Honorius died, the succession of Augustine's companions
died with him. It had been an interesting half century, dominated
by Roman-born or Roman-trained clerics who had managed to
fulfil that part of Pope Gregory's vision relating to a south-eastern
Anglian bloc swept clear of paganism, but had failed to bring the
western and Irish Celtic Christians within the ambit of Rome's
supremacy. Honorius's death, too, issued in a vacancy of almost eighteen months in the office of archbishop, and when this was filled in
655, it became clear that the original pool of Roman talent was either
exhausted or had been passed over. Nevertheless, the habit of having
a Roman archbishop proved too strong to discard entirely, and the
name 'Frithona' was discarded in favour of 'Deusdedit', a form of the
Papal name 'Adeodatus' (who had reigned from 615 to 618).

The high point of Deusdedit's period in office was the Synod of
Whitby (664), called to resolve disputed questions between the Celtic
and Roman congregations over such points as the date of Easter and

the form of clerical tonsure. Roman practice prevailed, but Deusdedit
was not there to see it. He may have been on his deathbed, for he died
of the plague that same year; but in any case he seems to have been an
ineffectual prelate. Bishops of other sees sought consecration abroad,
and when he died there was only one remaining Anglian bishop who
had been canonically ordained. His baleful luck or influence lasted
even beyond his grave, for his intended successor, Wigheard, went
to Rome to be consecrated and died there of the plague before the
ceremony could take place. A vacancy thereupon stretched out for
about three years until Pope Vitalian appointed a Greek, Theodore,
to the Canterbury see.

   Theodore (668–90) was the first undoubted scholar to occupy the
archbishopric. He was born in a Greek-speaking province of what
is now Turkey, in the city of Tarsus which had long been famous for
the quality of its Biblical scholarship, and at some point in his early
life he is likely to have travelled to Antioch where he received part
of his education and learned (or at least picked up some knowledge of) Syriac. From there he went first to Constantinople, and
then to Rome where there was a monastery of Greek-speaking
monks from Cilicia, and it makes sense to suggest he may have lived
there until his translation to Canterbury. He was not, as it happens,
Pope Vitalian's first choice. Vitalian wanted to appoint a friend and
councillor of his, Abbot Hadrian from Naples. But Hadrian quite
understandably declined and suggested first Andrew, an older monk,
who turned it down because he was ill, and then Theodore. Was this
out of malice – monastic politics and rivalries could be bitter and
very worldly – or because he actually thought Andrew or Theodore
would do a good job? A sick older man and a Greek-speaking
Biblical scholar who had spent a good part of his life in the eastern
Mediterranean are scarcely the first candidates who spring to mind
to go to a northern Germanic see which was still having difficulty
in holding its own amid pagan tribes and a hostile Celtic tradition
of Christian practice. Bede tells us that Theodore was sixty-six when
Vitalian consecrated him. Maturity is one thing, old age another.
Why did Hadrian recommend and Vitalian appoint someone who,
in the normal course of events, could not be expected to last long in

the post? The fact that Theodore lived for another twenty-two years could not have been foreseen; so unless we attribute his appointment to divine inspiration, the reluctance with which the Pope actually viewed the suggestion before acceding to it suggests that Hadrian's was the moving force behind Theodore's consecration, and the possibility of monastic bitchiness lingers in the background, like a touch of sulphur.

Still, if that was indeed the case, Theodore managed to turn the tables on his patron, for Vitalian insisted that Hadrian should follow him to England, presumably to act as a brake on any untoward Greekish practices he might try to foist on his flock, and as a spy in the faraway camp, who would report to Vitalian whether his choice had been a complete mistake or not. Theodore's setting out, however, was delayed. His head was completely shaven in accordance with what was then the customary Greek tonsure, and he had to wait for four months for a full head of hair to grow which he could then have shorn in the appropriate Roman way. This was at Vitalian's insistence. Clearly Latin spoken with a Greek accent could be tolerated in Anglian Kent; a skinhead look could not. Theodore finally arrived in May 669 and Hadrian a few months later in 670, both having been detained for a while in Gaul, Hadrian (perhaps appropriately enough) on suspicion of being a spy. But once arrived in Canterbury, they set about a tour of the archdiocese, and the immense vigour which was to mark Theodore's period in office had begun.

Theodore proved a great administrator. He divided a number of sprawling dioceses into more sensible territories and appointed new bishops to look after them; and this, repeated over the whole of his twenty-two years as archbishop, created a structure which not only began to unify what had been for so long a disparate body, but also planted the notion that this unity owed some kind of obedience, in English matters, to Canterbury. Theodore may thus be credited with doing much to ensure that there was such a thing as the English Church. His accomplishment could not be completed without trampling on toes, of course, and the most famous feet he stood on belonged to Wilfred of Northumbria. From 669 until 677, Wilfred exercised ecclesiastical sway over the entire unwieldy diocese which was coterminous with that kingdom. Then he quarrelled with King Egfrith because he had encouraged the Queen to leave her husband and become a nun. Meanwhile Theodore, too, had become suspicious of Wilfred's ambitions to establish another archbishopric in the far north; so he came to Northumbria, divided it into three, and appointed bishops for each area, thereby effectively depriving Wilfred of his see. Wilfred, however, decided to appeal to Rome and set off across the Channel in the winter of 677 for a host of adventures which saw him preaching Christianity to the Frisians and suffering amicable detention first by the king of Austrasia and then the king of the Lombards, who told him that someone in Britain had tried to bribe him to delay Wilfred's journey to Rome. The king grandly let Wilfred know he had refused the money, but detained him neverthe-less; so it was not until summer 679 that Wilfred eventually arrived in Rome. He had not had an entirely fruitless journey. In spite of a prior account of the case, sent by Theodore, Pope Agatho sided with Wilfred and restored him his bishopric; but the Pope was obviously ill at ease with the situation.

Theodore had little patience with people who did not do as they were told. He appointed the saintly Celt Chad to be bishop of Lichfield and forbade him to continue the usual Celtic custom of visiting his diocese on foot. Chad demurred, so Theodore picked him up and shoved him on a horse. He also deposed Chad's successor for disobedience, and insisted that all bishops consecrated according to Celtic tradition be reconstituted by a Catholic bishop. So although none of our sources expresses it in simple, unvarnished language, Theodore was clearly given to authoritarian ways and was not a man to cross. It may well be, of course, that this was the temperament needed for the moment. If the great sprawling dioceses were ever to be governed properly, they had to be split into manageable areas, and such splits would almost certainly cause resentment. If the bishops were not to become mini-monarchs in their own territories, they had to be curbed by some kind of central discipline relatively close to home. Canterbury might be far from Northumbria, but Rome was even further. Theodore's high-handedness is therefore understand-able, as is the grumbling reaction to it.

But Pope Agatho – possibly another Greek, or at least someone of Greek descent, from Sicily – was not prepared to allow Theodore to exercise unfettered sway in England, and told him (via a council) that the maximum number of bishops there, including himself, was to be twelve. After several more years of adventures, Wilfred and Theodore were reconciled in a scene which smacks somewhat of theatre. Theodore apologised for ruining Wilfred in the first place and said he would like Wilfred to succeed him at Canterbury – an abasement which may, of course, have been genuine (Theodore did become Saint Theodore after his death, although, interestingly enough, doubts have been expressed on that point) but which may also have been an old man's tacit acknowledgement that he had lost his long duel with Wilfred, a defeat which a show of humiliation would, by its very theatricality, help to cover.

The scholarly side of Theodore can be seen both in changes to the liturgy – Gregorian plain-chant was adopted in English churches for the first time, and a litany of the saints translated from a Greek original – and in education, which both he and Hadrian, now abbot of the Monastery of St Peter and St Paul in Canterbury, promoted and directed themselves. According to Bede, they not only expounded the Scriptures to their audiences, but also trained them in the skill of versifying, astronomy and 'Church arithmetic', that is, the calculation of the ecclesiastical calendar.[1] The day-to-day problems facing a bishop at this time are illustrated by a penitential appearing over Theodore's name, actually a compilation of his answers to questions put to him during his period in office. Perhaps significantly, given Germanic tribes' reputations as heavy drinkers, the penitential begins with 'The effects of intoxication and addiction to alcohol'. It then goes on to deal with fornication – adultery was four times more serious a sin than having sex with a virgin – sacrilegious theft, murder and manslaughter, before coming to heresy, perjury, and various other evil acts. These are extraordinarily diverse, and cover stealing money from a conquered enemy in a district not one's own; drinking blood or semen (a probable reference to love-magic in which these and other substances were put in food or drink); and a surprising number of separate points dealing with unclean or contaminated liquid. What should one do, for example, if a mouse or a weasel falls into one's soup and is drowned, or if birds let their droppings fall into it? (Skim off any impurities and sprinkle the soup with holy water before eating it).

One section is devoted to possible failings, principally sexual, by priests or monks, and another to what he calls the worship of idols, but which actually deals mainly with magical practices:

> If a woman places her daughter on the roof or into an oven in order to cure her fever, she should do penance for seven years. If someone burns seeds in the place where someone has died in order to keep the living and the house safe, he or she should do penance for five years. If a woman performs devilish incantations or divinations, she should do penance for one year, or three times forty days, or forty days, according to the nature of the offence.

The second volume deals largely with questions related to the sacraments, especially marriage – and one can see from this how difficult the Christian Church in England was finding it to impose strict conduct on converted couples: 'a husband who has slept with his wife should wash before entering a church: a husband ought not to see his wife naked'. On the other hand, Theodore's judgements could be understanding, as when he said that 'if someone has been harassed by the Devil and doesn't know what to do, other than run about all over the place, and, for whatever reason kills himself, prayers should be offered for him, if he was a devout person [before he was possessed]'.[2]

Theodore died on 19 September 690 and was succeeded by English-born archbishops about whom little need be said. *Behrtwald* (693–731) was learned and managed to retain Theodore's control over the other English bishops, always with the exception of the tiresome Wilfred who continued to plague both Canterbury and Rome in pursuit of his ambition to exercise unfettered control over Northumbria. When he died in 709, a sigh of relief may well have been heard in both cities, although in fairness it should be said that he had his supporters as well as opponents. Behrtwald seems to have been the first Archbishop of Canterbury not to be declared a saint after his death, an omission which set a precedent, because we have to wait over 200 years for the next one. *Tatwine* (731–34) is notable principally for his composing a Latin grammar and a stunningly complex, and often incomprehensible, set of forty short poems, each dealing with some aspect of the Christian life and taking the form of a riddle – the kind of verbal puzzle which would appeal to his learned Saxon readers. *Nothelm* (735–39) was one of Bede's informants, especially useful for transmitting a number of Papal letters he had copied during a visit to Rome during the Papacy of Gregory II, for which Bede was duly grateful, dedicating his *Thirty Questions on the Books of Kings* to him. *Cuthbert* (740–60), like Tatwine and Nothelm, probably came from Mercia, whose king, Aethelbald, was dominant well beyond his own borders. Archbishop Boniface of Mainz complained of the English at the time that they were drunken, superstitious and immoral, especially the women when they came abroad; so it is interesting not only that history repeats itself, but also that Cuthbert should apparently stand in need of being given advice by a foreign bishop (albeit of English birth) to reform his unruly flock. The correspondence did not come out of the blue. Boniface had exchanged letters with Behrtwald and Nothelm, too, but his tone with Cuthbert was different. Clearly he thought that his colleague in Canterbury needed to pull his socks up. Cuthbert left his mark on Canterbury itself by building the Church of St John the Baptist just to the east of the cathedral. Otherwise, his twenty-year period in office is obscured by later myths and stories intended to make him appear more significant than he was.

Bregowine (761–64) and *Jaenbehrt* (765–92) are personally obscure, although the latter had his name and title struck on one side of the Mercian coinage. Both had uneasy episcopates, Bregowine under the dominance of King Ethelbert II of Kent, Jaenbehrt under Offa, King of Mercia. *Aethelheard* (793–805) seems to have been yet another Mercian, his elevation to the episcopate an apparent tribute to the continuing power of King Offa who had been able to persuade the Pope to diminish the extent of the episcopate of Canterbury and elevate Lichfield to the same ecclesiastical status. But this Mercian dominance was deeply resented by the inhabitants of Kent, and when Offa died in 796, they rose in rebellion. Aethelheard, perhaps fearing for his life, fled to Ecgfrith, Offa's son, with whom he stayed in relative safety until a counter-movement restored him to Canterbury in 798; but it took a personal journey to Rome by Aethelheard to get back those parts of his province which Hadrian I and Offa had removed from him. *Wulfred* (805–32) is interesting, partly because he was rich and ruthlessly accumulated estates both for himself and for the monastic community of Christ Church (the cathedral), partly because two charters written in his own hand reveal that his Latin was atrocious, full of grammatical mistakes and misspellings. His acquisitive, not to say greedy, temperament clashed with the Mercian king Cenwulf over the administration of certain properties, a quarrel which escalated to the point where the king got Wulfred suspended from office. Wulfred, however, perhaps true to form, forged charters which he attributed to earlier Kentish and Mercian kings, purporting to grant Archbishops of Canterbury control over monastic elections and property – the very points of dispute he was having with Cenwulf – and it was not until just before he himself died that the king conceded, although he made Wulfred pay heavily for the settlement. Evidently Cenwulf knew how to make Wulfred smart.

After the tempestuous Wulfred came *Feologeld* (832), and it must be said that if Feologeld was born to be obscure, he succeeded admirably. Indeed, it seems his imperceptibility extended decades into the future, for under his immediate successors *Ceoluoth* (833–70) and *Aethelred* (870–89) the archbishopric fell further under royal control, this time of the kings of Wessex, who supplanted those of Mercia as rulers of Kent; suffered the loss of several coastal monasteries such as those at Dover, Folkestone and Thanet at the hands of successive waves of invaders from Scandinavia; and lost much of its command of learning, the Latin of the monks of Christ Church having degenerated to such an extent that many of them were incapable of translating documents into English. In fact, it was not until *Plegemund* (890–914) took over that some of these problems eased, although a measure of the desperate state to which the English Church had been reduced by constant influxes of pagan invaders can be gauged from a letter to him from Pope Formosus, who said that, had it not been for Plegemund's efforts to keep the Church intact and viable, he would have excommunicated the English bishops for their failure to stem the tide of resurgent paganism in the country. Plegemund had not been King Alfred's first choice for archbishop, but what seems to have been a personal holiness – there is a fairly reliable tradition that for several years he had lived as a hermit on an island in Cheshire – may have persuaded Alfred to recommend him to the office after all. *Athelm* (914–23) may have composed a coronation service for English kings, introducing the actual crown in the ceremony for the first time. *Wulfhelm* (926–41) seems to have become a noted political figure. His regular attendance at royal councils, and King Aethelstan's gift of two Gospels to Canterbury, suggest that the two men worked closely together, although whether this was a harmonious arrangement or one of political necessity for the archbishop is hard to tell.

With *Oda* (942–58), however, we return to sanctity, for he was the first archbishop to be declared a saint since Theodore (or perhaps Deusdedit) in the mid-seventh century, a reputation he seems to have earned by being called 'the Good' during his lifetime and, more importantly, by his miracles, of which three are recorded in Byrhtferth's *Life* of his nephew, St Oswald. Oda's father was a Dane, a pagan, who disliked Oda's penchant for Christianity but permitted him to join the household of a Christian Anglo-Saxon nobleman, Aethelhelm. Oda eventually became a priest and accompanied Aethelstan on pilgrimage to Rome, but while they were on their way Aethelhelm suffered 'a sudden weakness of the heart', with the result that he could scarcely breathe. This Oda cured, partly by prayer and partly by making the sick man drink a 'cruet of wine' (probably communion wine already poured into the *fiala* in preparation for Mass), over which he had made the sign of the cross. A second miracle happened one day while Oda, now Archbishop of Canterbury, was celebrating Mass; for as he was handling the consecrated Host, a drop of Our Saviour's blood flowed from it, at the sight of which he was both astonished and afraid until he was reassured by a priest who was at the altar with him. The third miracle was less awe-inspiring. Oda undertook repairs to the cathedral, re-roofing it and raising the height of its walls, and while this work was going on no rain fell on Canterbury.[3]

Hagiographical concretions such as these serve as polite salutations by the future to the past, but if Oda deserved respect, *Aelfsige* (958–9) did not. Later monastic writers claimed he had bought the archbishopric and scorned his predecessor, beating his tomb with a stick. St Oda got his own back, though. He appeared three times to a priest, telling him to go to Aelfsige and give him a message. After first forgetting the message, and then dismissing the vision as of little account, the priest plucked up courage and went to Aelfsige. 'There has come to me', he said, 'not the supreme Bridegroom's friend, Gabriel, but the glorious Oda, your predecessor, who angrily instructed me to deliver to your reverence the following words. "Because you treated me with contempt yesterday in word and in deed, I predict you will be able to sail across the sea and climb mountains, but that there is no way you will sit on the archiepiscopal throne"'. Aelfsige dismissed the whole thing as nonsense, but at the end of 958 he set out for Rome to collect his *pallium* from Pope John XII, and froze to death in the Alps before he could do so.[4] *Byrhthelm* (959), by contrast, was mild and meek, so mild and meek, in fact, that once King Eadwig, who had brought him to Canterbury from Wells where he was bishop, was dead, his son King Edgar sent him back there and appointed Dunstan in his place.

St Dunstan (959–88) was well connected. His uncle, Archbishop Aethelm, introduced him to the royal court in Kent, a well-meaning gesture which failed to engage his scholarly disposition, and so he returned to Glastonbury near which he had been born in *c.*909, and became a monk in the Benedictine community there. A second stint at the Kentish royal court brought complaints, once again, that he was boring and reserved; so, once again, he was sent away. Installed as abbot of Glastonbury, he governed the community quietly through the rest of King Edmund's reign and that of his brother, King Eadred. But the accession of King Eadwig saw him out of favour for a third time in his career and he went into exile in Ghent, where he absorbed and was excited by the Cluniac reforms of the Benedictine Order, reforms which he brought back to England

and implemented once he was in a position to do so. Reform, however, was not enough and he also endowed various monasteries,
including that at Malmesbury, one of whose monks, William, later
wrote a biography of him. From this and other available sources,
we learn that Dunstan was a competent musician, wrote passable
verses in Latin – when he gave Malmesbury an organ, a holy water
stoup and a little bell for the refectory, he inscribed each of them
with a distich of his own composition – while a surviving drawing
attributed to him suggests he was also an able draughtsman. We are
told he painted and embroidered, too, but no example of the latter
survives, so it is difficult to tell whether he actually did enjoy this
accomplishment or not. But there is no particular reason to dismiss
it as unlikely. It is remarkable how many men in the trenches during
the First World War embroidered pictures and samplers in what spare
time they had, so skill with a needle has never been a purely female
occupation.

But education, especially important to the Benedictines, he certainly encouraged both at Glastonbury and at Westminster, where
he refounded a monastery which had been destroyed during
Danish incursions. So we should picture him as a scholarly man,
eager and able to promote monastic and ecclesiastical reform,
with a mind of his own and a personality sufficiently engaging,
in spite of his three dismissals from Court, to capture the interest
and support of the powers which mattered. His independence of
spirit can be gauged from an incident at the coronation banquet
of King Eadwig. The new king walked out of the hall in order
to flirt (which may be putting it kindly) with a noblewoman and
her daughter. This was insulting to his guests, so Dunstan went to
find him and more or less dragged him back into the hall, thereby
creating three enemies for himself. But relations with King Edgar,
Eadwig's younger brother, were entirely different and the two
co-operated to a quite remarkable extent, Dunstan's hand being
perceptible in almost every aspect of Edgar's government. He was
thus a forerunner of those powerful Archbishops of Canterbury
who sailed high in the fortunes of the English state, advising,
directing, promoting, in many ways governing, but always subject

to the monarch's favour or whim, a supper with the Devil at which the spoon could never be long enough.

Indeed, according to Byrhtferth's *Life of Saint Oswald*, Dunstan was no stranger to the actual Devil, who appeared to him one night while he was praying – 'standing' in prayer, which perhaps suggests he may have been engaged in reciting the Divine Office in church – seized hold of his hands, and began to wrestle with him. Dunstan, however, called upon God for help, borrowing the opening words of Psalm 67 (Vulgate), 'Let God arise and His enemies will be scattered', whereupon his adversary took flight. He was also subject to visions on more than one occasion, fighting with parts of Behemoth made visible at one point, and hearing a most melodious hymn sung by the souls of those dead who were buried in the cathedral.[5] He died on 19 May 988 and his name was immediately written into the liturgical calendar, the usual fashion at the time of acknowledging someone as a saint. Biographies were soon composed, but unfortunately they are not much use to a modern historian, being largely (as one might expect) hagiographies rather than memorials of other aspects of the man's career. St Dunstan, therefore, is at once the most popular Anglo-Saxon saint, and yet someone about whose secular achievements we actually know very little from first-hand evidence.

3

Surviving the Millennium and the Conquest

Aethelgar to Lanfranc (988–1089)

What had the Archbishops of Canterbury achieved in the four centuries since Augustine came to Kent and founded the office? Perhaps the first and most obvious answer is that they had survived. The triumph of Christianity in the various parts of Europe seems inevitable from the standpoint of a millennium and a half later, but in fact Europe as a whole cannot be said to have taken on its Christian appearance until the twelfth or thirteenth century. That appearance in Canterbury would have been assisted, however, by the building and adaptation of structures intended for Christian worship. St Augustine, as we have seen, made use of a Romano-British Church already in existence, but founded a monastery and, if he followed the advice of Pope Gregory, took over pagan sacred places and turned them to Christian use. Whether the cathedral which existed in Archbishop Oda's time was the same as that consecrated by Augustine is open to debate, but we do know that the original Christ Church cathedral was probably built of wood, like so many other buildings in Anglo-Saxon Canterbury, and it is a fair guess that it was destroyed with much of the rest of the town in a disastrous fire in 756. The cathedral complex at this time consisted of Christ Church, the Church of St John the Baptist, built by Archbishop Cuthbert, and the Monastery of St Peter and St Paul. Visitors and townsfolk would thus have been impressed by an extensive, almost sprawling set of edifices, each of which proclaimed the majesty and therefore the power of the Catholic religion.

Gradually the archbishops acquired control over the Church in kingdoms of England other than Kent, and with that control gained a measure of influence and power and wealth. This growth in secular significance was, of course, difficult to live with. Some archbishops were strong enough to withstand as well as to co-operate with the reigning monarch. Others were not, and sought refuge in introspection. Most reflected the monastic origin of their office and encouraged fidelity to the monastic ideal, as well as care in the performance of the liturgy and the transmission of education to the young. Many were acclaimed saints, the signs and miracles which had attended their Gospel witness carefully recorded, and often embroidered, for the edification of the community at Canterbury itself and for the wider English Christian fellowship which, for a long time, faced claims by a Celtic tradition opposed to their own, equally supported and verified by signs and miracles. But by 988, Dunstan must surely have felt satisfied that the modified Roman style set by Canterbury had prevailed, and that his own remarkable position as first councillor to the king as well as first cleric in England would be enjoyed without hindrance by those who came after him.

Aethelgar (988–90), *Sigeric* (990–94) and *Aelfric* (995–1005) soon proved him wrong. All were monks, the first two from Glastonbury, the last from Abingdon, and seem to have become archbishop late in life. Aethelgar lasted long enough to go to Rome, collect his pallium, and bring back large gifts for the monastery of St Bertin near Omer, which he visited on his outward journey. Sigeric replaced the secular clerics of Christ Church with monks and advised King Etheldred to pay tribute to the Danish raiders still harassing Kent in 991, advice which may have sprung from timidity, but was perhaps more likely to have originated in concern for estates belonging to the see, spread out over much of the south-east of the country. Huge sums – £16,000 in 994, for example – were being paid as protection money, thereby creating a severe drain on the available cash throughout the southern and eastern kingdoms. Aelfric had to help the king pay even more – £24,000 in 1002 – but no doubt these increasing demands on both ecclesiastical and secular purses paled beside the most dreadful event of Archbishop Aelfric's period in office, the advent and passing of the year 1000.

The number one thousand had both frightening and uplifting resonances for Christian Europe, the key to these responses being *Apocalypse* 20.2-3 and 7. St John in his vision saw an angel coming from Heaven, binding Satan and confining him in a bottomless pit where he was to remain for a thousand years, 'until the thousand years are completed: and after this, it is requisite he be let loose within a short space of time' (verse 3). In the year 1000, therefore, there was every chance that this period of Satan's imprisonment would be over and that the end of the universe would be ushered in by his releasing, followed by the judgement of the living and the dead and the start of Christ's thousand-year rule. Signs of the End would occur – wars, famine, plague and death – all of which were easy to discern in the upheavals troubling many places in Europe. 'This earth must of necessity come to an end in this age which is now present', declared a tenth-century English preacher, 'for five of the [fore-tokens] have come to pass in this age; wherefore this world must come to an end, and of this the greatest portion [already] has elapsed, even nine hundred and seventy-one years, in this very year'.[1]

Aelfric will thus have had the uncomfortable task of guiding his clergy and his flock through expectations of impending doom, made constantly worse with each Danish incursion and each outbreak of disease, expectations which may have diminished slightly once the year 1000 had passed, but which could not disappear entirely because no one was quite sure exactly when the thousand-year period had begun and therefore when it was due to end. But Aelfric's will contained one provision which, given the apocalyptic times in which it was written, had symbolic resonance; amid the bequests of lands and ships and armaments, books and Christian artefacts and personal ornaments, slaves were to be freed, the clink of psychological chains thus chiming with that of the spiritual chains which were falling from Satan.

The waves of Danish marauders continued to plague the south under *Aelfeadh* (1006–12). He, like his immediate predecessors, was a monk and had gained experience of administration partly by becoming abbot of his own community at Deerhurst (or, possibly, Glastonbury), and partly by being bishop of Winchester, where he also undertook extensive remodelling of the cathedral in order to give the relics of St Swithun a suitably impressive shrine. It was while he was at Winchester that Aelfeadh had to cope with renewed Danish attacks, greeted as usual by the offer of large sums of money, and things did not improve for him after his translation to Canterbury. In 1011 Thorkell the Tall and his brother Hemming were admitted into the town by treachery, and proceeded to plunder and burn it, capturing the archbishop and taking him back to Denmark. The *Anglo-Saxon Chronicle* broke into a lament:

> Then was he a captive, he who had been
> The head of England and of Christendom.
> There might be seen wretchedness
> Where often was seen bliss before,
> In that unhappy city, whence came first to us
> Christendom, and both spiritual and earthly bliss[2]

Even if one makes allowance for the rhetorical exaggeration of Aelfeadh's perceived importance – it is possible that the information and therefore the tone derives from the abbey of St Augustine in Canterbury – there can be no doubt that the forced removal of the archbishop was a devastating blow to both the religious and secular communities of southern England. An immense tribute, in effect a ransom, was demanded – £48,000 – and although a slightly later historian, Thietmar of Merseburg, tells us that Aelfeadh was adamant he did not want any ransom to be collected for him, money was gradually found, although it took months to scrape together.

Meanwhile, the archbishop was dead. The Danes had brought him back to England, and on Easter Sunday, 19 April 1012, they were holding a feast in Greenwich during which a great deal of alcohol was consumed and the archbishop brought out to provide some rough entertainment. According to Thietmar (who is clearly writing in those terms of pious fiction appropriate to certain key moments in hagiography), Aelfeadh made a speech in answer to rough demands for immediate payment of his ransom, that he could not pay because he was too poor and that he was ready to die if that was what they wanted. 'While he was saying this, a mass of heathen surrounded him and repeatedly hurled various weapons [at him] with a view to killing him'. Their leader, Thorkell, tried to dissuade them from doing so, but they were too inflamed to take any notice.

> [His words] did not soften the unbridled anger of his companions, which was less inclined to take an impression than iron and rocks, and was to be appeased only by the spilling of innocent blood; and this they immediately spilled together, [using] the heads of cattle, showers of stones, and a flood of sticks.[3]

Consequently, Aelfeadh died under their blows and was at once justified as a saint and martyr by a miracle, for, we are told, one of the ringleaders suddenly found himself crippled. Thietmar's account makes vivid and uplifting reading, as it was meant to do; but as he calls Aelfeadh 'Dunstan' throughout, his accuracy as an historian is not as sharp as one would like. We are therefore left principally with pious afterthoughts and nothing of his personality.

Lyfing (1013–20) was the first bishop of Canterbury to receive formal Papal authorisation as an archbishop. He went to Rome, as was customary, to receive his pallium and to report on the state of the English Church, and returned in 1018 with a letter from Benedict VIII to King Cnut, urging the fairly new monarch to protect the Christian religion and bring order and justice to his kingdom. Cnut, who should perhaps be known as 'Lambert', since this is the name he had taken at his baptism, was certainly keen to govern as a Christian monarch, and his accession, of course, more or less put an end, for the time being, to the constant invasions from Scandinavia which had bloodied the long reign of King Ethelred, his predecessor. But the army with which he had established himself as king almost certainly contained a large number of heathens, and so Archbishop Lyfing was faced with a pagan influx unlikely to make his task as pastor any easier. On the other hand, it is also true that Cnut needed English officials to help him govern effectively, especially since he himself was not continuously resident in England, and those officials would be supplied largely by the English Church. So Cnut actually depended on Lyfing's co-operation to get himself established and continue successfully thereafter, acknowledgement of which can be seen in the generous gifts he made to the church in Canterbury. It is therefore an interesting, if unanswerable, question why Lyfing did co-operate with Cnut. The *Chronicle* by Florence of Worcester tells us that not long after 30 November 1017, 'Cnut commanded all the bishops and ealdormen, and the chief men and magnates of England, to assemble at London' to get them to swear fealty to him as king, and that they did so. If 'all' means 'all' – and there is no reason to suppose it does not – presumably Lyfing must have been there and added his voice to their deliberations. He may have thought that accepting the foreign invader as king would prevent further bloodshed; he may have surrendered to *vox populi*; he may have welcomed the Danish intervention as a guarantee of his own property and that of the Church; he may simply have accepted the situation in the spirit of Alexander Pope: 'And, spite of Pride, in erring Reason's spite, / One truth is clear, whatever is, is right'.

Cnut's favour was also extended (perhaps partly stimulated by his Norman wife, Emma, Ethelred's widow and mother of the king later to be known as 'Edward the Confessor') to *Aethelnoth* (1020–38), who is recorded as being 'a man endowed with great courage and wisdom'. Aethelnoth, another monk, who was dean of Christ Church at the time of his elevation, received the distinct privilege of having his extensive secular holdings and judicial powers broadcast to the English in a writ issued by Cnut, a document carefully preserved in a book of Gospels belonging to Canterbury, which we may take as a sign of Cnut's eagerness to have his rule endorsed by one of God's representatives, an eagerness by no means free of political calculation, since Aethelnoth consecrated bishops, and if he could be persuaded to consecrate bishops the king considered trustworthy representatives of his rule in some of the further reaches of his kingdom, that could only be desirable and useful to the Crown. *Eadsige* (1038–50), who had become a monk of Christ Church in Canterbury only about eight years before he was chosen archbishop, had a somewhat difficult time in office. He managed to collect his pallium from Rome in 1040 and crown Edward the Confessor in 1043, but soon after that he fell ill, so ill that he was unable to function as archbishop. The *Anglo-Saxon Chronicle* and William of Malmesbury tell us that, in consequence, he secretly appointed the abbot of Abingdon, Siward, as his successor, informing only the king and Earl Godwin that he had done so. His motive was intriguing. He was afraid that some improper individual might persuade King Edward to recommend him for the post, or successfully bribe his way into it – neither of which consideration says much for Eadsige's opinion of the king. But in any case, his action was entirely uncanonical and, in view of the disputable legality of anything Siward may have done while acting as 'Archbishop', it is probably fortunate that Eadsige managed to recover his health in 1046. His fears that King Edward could be open to bribery may have sprung from recognition of a similar defect in his own character, for the historian Eadmer tells us that Earl Godwin got hold of the manor of Folkestone (the property of the Church) by bribing the archbishop. One has the impression (perhaps mistaken, but perhaps not) that both Aethelnoth and Eadsige folded in the face of *force majeure*, and that neither was capable, for whatever reason, of resisting a strong and ruthless layman.

When Eadsige died, this incapacity seems to have been mirrored in the failure of the monastic community of Canterbury to get the king to accept their preferred candidate for archbishop, a relative of Earl Godwin, Aelric. Their proposal was a bad miscalculation. King Edward was scarcely going to allow Godwin the immense privilege of shoehorning one of his own family into the first ecclesiastical office in England and thus creating an extra mouthpiece for the earl in the king's council. What they got instead was *Robert of Jumièges* (1051–52), the Norman bishop of London, who had met Edward while Edward was in brief exile in Normandy, and who entered the maelstrom which was the English Court at the time as an obvious ally and placeman of the king. For a short time Edward was able to rid himself of the whole Godwin faction by driving them out of the country; but after only a few months they were back, seemingly more powerful and contentious than ever, so Edward was obliged to restore them to their former privileges and the archbishop fled to France. He was replaced by *Stigand* (1052–70), a man about whom there is little if anything to be said by way of compliment. The account of him given by Gervase of Canterbury, an obviously hostile source, is worth giving almost in full, since much of it seems to have been true.

> Stigand, King Edward's chaplain, who had at one time abandoned the see of the southern Saxons and laid hands on the church of Winchester, was not afraid to seize hold of the archbishopric of Canterbury too, make himself master of it, and put on the pallium belonging to Robert who was still alive, without, however, letting go of Winchester, the reason being he was arrogant and [a man] of incalculable effrontery... He received the pallium from the antipope Benedict... This man was the first wearing clerical attire to take it upon himself to lay hands on the bishopric of Canterbury... Once Benedict had been forcibly removed from his 'Papal' office, Stigand was suspended by Pope Alexander; and after the death of the holy King Edward, a council was held at Winchester, under King William

where, by consent of Pope Alexander and King William (who added England to his possessions), Stigand was deposed by two cardinals [sent as] legates to England. He was thrust into prison, suffered dreadful punishments for his untameable effrontery, and died in that same place.[4] However, upon his death they discovered a little key among his private papers, and when they put this to the lock of a small chest in his bedroom, they gained sight of a very large number of precious objects. They also found documents in which were noted down the value and weight of the metals he had buried throughout all the estates he had stolen.

News took a long time to travel, so the advent of Benedict, his deposition and the election of Pope Nicholas will not have reached England for several weeks after the event. Even so, Stigand was able, relying upon his supposed authority from Benedict, to consecrate several bishops whose subsequent positions must have had a cloud looming over them as a result, and when it came to the coronations of both King Harold and King William in 1066 it was to the Archbishop of York the two monarchs turned, so as not to cast a possible similar shadow over their title to the throne. The implication of personal greed levelled against Stigand by Gervase seems to be borne out by the contrast between his apparent lack of effort to obtain further endowments for Canterbury, while building up his own fortunes by amassing sizeable quantities of land in Gloucestershire, Suffolk and Norfolk, and estates and manors aplenty elsewhere; and Nicholas Brooks's summary is just and measured:

> The 18 years of Stigand's pontificate, when the metropolitan author-
> ity of the archbishop was in abeyance, when spiritual leadership was
> absent, and when the landed interests of the church of Canterbury
> were largely ignored, created a host of problems for Stigand's Norman
> successors. It was a great misfortune that he was still holding the see
> when the Norman conquest brought revolutionary changes to the
> English political and ecclesiastical establishment. In 1066 the church
> of Canterbury was in a weak position to defend its interests.[5]

That major event, the invasion and conquest of England by the Norman claimant to the throne, must have presented Stigand with a problem and an opportunity. He had briefly supported the cause of a Saxon, Edgar Aetheling, to succeed the defeated Harold, but then saw that the Norman victory was different in kind from the various Danish incursions to which the south of England had become wearily accustomed over so many decades, and decided to follow most others and do homage to the new king, William. (It is perhaps a measure of how completely William has been absorbed into the English historical record that he is more frequently known as 'the Conqueror' than by his regnal number I, and that he is always anglicised as 'William'. Yet he should be known as 'Guillaume', and for the sake of emphasising the strangeness and foreignness he would have represented to the English at the time I shall refer to him by his own rather than by his translated name).

Guillaume was crowned by the Archbishop of York on Christmas Day 1066 and then returned to France, taking Stigand along with him. Why did he do so? Stigand's position as archbishop was uncertain and uncanonical, but it could be rectified by the Pope if the Pope so chose, and even if he did not, Stigand was a great southern magnate by virtue of his landed possessions. Better, therefore, to have him at hand and keep an eye on him than alienate him unnecessarily. But as time passed and Guillaume consolidated his rule, Stigand became more of an encumbrance than a political help. Having an uncanonical primus was too uncomfortable, and if he were ousted from his dubious position, Guillaume could not only appoint an archbishop he could trust and use, but also gain materially from the confiscations of property which would result from Stigand's fall. Pope Alexander II would undoubtedly concur and co-operate. Stigand owed his position to an antipope, and Alexander could scarcely be seen to uphold an appointment made by a schismatic predecessor. So all in all it was in the combined interests of both the Pope and the new king of England to get rid of an anomaly. Charges of expelling Robert of Jumièges by force, stealing his pallium and wearing it as his own and accepting a pallium from a 'Pope' who was as uncanonical as himself were thus easy to bring and prove against Stigand, who thereupon suffered more or less the fate described by the monk Gervase. One says 'more or less' because he did not die in prison but in detention, receiving a very small pension from the Crown and the occasional letter of sympathy from Edith, the widow of the conquered King Harold. Allowances must be made for a deliberate *post eventum* blackening of Stigand's reputation by the chroniclers. Nevertheless, no amount of allowance can disguise the fact that he seems to have been a Wolsey in the making, but without Wolsey's self-evident talent.

New king, new archbishop. *Lanfranc* (1070–89) must be accounted one of the most significant appointments to the see of Canterbury, the foundations for which were laid during his youth in Italy. He was born in Pavia at some time between 1000 and 1020, and concentrated his studies upon both Roman and Lombard law, a subject which seems to have appealed to his temperament and suited his intellectual capabilities, for he was to display great forensic skill for the rest of his life. At some point in his youth, however, he dropped his career in this discipline and went to Normandy where theology rather than law was queen, and it is at this point he must have become a cleric. For a while he attended the lectures of a controversial theologian, Berengar, in the cathedral school of Tours. Berengar became embroiled in a major controversy about the Real Presence in the eucharist: did the bread and wine substantially change into the body and blood of Christ, or was the change symbolic only? The latter, heretical opinion was the one Berengar adopted and persisted in advocating for nearly four decades, despite more than one condemnation by the Church; so anyone who associated with him, either as colleague or pupil, was apt to be tainted and find himself, at least potentially, in trouble too. Lanfranc therefore left Tours and settled in Avranches where he taught, probably grammar and rhetoric, in the cathedral school there, and acquired the Norman-French which would be so useful to him later on.

What might be described these days as a mid-life crisis appears to have overtaken him while he was in Avranches, and he began to think about becoming a monk. The *Chronicle of Bec* tells us that an incident on the road from Avranches to Rouen, where he was hoping to find a suitable monastery, proved decisive in his search. He and a young companion were attacked at night by footpads on a bank of the River Rille, robbed, and tied to a couple of trees. Lanfranc realised he could not remember the office of Lauds which he was trying to recite for comfort, and thereupon promised God to serve Him if He would rescue the two of them from their plight. Dawn came; some travellers passed by, cut them free and led them back on to the road, and then, in reply to Lanfranc's question, directed them to the nearest monastery. This was Bec, a recent Benedictine foundation, strict and simple in its style, and here Lanfranc became a monk and three years later, in *c.*1044, prior. His reputation as a teacher of theology attracted students from all over Europe, so it is not surprising that his name came to the attention of the reigning Pope who, in 1059, summoned him to take part in a council which sought to implement a programme of reform, and particularly to condemn both simony and clerical marriage. But it was at this council that Lanfranc's former brief acquaintance with Berengar returned to bite him, and he was obliged to use his knowledge of the law and his forensic ability to distance himself from the heretic and ensure that he was not caught up in Berengar's inevitable condemnation and excommunication.

Lanfranc's first dealing with Guillaume, however, was not so felicitous. In 1053 Guillaume had married against the express orders of Pope Leo IX, and when he sent his chaplain to Lanfranc to try to win the prior over to his side, Lanfranc thought the priest so remarkably stupid that he presented him with a child's spelling-book. It was an act of tactless arrogance (or possibly a stupid joke), which alienated Duc Guillaume and produced an immediate instruction that Lanfranc leave the country. One of the monastery's farms was burned down, too, as a warning to the other monks not to presume above their station. We are told that Lanfranc and Guillaume met while Lanfranc was on his way out of Normandy, a story which may be true but sounds just a touch *ben trovato*. Still, the fact remains that the two men must have met at some point, and that Lanfranc must have thought better of his original support for Pope Leo's view of the duke's marriage, because the two men were certainly reconciled, and Lanfranc went to Rome, intending to ask the new Pope, Nicholas II, for a dispensation which would give canonical recognition to the union. Since the dispensation was granted, the duke continued his favour and appointed Lanfranc to be the first abbot of a new monastic foundation at Caen; and it was from here he was translated to Canterbury – much against his will – to be consecrated archbishop in a temporary wooden structure, the equivalent of a modern marquee, because the cathedral was in ruins after a disastrous fire.

We may discern two experiences which imprinted themselves on Lanfranc's character and helped to mould his actions as archbishop: his legal training, and his years as a Benedictine monk in a strict establishment. The latter obviously informed his revitalising English monastic life, gradually appointing capable Norman managers as abbots – a move not free from political considerations, of course – who set about huge building programmes which gave England the kind of spectacular religious houses more common in Normandy, and establishing monks at Durham, which turned into a model observant Benedictine community. (Lanfranc's own building programme began, as it had to do, with Canterbury itself, but extended also to restoration work at Rochester and St Albans). His legal training and interest can be seen in his introduction of canon law into England, and his provision for the celibacy of the clergy. Pope Gregory VII was eagerly promoting ecclesiastical reform all over Europe, and one of the changes he was keen to make was the adoption of a celibate priesthood which would be free to devote itself entirely to the functions of its office without the distractions of personal secular concerns, hereditary interests, acquisition of property, and so forth. Priests were now to disencumber themselves of their wives, and anyone coming forward for ordination would remain unmarried. Lanfranc tiptoed his way through the practical difficulties. Canons were to put away their wives at once, but parish priests already married would not be harried. Sooner or later they would be replaced with by celibate clergy. It was a compromise which a lawyer might argue was in conformity with the spirit of the Pope's requirements and therefore not disobedient to his wishes.

Nevertheless, however practical the solution, one cannot help wondering about that streak of arrogance in Lanfranc's character which flashed out in his dealing with Guillaume's unfortunate chaplain. When the English clergy met in synod, only bishops and abbots were to be permitted to speak freely. Is this because Lanfranc considered the parish clergy too stupid to be able to express their opinions, or even to have opinions worth consideration? Similarly, did he allow married parish priests to continue living with their wives because he thought them incapable of a higher discipline? Was his apparently understanding gesture in fact merely one of contempt? In 1070, the Archbishop of York had been chosen but not consecrated. Lanfranc took the opportunity to ask the candidate, Thomas of Bayeux, to give him a written guarantee that the see of York would acknowledge itself subordinate to the see of Canterbury and render the primus obedience – a request which Thomas refused. Lanfranc had blundered badly. Written professions of obedience to Canterbury from suffragan sees certainly existed, and there had been for some time a traditional acknowledgement by York of Canterbury's claim to primacy. But Lanfranc's attempt to get this put into legal form – hence the request for a document – suggests something rather more than a desire to unify the English Church under a single discipline for purely practical purposes. This is the essence of the argument he put forward to King Guillaume, who immediately saw the political danger in having a second equal and independent archbishopric in the north, which might choose at any point in the future to crown a rival king to the one in London. Thomas was therefore commanded to do as Lanfranc wanted and, faced by the king's threat to expel him from the country and his relations from Normandy if he refused, Thomas reluctantly gave in and was then consecrated.

But why was Lanfranc so overbearing and insistent? When he reported his actions to Pope Alexander II – a former pupil of his, and therefore someone he might expect to be sympathetic – the Pope refused to confirm Canterbury's primacy, almost certainly because he had his suspicions that Lanfranc was aiming at something more than an archbishopric: a patriarchate in the west. Neither Lanfranc nor Guillaume took notice of the Pope when it suited them not to do so. Guillaume asserted, for example, that Papal letters must not be received in England without his permission, and that any act of ecclesiastical legislation must have his approval before it could be put into operation; and he also refused to do homage to the Pope for his kingdom. As for Lanfranc, his attitude to Gregory is revealed in a letter, dated summer 1080, sent in reply to a complaint from the Pope that he seemed to have lost his respect for the Holy See. Amid protestations of gratitude for his elevation to the archbishopric, he introduces a qualification: 'My will submits to your instructions in all matters and in every respect *in conformity with the instructions of canon law*' (my italics). Guillaume's reservations about the Pope's ability to exercise actual, practical powers in the conduct of English secular life had either rubbed off on Lanfranc, or the two men were more or less of the same mind – that the king was of greater immediate importance in England than the Holy Pontiff. But it is also important to remember that, like Augustine, Lanfranc was a foreigner, initially at least somewhat reluctant to be exiled to England and live out the rest of his life among strangers, speaking a foreign tongue and coping with foreign customs; so a part of his assertiveness may therefore have stemmed from residual trepidation or even resentment.

The England to which he came was also in a somewhat peculiar state of transition. Guillaume, having become its king, was busy throughout his life imposing Norman ways upon an Anglo-Saxon populace; and while Lanfranc would have been familiar and, probably, more or less comfortable with that Normanising, the distance between the élite and the rest of the people was still immense – was Lanfranc able to communicate in English, for example? – and his foreignness would inevitably have reminded anyone who saw and heard him that he was yet another imposition from abroad. Does some such reaction to him lie behind the difficulties he had in getting some English monks to do as they were told? Even those under his own nose in Canterbury were fractious, rebelling against his orders that they attend Church synods to hear him preach, and refusing to accept a new abbot in 1087 because he had been appointed by Lanfranc and not elected by them. Lanfranc replied by giving them the choice of accepting the new abbot or leaving the monastery, whereupon most of the community left. Some came back later and submitted, others were sent to other religious houses and placed under strict discipline, some were imprisoned. A final attempt to rid themselves of the new abbot by murdering him resulted in Lanfranc's ordering the ringleader to be flogged in public and then driven out of the city. It had been a situation precipitated partly by Lanfranc's high-handedness, but one which he then handled with a combination of firmness and restraint. The restlessness of the community, however, sprang from many of its members, and from them alone, and one cannot help wondering how far it was exacerbated by the tacit complaint 'bloody foreigner!' echoing through their heads as they stood on their petty privileges, and sought to defy the perfectly reasonable instructions of their father in God.

Lanfranc died at Canterbury on 28 May 1089, at which time, says Florence of Worcester, there was a great earthquake throughout the whole country. He had been ill for several weeks and, according to William of Malmesbury, refused to take medicine until he had received communion. The medicine meanwhile turned rancid and, when Lanfranc eventually drank it, brought on his death more quickly – in simple terms, poisoned him – a sad fate which reminds one of Robert Herrick's lines on the doctor in his *Litany to the Holy Spirit*:

> When his potion and his pill
> has or none or little skill,
> meet for nothing but to kill,
> sweet Spirit, comfort me.

4

Who is the Greater Primate?

Anselm to Becket
(1093–1170)

If Lanfranc had been a most capable organiser of the English Church, laying down foundations which were to persist for centuries, his character missed those qualities needed for sanctity. Not that people did not feel his absence. The *Register* of Henry de Estria, Prior of Christ's Church in Canterbury, devotes a lengthy paragraph to describing Masses which were to be celebrated each year in his memory, and Ingulf, the abbot of the monastery of Croyland, who wrote a history of the Mercians and of his own religious house, lamented the death of someone he described as the only friend left to him, and recorded an epitaph written by one of his monks which called upon all the nations of the earth, but especially those of Italy and England, to bewail the loss of Lanfranc, 'the apostolic man'. But his successor, *Anselm* (1093–1109), is an interesting contrast. The office of archbishop lay vacant for four years while William II, according to Gervase of Canterbury, ravaged the Church in England and wallowed in every type of depraved and wicked behaviour; so when Anselm was called from Bec to Canterbury, one can easily understand his reluctance to undertake what may have appeared to be the unpleasant task of cleaning its Augean stables.

But Anselm's methods were not those of his illustrious predecessor. Contrast, for example, his relations with the monks of Canterbury. Where Lanfranc had sought to impose his will from a lofty Norman height, Anselm wooed by placating Anglo-Saxon sensibilities, a strategy which was not dictated by political calculation but by a genuine interest stemming from long conversations with one of Lanfranc's bugbears. Among the rebellious Canterbury monks Lanfranc sent to other houses for discipline was one Osbern. Lanfranc despatched him to the monastery of Bec where Anselm was abbot, and the two men seem to have taken to one another, Anselm learning from Osbern how high-handedly Lanfranc had treated Anglo-Saxon saints, removing their bodies to less exalted burial places or excising their names from the liturgy. So impressed was Anselm by Osbern's account that he actually persuaded Lanfranc to restore Archbishop Aelfeadh, regarded by the English as a martyr, to a place of honour in the cathedral and the liturgy. Thus it is scarcely surprising that when he became their archbishop, the monks of Canterbury gave Anselm their affections as well as their obedience.

Does this relationship tell us anything profound about his character? Frequent points of contrast between him and Lanfranc are illuminating. Both were born in Italy, both were of Lombard extraction, both left Italy (Anselm after an unhappy childhood in which he lost his mother early and suffered at the hands of his father), both made their way to Normandy and ended up at the monastery of Bec. It was there that they met. Anselm assisted Lanfranc in the school, and when Lanfranc left to become abbot of Caen, Anselm succeeded him as prior of Bec, now devoting himself particularly to the rigours of the contemplative life and to a spiritual quest for truth, conducted by means of constant questioning whose answers were meant to produce not merely answers, but proofs of those answers, which would make them irrefutable. It is thus interesting to see another factor in common between him and Lanfranc, and how that common starting-point sent them in different directions. Close scrutiny of a proposition requires forensic skill and both men were clearly good at it, Lanfranc by early training, Anselm by natural linguistic sensibility. But where Lanfranc applied his skill to the management of ecclesiastical affairs in the secular world, Anselm translated his into intense self-scrutiny and the more refined reaches of the moral theologian, a spiritual exercise which made him acutely aware of sin, especially his own grave sinfulness, and taught him to seek ways of redemption by prayer outwith as well as inside the Church's formal devotions. Out of these interior struggles came several books of meditations and theological speculation, the latter skirting the edges of acceptability – neither Lanfranc nor, later, St Thomas Aquinas liked what they read; but they also produced a man who clearly had the gift of talking to individuals and making them feel as though they were the absolute focus of his attention, and affecting them profoundly by what he said.

Needless to say, these personal qualities produced recollections of signs and wonders later on. Eadmer, one of Anselm's biographers, tells us that on one occasion he cured a young man of a sexual ailment merely by looking at him; on another, he exorcised demons in the form of wolves which were gripping a dying monk by the throat, 'and when he stretched out his hand to make the sign of the holy cross, [a witness] saw a flame of fire coming out of his mouth in the manner of a lance hurled at the wolves, which terrified them and drove them off: and they melted away in the midst of their rapid flight'. A monk called Riculfus saw Anselm one night, standing at prayer in the chapter house of the monastery, 'girded about with a huge ball of shining flame'; and a fisherman, ordered to catch enough fish for Anselm and his companions, threw his net into a river and immediately caught an unusually large trout – a wonder curiously reminiscent of one of Jesus's miracles (*Luke* 5.4-6). But all these had been presaged, as one might have expected of a future saint, by a vision Anselm had had when he was a boy. One night he saw himself climbing a high mountain into the presence of God, who thereupon fed him with bread which was radiantly bright and sleek and shining (*nitidissimus*).[1] So one is therefore not altogether surprised to find that Anselm's two principal theological works, *Monologion* and *Proslogion*, are devoted to demonstrating by logical argumentation the existence of God and the nature of the Trinity. They both generated criticism, fairly superficial from Lanfranc, to whom Anselm sent the *Monologion* before he released it to a copyist, intelligent from a monk, Gaunilo, whose critique of the *Proslogion* Anselm directed should be included, along with his known reply, in the 'published' version.

Anselm's lack of self-importance, as revealed by this last arrangement for the *Proslogion*, seems to have been typical of the man. Stories of his care for the sick (quite apart from any miraculous cures attendant on that concern) and his eagerness to instruct and assist the young help to confirm the impression that he was a man of genuine holiness of life and sweetness of disposition, without being on the one hand disconcerting, or on the other sickly-pious. But he was no administrator and found that essential part of his role as prior, then abbot, of Bec a trial and a distraction – not altogether a comforting omen for his time in the office of archbishop. 'Comfort', however, was scarcely what was being offered him when he attended William II in what the king thought might be his final illness, and found himself forced, quite literally, into the primatial seat. Eadmer tells us he resisted the appointment 'virtually to the point of losing consciousness', but that he was seized – *rapitur*, the verb is used of sacking a city or ravishing a virgin – and violently *carried* into the nearest church where he was consecrated without further delay. Such an appointment and investiture, of course, rendered his occupation of the archbishopric uncanonical, a consideration which weighed as little with William II as it would have done with his father. Sally Vaughn, however, regards Anselm's reluctance as little more than the kind of routine protestation which by now was traditional, almost a polite requirement, upon a person's elevation to high office. She points out that there is evidence to suggest that Lanfranc had actually been grooming Anselm to be his successor, and that Anselm's visits to England in 1079 and again in the autumn and winter of 1092–93 were used by Lanfranc to make Anselm increasingly familiar with the ecclesiastical affairs of England, and that Anselm could scarcely have been unaware of what Lanfranc had in mind.[2]

Was his expressed reluctance to become archbishop therefore akin to hypocrisy? Not necessarily. At some point, Anselm clearly became convinced that God intended him for that office; otherwise he undoubtedly would not have accepted it. But the violence of his refusal expressed two important points: first, his personal aversion to the wealth and worldly honour attendant upon the archbishopric, and secondly, his own genuine recognition that in certain respects he was not competent to hold it. If the position were forced on him, however, he could argue that he was no power behind the throne, as Lanfranc had been at the beginning of William II's reign, and that any inadequacies revealed during his tenure of the office should be excused, at least in part, because he had tried to warn people not to invest him. It is an explanation of his actions which perhaps makes him sound cynical and worldly, but there is really no good evidence that he was either. As Vaughn puts it, 'Anselm [was] functioning on two distinct levels of reality: the ideal level, where his actions perfectly reflect the due order of God's kingdom and the behaviour appropriate to a holy prelate, and the more disorderly level of everyday events'.[3]

One feature Anselm seems to have shared with Lanfranc is his attitude to the Papacy. The irregularity of his election and investiture should have been made good by the Pope, but Anselm failed to write to him about it and was happy to exercise archiepiscopal authority for nearly two years without having received his pallium, the symbol of that authority conferred by the Pope. Indeed, he made it clear in letters he wrote to some of the Irish bishops that they were obliged to offer him obedience as their archbishop, a tacit assumption of ecclesiastical superiority over the whole spread of English and English-held territories, an assumption extraordinary in view of his own possibly flawed title to office in the first place. The situation was exacerbated by the existence of an antipope, Clement III, whose claims had reduced the pontificate of Victor III to a shambles, and threatened to do the same for Urban II. By 1093, however, Urban managed to exert his proper authority, and Anselm should have been urging King William to recognise Urban as the legitimate pontiff and should himself have gone to Rome to be invested properly. The fact that he did neither suggests he had succumbed to the English king's view that in England the monarch could appoint ecclesiastics without necessary reference to Rome, a submissiveness to royal pretension symbolised by his doing William homage, an act specifically prohibited to ecclesiastics by Papal legislation.

What is more, Anselm appears to have developed a remarkably exalted view of his new position. Paschal II had succeeded Urban II in 1099, and two years later received a letter from Anselm in which the archbishop expressed a notion he had first put to Urban in 1098 or 1099, that the Archbishop of Canterbury was also, by virtue of his position, a Papal Legate. This status he now found, to his distress, had been transferred to the Archbishop of Vienne, and Anselm wanted it back.[4] Are there here faint echoes which would have sounded to the Pope's ears like a revival of a possible desire on the part of Canterbury to advance itself to a patriarchate? Henry I, who succeeded William as king, wrote an arrogant letter to Paschal, overtly offering him the honours and obedience he had had in England during King William's time (an offer in itself somewhat less than wholehearted), but adding that 'Your Holiness should be aware that as long as I am alive, with God's help the privileges and customs of the kingdom of England shall not be diminished'. The letter ended with a threat. The Pope should act with very great circumspection towards England, otherwise Henry would withdraw the kingdom's obedience from the Papacy.

This pride Anselm resisted, but only to a certain extent. Having collaborated, whether knowingly or tacitly, with Lanfranc and then

William II in becoming Archbishop of Canterbury, he had in effect supped with the Devil and his spoon had not been quite long enough. King William endlessly demanded money from the English Church and interfered in purely ecclesiastical affairs. The result was that Anselm went into voluntary exile in Rome from November 1097 until September 1100. On 2 August 1100, King William was killed and the new king sent messengers asking Anselm to come back to England. But the situation there had scarcely improved. King Henry continued, for example, to invest bishops and receive their homage, both acts, as I said, specifically forbidden by Papal decree, and Anselm made no objection. He busied himself with two ecclesiastical councils which dealt with a wide variety of business but left the sore points of regal investiture and episcopal homage unresolved, points which the king had taken up directly with the Pope and which Anselm, had he been as effective a politician as Lanfranc had been, should have dealt with himself, as matters of urgency.

In 1103, however, he was despatched to Rome as the king's man to put before the Pope the king's wishes for relaxation of the relevant Papal decrees in favour of royal pretensions. It was, in effect, a second exile and lasted from April 1103 until August 1106. Pope Paschal would not budge, so Anselm's journey was fruitless except for one tiny consolation: the primacy of Canterbury over the other English bishoprics was now confirmed *in perpetuum*. A somewhat hostile letter from the king (who had confiscated the archiepiscopal revenues of Canterbury to his own use) made Anselm pause before he returned to the frustration of political life in England. He was staying with the Archbishop of Lyon, where he was able to take up his pen once more to produce a definitive edition of his prayers and meditations for Matilda of Tuscany, whom he had met during an early stage of his return. It was all quite peaceful and agreeable, but then Anselm decided to take sides and chose to side with the Pope. The 'sides' involved the king's excommunication. Paschal had written to Henry three times already, in 1103, 1104 and 1105, announcing excommunications of certain of Henry's advisers, clearly a preliminary to the possible excommunication of Henry himself on the grounds of his constant misdeeds and confiscation of Church property. Since Henry was in Normandy in 1105, asserting his right to rule the dukedom, Anselm could reach him quickly and therefore set out from Lyon with the openly expressed intention of carrying out the Pope's threat. His journey was, of course, a feint. He could easily have excommunicated the king from Lyon, so his object in making the journey to the king's camp was to allow Henry time to reflect upon the course he was taking. Procrastination worked. The two men met at L'Aigle in southern Normandy; the king gave back Anselm his archiepiscopal revenues; the king and the Pope reached a compromise on the principal matter of contention between them. Henry would no longer nominate or invest bishops, but bishops would do him homage for their lands. This done, Anselm returned to Canterbury. But although he was able to preside over what appears to have been a somewhat ramshackle ecclesiastical council in May 1108, he was obviously a sick man and during the succeeding months grew increasingly feeble. His last major concern was to make sure that a new Archbishop of York should not be consecrated until he had acknowledged, in writing, the superior status of Canterbury – a worldly, not to say somewhat vainglorious, occupation which one hopes did not cloud his final hours.

Anselm died on 21 April 1109. There was the expected acclamation of sainthood, and various attempts were made, notably by St Thomas Becket, to have his canonisation confirmed in the universal Church. But nothing actually happened and so Anselm remains a saint by default, included among the Doctors of the Church by Benedict XIV in the mid-eighteenth century, which may count as a tacit acknowledgement of his elevation. The gentleness and compassion he is credited with showing towards the sick and the young in particular, and the intellectual acuity he brought to his theological speculations, must be accounted gifts of a high order. But there are also indications that he was not altogether removed from worldly affairs, and his complaisance over the pretensions of the English Crown to be master of its ecclesiastical as well as its secular house, and his preoccupation with Canterbury's primacy over York, while perfectly understandable in the context of twelfth-century England, sit uneasily alongside his miracles and his marvels and his prophecies, and introduce something of a sour note into the sweetness of his character.

Poor *Ralph d'Escures*, who followed him (1114–22), suffers, of course, by comparison. His time in office was dominated by his own bad health – he suffered an ulcer on the face in 1116 and a stroke in 1119 – and by the protracted wrangling about superiority and obedience between Canterbury and York which had embittered Anselm's last weeks and days. Thurstan, the Archbishop-elect of York, flatly refused to give a written guarantee of obedience to Canterbury, and Ralph refused to consecrate him until he did so. Thurstan had the support of three successive Popes – Paschal II, who was on poor terms with England anyway, Gelasius II and Calixtus II – partly, perhaps, because Ralph was always too ill to be able to go to Rome and plead his case, whereas Thurstan could and did go there. But in the end the matter was resolved by the highest authority. Pope Calixtus himself consecrated Thurstan and King Henry, filled with unjustifiable temper as was frequently his wont, forbade the new archbishop to enter England, and dispossessed him of his estates. Calixtus retorted by threatening Henry with an interdict, so Henry gave in and Thurstan came back in triumph.

It had not been a successful period for Canterbury, and the efforts of *William de Corbeil* (1123–36) to ride the storms of an English civil war and the reactions to his own attempts to reform the English Church were repaid by most chroniclers with unrestrained criticism. William, like Ralph, was French and, although a canon, was not a monk. This did him no good in the eyes of the monks of Christ Church who were always keen to see a monastic archbishop, since he would be better able to articulate their needs in the political community and safeguard the estates which had been given, and continued to accrue, to Christ Church. Like Anselm, he too had a vision when he was young. He was twice attacked by demons, he recalled in his own account to Alexander of Canterbury, but was rescued by the Virgin Mary and three archangels, an experience which much increased his religious devotion. His election to Canterbury was in the nature of a compromise. A council called for the purpose by Henry I was evenly divided, the bishops wanting one type of candidate, the monks of the Christ Church another, and after two days' wrangling they agreed on William. In effect, therefore, William would always have difficulties, because neither party to his elevation was entirely satisfied and would thus blame him for any of his subsequent actions they did not like; and sure enough, the disputes and discontents he had inherited from his immediate predecessors soon rose up to bite him.

The most obvious example is the tortuosity of the continuing claim by Canterbury to be superior to York. Because Thurstan of York refused to give him a written guarantee of obedience, he was not allowed to assist at William's consecration as archbishop. So both men went to Rome to complain to the Pope, Thurstan objecting that William's election had been uncanonical, and William presenting the Holy Father with a bundle of documents purporting to be Papal privileges, which had long conceded Canterbury's case for primacy. These papers were read in a full meeting of the Curia. Questions were asked. Did these documents have their Papal seals attached (otherwise they would not be valid)? No, apparently the English had left the originals at home and simply brought copies with them. Would the English swear they actually had the originals with the seals attached? This threw the English into confusion and they retired to consider. They agreed none of their documents had any seals attached, but one of the party urged the others to swear anyway. This they were unwilling to do. They were prepared, however, to say that the lead seals had either perished or been lost – at which the Curia was much amused. 'Some smiled', records Hugh the Chanter, 'some wrinkled their noses, others emitted a guffaw, mocking them and saying it was an extraordinary thing that lead should perish or be lost and parchment survive'. Did William know the documents were false? It is difficult to see how he could not have done, especially when his party then tried to bribe the Papal chamberlain to influence Pope Calixtus in their favour. The incident therefore suggests that William was a less than adroit politician, an impression which seems to be confirmed by his behaviour in the Stephen-Matilda crisis.

Henry I died in December 1135. Eight years previously, William had sworn, with the rest of the English political and religious establishment, to acknowledge Henry's daughter, Matilda, as heir to the throne. But when Henry died, Matilda was out of the country and her husband, Stephen, seized the opportunity to declare himself king in her stead. The establishment was split and William allowed himself to be persuaded to accept Stephen's *coup d'état* and crown him king. It was a piece of perjury which does him no credit and makes one ask oneself who was the person at Rome who suggested to the English that they forswear themselves over the existence or non-existence of the Papal seals. Still, against this, and the obvious prejudice of some of his monastic chroniclers, we should perhaps bear in mind the judgement of the Archbishop of York who, according to Hugh the Chanter, thought William 'a good cleric, and a straightforward,[5] fair man', although this could have been a diplomatic opinion, since it was offered to the Pope and was meant by Hugh to show York's generosity of spirit rather than provide any kind of compliment for Canterbury.

Theobald (1138–61), Abbot of Bec, was made archbishop by King Stephen, as the chronicler baldly puts it. This is, as we have seen, how the appointment usually happened, although by the fourteenth century the Pope was more frequently exerting his right to fill a vacancy or arbitrate when an election was disputed. In Theobald's case, King Stephen's swift insistence was dictated by what he saw as his brother Henry's ambition to become the most powerful man in England, and since Henry was already bishop of Winchester, a rich and important see, his elevation to Canterbury would have translated him into a position too potent for the king to stomach. Theobald thus began his period in office with a redoubtable enemy who had been rendered even more powerful by being created a Papal Legate. It was Henry's consolation for being deprived of Canterbury.

Theobald was a Norman of good family, perhaps related to St Thomas Becket's father, and entered upon the religious life somewhat late, when he was about twenty-seven, becoming abbot of his monastery (Bec) in June 1136. Two and a half years later he was

Archbishop of Canterbury, and set about imposing discipline on an English Church, and especially an English monastic community, which had lacked for too long the smack of firm government. The monks of Christ Church in particular were inclined to rebelliousness, but when Theobald tried to contain them by promoting his chaplain, Walter Parvus, to be their prior, he soon realised he had made a bad mistake. Walter was worse than useless. He was quite incapable of management and let the monastic estates run into such debt that the monks asked Theobald himself to take over the running of them. This he did and restored them to good order, only to have some of the monks accuse him of peculation. Now Theobald was the villain in their eyes, and they appealed to the Pope for redress – something which English monks were doing more and more, thereby attempting to bypass their legitimate English primate and undermine his authority.

In 1151 the envoys from Christ Church set out for Rome, but were stopped by Theobald's soldiers, arrested, and put in prison. Their written complaints were confiscated and the monks left to contemplate their unhappy position for eighteen days, after which Theobald let it be known that he was prepared to be clement and reasonable. Now that he had demonstrated his authority Walter Parvus should resign as prior, as a polite gesture to that authority, after which Theobald would reappoint him at once and everything would go back to normal. Walter was foolish enough to believe him. In a full chapter of the monastery, with the archbishop in the abbot's chair, Walter resigned his priorate and was told that, on the contrary, he was deposed. Ordered to follow Theobald to Lambeth (where he did not have any friendly monks on hand to support him), he was there arrested and taken to Gloucester, whose abbot received instructions to keep him prisoner. It was an authoritarian display worthy of Lanfranc, although the deviousness attendant upon it perhaps belongs especially to Theobald. Canterbury had acquired both a master and a politician, and it is notable that Theobald was prepared to brook no nonsense where obedience to his authority was concerned. When the prior and sacrist of St Augustine's in Canterbury refused to observe an interdict placed on England by

Pope Eugenius III in 1149, for example, Theobald had them excommunicated and then publicly flogged. All in all, therefore, the man who had entered on his archbishopric as a relatively obscure French monk was turning out to be the formidable governor the English Church needed during this time of what was effectively civil war.

He was faced by Bishop Henry, however, who was equally determined to carve out for himself an archiepiscopate based on the west of England. Fortunately for Theobald, Pope Eugenius disliked Henry and therefore thwarted his ambition; but in 1141 Henry took advantage of King Stephen's capture by forces loyal to Matilda and swore fealty to her in return for her appointing him her chief adviser. Theobald, ever practical, also offered his services to Matilda in spite of his sworn obligations to Stephen – although he was acute enough to protect himself against repercussions should Stephen return to power, by visiting Stephen in prison and asking his permission to perjure himself. Sure enough, given the turns of war and fortune, Stephen was restored in December that same year, and Theobald apparently suffered no immediate diminution of his influence with the king. But Stephen was not altogether forgiving. When Theobald wanted to attend a council called by Pope Eugenius at Rheims in 1148, for example, Stephen refused to let him go, probably because he was suspicious of English ecclesiastics' frequent toing and froing between England and Rome, which meant that the Pope was exercising more direct control over the English Church than the king felt was comfortable. The two men also had their political differences. In 1152, Stephen wanted to have his heir, Eustace, crowned king while he himself was still alive – a device to ensure a smooth succession, understandable in view of the civil war which had shadowed his footsteps throughout his reign. But Pope Eugenius and Theobald would not co-operate and it was only Eustace's death which broke the impasse. The heir was now Matilda's son, and Theobald brokered a deal which had Stephen recognise the young Henry as his heir and associate ruler, but which did not involve his coronation during Stephen's lifetime. Once again, then, the archbishop had shown himself to be singularly adroit.

He lived long enough to crown Henry II and to see three more pontiffs in Rome: Anastasius IV, Hadrian IV and Alexander III, the last of whom had to withstand a whole series of counter-claims to the Fisherman's ring from as many as four antipopes. But in persuading King Henry to recognise Alexander as Pope, rather than a certain 'Victor', Theobald had come to the end of his strength. He died in Canterbury on 18 April 1161. One of his most notable successes was entirely personal. When he became archbishop, he created a quite remarkably distinguished household about himself, consisting partly of his own family and partly of learned clerics with a European-wide reputation, of whom perhaps John of Salisbury would prove to be the most famous, and St Thomas Becket the most illustrious. But it was as a politician rather than as a patron that Theobald made his more immediate mark on the English Church. He had fought for Canterbury's supremacy over all other British bishops ('British' because we must include Welsh, Irish and a number of Scottish bishops, too); had weathered his rivalry with Henry, Bishop of Winchester; survived the civil war; and imposed a fairly strict discipline over the English monastic body, this last being so disgruntled, self-obsessed and pettish that had he done no more than bring it to heel, he would have done the English Church a major service.

Theobald's reputation, however, has been quite overshadowed by that of his successor, *St Thomas Becket* (1162–70). Becket is the first Archbishop of Canterbury it is possible to describe in any detail. A composite portrait, put together from English chroniclers and a late thirteenth-century Icelandic saga, has him over six feet tall, slim, good-looking, with an aquiline nose, charming in conversation, perhaps with a slight stammer or hesitation, an acute intelligence, and a remarkable memory. The last two enabled him to learn quickly and retain what he had learned, both essential to his advancement, since his initial, formal education was somewhat poor.

Becket's history is very well known, and there is no point in repeating much of it here. He was born in London of Norman parents and began his working life as a clerk in a banking office before being introduced into Archbishop Theobald's household in

1145, where he could find plenty of stimulus to improve the state of his learning and to acquire the graceful manners of a courtier. Nine years later, he was appointed archdeacon of York, a position which gave him several benefices and set him up as a fairly wealthy man. English politics being what they were at the time – volatile, but filled with opportunities for anyone acute enough to take advantage – the same year (1154) saw him acting as Henry II's Chancellor and constant companion, an association which made him very rich indeed and also gave him almost limitless experience of the young king's notorious autocratic and anticlerical disposition. It was Henry's misunderstanding of Becket's character which led him in 1161–62 to push for Becket's elevation to Canterbury. Becket was, at bottom, as autocratic as Henry himself, and so far his tendencies had been content to run alongside those of the king. Were they to diverge, however, an irreconcilable clash between the two men would be inevitable.

Becket was not really suited to be archbishop. He had little if any calling to the priesthood (it was not until 2 June 1162, after his appointment to the archbishopric, that he was ordained); the monks of Christ Church were opposed to his election; other, better-qualified candidates were available; and the appointment was too obviously one which declared that Becket was Henry's man, not to say puppet, and that the principal religious office in England belonged to the Crown. But Henry's will prevailed and Becket was consecrated the day after his ordination as a priest. He did not slip into his new life immediately, although William of Canterbury gives the impression that he was transformed almost at once and 'put on the monastic habit with the hairshirt', an impression and a phraseology repeated by John of Salisbury. That there was a transformation, however, is undeniable, and it seems to have happened when he received his pallium at a ceremony in Canterbury Cathedral on 10 August 1162. Before it was placed round his shoulders, he took the usual oath which bound him to the Papacy, an oath which made him, in effect, the Church's man, not the king's; and it was probably at this moment he decided to resign his office of Chancellor and devote himself wholly to his ecclesiastical office.

The resignation sent a signal to the king, of course, and should have warned him that his plan for Becket was not going to work as smoothly as he had supposed. Combining these two great offices of state should have made the king complete master in his own realm and given him (if only in his own eyes) a status equal to that of the Holy Roman Emperor, who also had an archbishop as his Chancellor. Becket's undermining this piece of vanity had the effect one might have anticipated. He and the king began to clash over the rights and privileges of the Church, especially those involving money or legal jurisdiction, with Becket determined not to concede an inch to lay pretension, even if, in the calm light of moral reflection, some of the ecclesiastical practices he was defending were not really worth his effort. But a principle is a principle, and once he gave way to Henry's egocentric arrogance he would lay the Church open not only to financial depredation but also to legal control by the state, thereby turning Henry into a latter-day Byzantine Emperor. Faced by Becket's intransigent opposition, Henry had no hesitation in becoming vindictive and, after depriving Becket of everything he had granted him while Becket was still Chancellor, set about trying to boost the status of the Archbishop of York so that he could use him, if necessary, as the alternative source of ecclesiastical jurisdiction in England.

In January 1164 there was a patched reconciliation of a sort. Actually, Henry had outmanoeuvred Becket over the central question of whether English clerics should be tried in ecclesiastical or secular courts for crimes which were essentially secular rather than ecclesiastical, and much to his chagrin Becket found that he and the rest of the bishops had, in effect, conceded the king's point that criminous clerics be tried in a secular court. So the reconciliation, if such it can be called, was entirely one-sided, and Becket began actively to consider seeking asylum in France, an impulse which turned into reality before the end of the year when Henry had him charged with embezzlement of royal revenues during his Chancellorship. In early November, Becket fled to France, appealing to the Pope for support and justification. The Pope, however, offered little comfort, in spite of the fact that much of what Becket was saying to him about Henry's trampling on canon law was perfectly accurate. So, with Alexander's permission, Becket retired, first to a Cistercian abbey in Pontigny, and then to the Benedictine abbey of St Columba not far from Sens, where he remained until 1170 when, after a series of attempts largely engineered by the Pope to end the feud between them, Becket and Henry at last agreed to exchange a kiss of peace, and Becket was thereby enabled to return to England in the November of that year.

His behaviour during this prolonged French exile was a distinctive mixture of the imperious and the humble. Edward Grim, who was present at Becket's murder and attempted to shield the archbishop from the swords of his assailants, later wrote a biography of the murdered man, in which he included details of Becket's life at Pontigny, details he must have got (since he is generally regarded as a sincere and careful biographer, not a fantasist) from one of Becket's household. The archbishop quietly restricted his diet to simple food and passed on delicacies from his table to the sick and poor; and he would immerse himself for long hours in the freezing, rushing water of a stream in an effort to rid himself of sexual thoughts. This last is one with the mortifications we are told he practised in Canterbury, the use of penitential whipping being a notable example. He wore a hairshirt which reached down to his knees and, as Walter Fitzstephen tells us, was crawling with maggots, ate very little food, and usually drank water in which fennel had been boiled.[6] None of these practices was at all unusual by the standards of the twelfth century. One has to turn to much earlier centuries to find saints practising far greater austerities, such as the fifth-century Simeon Stylites who spent years standing atop a pillar, or to the later fourteenth-century St Catharine of Siena, who once drank a bowl of pus in a hospital to teach herself not to be so dainty. By comparison, therefore, Becket's behaviour was scarcely exaggerated, and in consequence there is no call for us to exercise undue suspicion over the sources of this information. It is true that they were writing *post eventum* and thus intended to paint their subject with the lineaments appropriate to a saint; but the accumulation of miracles was much more important evidence of his sanctity, and the very fact that Becket's biographers have not chosen to credit him with any extraordinary acts of penitence or durance suggests that what they report of his personal austerities may well be true.

That said, however, can we acquit him of hypocrisy? During his period in England as archbishop, as well as during his long exile, he had no hesitation in striking out against those who opposed his will. In England his principal target was the king; in France, on a single day, he excommunicated ten individuals, including the bishops of London and Salisbury, and since the bishop of London, Gilbert Foliot, had always been contemptuously dismissive of Becket, this act could scarcely help looking spiteful in return. Again, King Henry wanted to crown his son king in his own lifetime and pressed ahead on 14 June 1170, using the Archbishop of York to do his bidding in Becket's absence. Immediately, Becket sought to move against the bishops involved, but not against the king who had thus knowingly ridden roughshod over one of Canterbury's most valued privileges. What was Becket trying to defend by these various fulminations against and excommunications of his clergy? The language he used in his letters to the people involved is violent and bitter and personal. Would he have ventured thus far in rebuking the king himself? The difference in behaviour is understandably politic, but does it sit well with someone whose private life is filled with austerities, and who is granted at least one vision of his own murder? There is a disjunction between the public man and the private which appears to be somewhat too great for comfort, as though the more exalted Christian virtue at which his austerities were intended to help him aim simply did not grow big enough or strong enough to master his pride and steel him to face down his secular superior as well as his ecclesiastical subordinates.

But is this actually evidence of hypocrisy? Perhaps we should consider that question in the light of his murder. Becket and Henry met at Fréteval in Touraine on 21 July 1170. There they papered over their differences and Becket was able to return to England. But Becket's relations with the king, fragile as they were, were further undermined by letters from Pope Alexander, suspending the bishops who had taken part in the young prince's coronation, excommunicating the bishops of London and Salisbury, and complaining about King Henry's crimes against the Church. Several English bishops were in revolt against Becket's authority as archbishop. So Becket's arrival in Canterbury was fraught with peril, although he was received politely by the monks and enthusiastically by the people even though he did not hesitate to set about disciplining those monks and secular individuals he considered had despoiled in any way the rights of the Church or stirred up discord between himself and the Crown. King Henry was still in France, and it was there he spoke the words which seemed to suggest to four of his knights that the royal honour had been violated and needed to be avenged. On 28 December they invaded Becket's presence and began to harangue him. Becket replied in kind and was then rushed by some of his household into the asylum afforded by the cathedral. Sanctuary, however, did not protect him, and in the evening of that same day, not long after Vespers, he was struck down and murdered. His death had not been quiet. The four knights had engaged him yet again in controversial demands and once again he had replied in similar angry terms. It was not until he collapsed under the first sword-blow that Becket ceased to wrangle and uttered a brief prayer, commending his soul to God.

It was no time at all before Becket was proclaimed locally as a martyr, and his cult, which was to grow immensely during the succeeding decades and then centuries, turned into a major reason for pilgrimage, drawing the devout from all over Europe to Canterbury. An anonymous curse expressed the immediate horror people felt at his sacrilegious assassination.

Woe to you, savage land of the English, spiteful region! When the world's disasters have been recalled, may you have a rapid death! Why do you destroy so many people, land which abounds in evils? Why do you slit the throats of saints, [land] hateful to the eyes of the gods? No law is acceptable to you. A futile departure from moral principles holds you prisoner. Your praise lies dumb, snuffed out by [your] sacrilegious deeds. Why do you rage against the gods? Alas, you cut down gentle people in a crime which cannot be pardoned. Canterbury weeps at a death of this kind.[7]

Fuelled by emotions similar to these, petitions soon cascaded into Rome, asking for Becket's formal canonisation. It is noticeable that none came from the English bishops. Death, hostility, Papal censure and partiality towards the king meant that Becket's reputation as a saint was left in the hands of certain cardinals, monks from Canterbury, and the English commonalty, and if their motives were mixed, the result was not in doubt. Miracles proliferated, pilgrims descended in droves, and Pope Alexander declared the archbishop a saint. As far as official recognition of Becket's sanctity is concerned, therefore, there is no room for further question. *Roma locuta est*, and this takes care of the hypocrisy which some people have claimed to detect in Becket's conduct during his exile. Saints are not perfect. They are ordinary human beings who exhibited greater than expected virtue while they were alive, and have had their essential sanctity confirmed by signs and miracles after their death.

The most notable fact about Becket – apart from his death – is that he held both the highest secular position (apart from the Crown) and the highest ecclesiastical office in England, and devoted himself wholeheartedly to each. The attractions of the secular life once tasted proved a perpetual source of seduction, and yet once he became archbishop he fought against them heroically in his private life. His election to that office opened the door to a kind of conversion and, as is well known, converts are often more emotionally charged by their new faith than those who were born into it. Something of such an emotional charge can be seen in Becket's often ill-judged defence of the rights of the Church over the demands of a secular monarch; and if his defence was often accompanied by actions which sometimes bore more than a trace of hot temper or personal dislike, his courage in the face of the fury roused by this essentially principled stand cannot be faulted.[8] But did he die – and embrace a death he clearly foresaw – merely to safeguard certain aspects of canon law, or to prevent Church lands from being pillaged or confiscated by the English king? Scarcely so. Different writers have expressed it in different ways, but their conclusions are in agreement: 'In dying for the claims of the *sacerdotium* as he understood them, he witnessed to another dimension of human experience, and kept alive an ideal of Christian society... Archbishop Thomas, at that particular moment, and in the largely accidental circumstances that brought about his murder, died for the freedom of the spiritual authority of the Church, and he died declaring that he knew this and was willing to meet death in this cause'.[9] A martyr, then, as well as a saint: just as the English people claimed on his behalf.

5

Saints, Scholars and Violence

Richard of Dover to Pecham
(1174–1292)

After the tempest, storms. One might have thought that so dramatic had been the relations between the Church and the English state, a period of calm would have been welcome. But that was not King Henry's way, nor, indeed, the way of his young son, who quickly embarked on a series of rebellious acts against his father. It took until 1173 for the immediate turmoil of St Thomas's murder to begin to settle and proposals for a new archbishop to come to the surface, and when they did, there was little but dissent. King Henry cast around for a suitable quiescent Norman; the

monks of Canterbury pushed forward their prior; the bishops, led
by the contumelious Foliot, Bishop of London, favoured *Richard
of Dover* (1174–84), a Benedictine monk and prior of St Martin's
monastery in Dover, whose social and intellectual obscurity held out
the promise of Church and state going their separate ways without
any overt threat of confrontation. Needless to say, young Henry
objected at once on the grounds that he had not been consulted,
and that Richard's election (along with that of four other episcopal
elections at which he demurred) was uncanonical. As usual, therefore,
appeals were made to Rome and Pope Alexander, brushing aside
these frivolities, consecrated the new archbishop himself, gave him
his pallium, confirmed the primacy of Canterbury within England,
and appointed Richard a Papal Legate into the bargain.

Richard, unlike many of his predecessors, was intimately acquainted
with Christ Church, since that was where he had become a monk
and St Martin's at Dover was a dependency of that religious house.
He had four main problems to deal with during his period in office.
One was the restoration of the choir of the cathedral, which had
been destroyed in September 1174 by a great fire caused by sparks
from a burning thatch in a nearby street. A second was the rapidly
burgeoning cult of St Thomas, which needed a grander shrine and
a bigger space to accommodate the flood of pilgrims who were
beginning to come from all over Europe; and for this purpose a large
new chapel, dedicated to the Trinity, was begun at the eastern end
of the cathedral in 1175. A third was his relationship with Henry II
in particular. This was the man publicly condemned as St Thomas's
murderer and someone known to have arrogant pretensions towards
Church lands, Church revenues and Church appointments. Yet
Richard acquiesced in Henry's deposing the abbot of Peterborough
and appointing abbots and bishops, and kept company with the king
far more frequently than duty required. Contemporaries thought
him weak and pliable – but why else would Henry have agreed to
his election? – and one anonymous comment damns him as 'unworthy of the name of archbishop, both in word and deed'. William of
Newburgh dismissed him as a man 'only moderately well-educated,
but praiseworthily inoffensive', adding that he avoided becoming

involved in matters which would be beyond his capacity, and was thus prudent enough to stick to those he knew he could handle.[1] Even Gervase of Canterbury could find little more to say other than that Richard was a man of good character, and that he was courteous, which created a good impression.

Nevertheless, like many before and since, Richard was acutely aware of what was due to his position. Gervase of Canterbury and William of Newburgh describe what appears to us a ludicrous scene at a council held in Westminster in 1176, to which the Archbishops of Canterbury and York were both summoned by the Papal Legate, Hugo of St Angelo. York arrived early and sat down in the principal seat, whereat Canterbury, once arrived, took serious offence, and the attendants of both clerics entered upon a brawl which had the Archbishop of York turfed out of his seat and a part of his clothing torn. Needless to say, both men threatened to appeal to the Pope for redress. This leads us to Richard's fourth problem, which stemmed from one of the bitterest points of dispute between St Thomas and King Henry, the relationship between canon and secular legal jurisdictions. Canon law was not an unchanging monolithic given. Controversy and dispute constantly battered against its sides, producing change and modification over the centuries. But during the eleventh and twelfth centuries in particular there emerged the basic principle of the judicial supremacy of Rome, with the power of dispensation (that is, the means whereby such legal conflicts could be resolved) invested in the Pope alone. This position was enshrined in the law-book used by everyone throughout Europe from the mid-twelfth century onwards, the *Decretum* of Gratian of Bologna; and the generally acknowledged supremacy of Rome explains why English bishops, archbishops, monarchs and indeed lesser individuals kept appealing to the Pope in cases of legal disagreement. It was a system which had its strengths and weaknesses. On the one hand, it supplied a source of authority which no one could easily gainsay, and the existence of specific legal procedures and the need for written decisions encouraged parallel developments in the secular judicial systems of Europe; on the other, it allowed frivolous appeals to flourish, because if anyone did not like a local decision, he could appeal to

Rome and be safe in the knowledge that for a good twelve months he would be beyond the reach of the ecclesiastical superior who had delivered the judgement to which he was objecting.[2] Now, Richard of Dover may not have been much of a canonist himself, but he did create an archiepiscopal household of highly reputable experts in canon law, and saw to it that Papal jurisdiction in England was both received and enforced. His obedient enthusiasm therefore allowed a flowering of the study of canon law in England, and the growth of written legal compilations of Papal decisions, which had an influence beyond the shores of England. His time in office may thus be regarded as worthwhile in this particular regard, whatever else may be said of his suitability for the task he had been given.

His successor, *Baldwin* (1184–90), was both more learned and more tactless. Giraldus Cambrensis, who knew him quite well and accompanied him on a preaching mission to Wales, describes him as a man of dark complexion, serious face, medium height, and inclined to be rather skinny. He spoke little, and it took a great deal to make him angry. Well-educated – we know he studied law in Bologna – he was appointed archdeacon of Totnes in 1162 before resigning the post to become a Cistercian monk in *c.*1170. His deep spirituality shines through his several theological works and sermons, and his zeal for the Christian faith pressed him into taking the cross as a crusader in 1185, preaching the Third Crusade in Wales during the spring of 1188, and finally setting off for the Holy Land in March 1190, only to die at Acre in November –'of sickness', according to Gervase of Canterbury. On the negative side, he indulged in a protracted and bitter struggle with the monks of Christ Church because he wanted to found and build a new collegiate church dedicated to St Thomas Becket at Hackington, not far from Canterbury, a proposal the monks feared would divert pilgrims and funds and prestige from their own establishment. They wrote to everyone they thought might listen and at last their persistence won. The Benedictines had thus seen off the Cistercians, although it would be too crude to view the quarrel in these simple terms. But Baldwin's method of expressing his spirituality was not the same as theirs, and he actually spent very little time in Canterbury; so if temperaments did grate, they did not have much chance to smooth each other's rough edges, since they scarcely came into contact while Baldwin was archbishop.

It is also disappointing to see that, in spite of his personal worthiness, Baldwin was trapped by his office into asserting the supremacy of Canterbury yet again, this time over the Welsh. It is perhaps difficult to put one's finger on the exact cause, but there is something unsatisfactory about the man, something Pope Urban III also noticed, since he is said to have addressed a letter to him as 'Most fervent monk, warm abbot, tepid bishop, and slack archbishop', a diminuendo which must have read more uncomfortably than we may realise, because *remissus* may mean not only 'slack' or 'casual', but also 'deceitful',[3] and perhaps we should understand this to be a reference not to any mendaciousness on Baldwin's part, but to the Pope's realisation that there was less to this learned, devout man than met the eye.

Unlike Baldwin, *Hubert Walter* (1193–1205) survived his crusading adventure. Not a man with much formal education, he had become adept in the law through long experience and seems to have been a natural administrator. In 1189 Baldwin consecrated him bishop of Salisbury, and the following year saw him with the crusading army which was besieging Acre. Here Bishop Walter not only fought with the troops; he reorganised the army's logistics and tended to everyone's spiritual needs, with the result that when Richard I arrived in June 1191, the army's morale had soared. During the next two years, Walter had many opportunities to display his personal courage and his gift for diplomacy, the latter culminating in a negotiated agreement with Saladin, the Saracens' leader, which permitted, among other things, free access to Jerusalem for Christians – an access of which Walter availed himself at once – and the preliminary bargaining for King Richard's release from captivity in 1193 (Richard having been taken prisoner on his way home by Leopold of Austria). Richard's gratitude for these efforts resulted in Walter's being elected and consecrated Archbishop of Canterbury in that same year. The absent king also appointed Walter his justiciar, and it was this role which characterised his period in archiepiscopal office. England had suffered chaos during the regency of Richard's brother John, and the efficient administration of justice was now essential for everyone's benefit. This Walter restored, partly by sending justices through every shire with a particular view to bringing order out of the mess into which finances and landownership everywhere had fallen during Richard's absence; partly by introducing a new system of recording and managing financial arrangements between English Christians and Jews; and partly by encouraging the development of highly specialised courts of justice to deal with specific matters, such as legal cases involving Jews.

To all intents and purposes, then, Walter was acting as King Richard's deputy, and when Richard died in 1199, King John recognised Walter's pivotal role in English government by appointing him Chancellor. The title may have been different, but the process of administration remained the same, and until the very end of his life Walter was a whirlwind of efficiency, improving, negotiating, instituting, supervising, demanding, investigating, recording, in what must have seemed at times a frenzy of management. It is interesting to note the difference in vocabulary used by Giraldus Cambrensis in his descriptions of Baldwin and Walter. Baldwin, he says, was distinguished by 'an innate apathy and lethargy', whereas Walter was conspicuous for 'his vitality and energy'. The contrast must have been startling to contemporaries. So too would have been their style of living. Walter, as Gervase of Canterbury points out, was lavish almost to a fault. 'He was so bountiful, generous, and munificent in the entertainment of his guests and of the poor that what he possessed seemed to belong to everyone'. But was he a religious man? He was certainly charitable and appears, in spite of the extraordinary lavishness with which he chose to live, a man without personal vanity. We are told, for example, that he was so struck by the exemplary conduct of a Carthusian monk in Witham that he went to the monk's cell, confessed his sins, and allowed himself to be whipped as part of his penance; and while sometimes embarrassed by his lack of formal education, he happily assembled an archiepiscopal household of talented men and allowed them a free hand to fulfil their offices. In sum, as Charles Young observes, 'Hubert's career… provides an indication that able men who rose to prominent positions might do so as the result of demonstrated ability and not as a matter of mere whim or favouritism on the part of a powerful ruler'.[4]

Walter died on 13 July 1205 and was succeeded by *Stephen Langton* (1206–28), about whom remarkably little is certain until his elevation to the cardinalate by Pope Innocent III in 1206. If Walter reminds us in certain ways of Lanfranc, Langton is perhaps closer to Anselm. He was a scholar and a theologian, producing several commentaries on the Old and New Testaments, many of which bear the mark of his studies in the schools of Paris, and a very large number of sermons. The latter are enlivened for his audience by all kinds of anecdotes, similes and references to everyday life, which will have been familiar and sharply pointed the lesson he wished to teach. 'In a ship, the prow and stern are narrow, and the keel is wide. The beginning of life is narrow, the end of it likewise… The middle of life is wider. At this point a person is physically strong, and just as all the cargo is in the middle of the ship, so a person bears his or her burden in the middle of life'. Over and over again, too, in the manuscripts, we find phrases such as *vulgariter dicitur, vulgo dicitur, usu vulgari*, 'it is said in the vernacular', 'it is said in common parlance', 'the usual vernacular expression is', showing that he was mindful of how unlearned listeners thought and spoke, and was keen to draw into his essentially learned discourse such illustrations as might illuminate his point by turning his clerical audience's eyes outwards, if only briefly, from the study to the marketplace. 'If someone wants to make his way safely through the kingdom of France and carries the king's seal with him, he will be safe anywhere in the kingdom. But suppose he were to throw away that seal and take some nobody's seal instead – he'd be regarded as a lunatic, wouldn't he? So how much more of a lunatic is someone who throws away the seal of the everlasting King and takes the seal of the Devil'. As Langton observed elsewhere, 'an illustrative anecdote [*exemplum*] is very often more effective than a polished, subtle phrase'.

Langton's life in France saw him a teacher as well as a student, and when one of his Paris acquaintance, Lotario di Segni, became Pope Innocent III in 1198, his reputation as a Biblical scholar induced

Innocent to send for him and create him cardinal. He was about fifty-one and had spent more than thirty years in France. Almost immediately his troubles began. Hubert Walter had died the previous year and, almost needless to say, the election of his successor was disputed. The monks of Christ Church chose their sub-prior, Reginald, but the election was irregular and the king objected, so they elected the bishop of Norwich instead. Both candidates then made their way to Rome but, for reasons which are not in the least clear, found themselves disregarded in favour of Langton who was elected by a deputation of Canterbury monks – their third candidate in less than six months – in the presence of the Pope himself. This election proved valid, and Langton was consecrated archbishop the following June in Viterbo.

Langton was in difficulties partly because the decade in which he attained this elevation saw the start of a turbulent period both in Europe and in England, partly because King John refused to accept as archbishop someone he regarded as a friend of his enemies – Normandy had been lost to the English Crown only a few years previously and the French kings were now John's rivals, not his associates – and partly because his long residence abroad meant he was unfamiliar with England and the English. From 1207 to 1213, Langton was unable to set foot in England, and interdict was pronounced against England and Wales on 23 March 1208, which meant that all sacramental life and ecclesiastical administration ceased, and King John was personally excommunicated in 1209 and in January 1213 threatened by the Pope with deposition. Recognition of Langton as archbishop was not, of course, the entire reason for this ever-deepening crisis. John saw the argument as essentially one of authority. Who was to be supreme in England, the king or the Pope? In 1213 he got his answer. In June or July that year, Langton landed at Dover to be greeted by King John who threw himself at Langton's feet and begged for forgiveness and absolution. It was a demonstration on a parochial scale of Papal supremacy which had been exhibited on a much wider, grander stage 136 years earlier when the Holy Roman Emperor had been forced to humble himself in the winter snows of Canossa at the feet of Pope Gregory VII.

One major reason for John's caving in to the Pope's demands was that he feared the English barons would seize upon England's dire situation and unite to oppose him, or even get rid of him. The huge increase in taxation under Richard I, made essential because of his crusading, his ransom, and a subsequent war with France, made the English nobility restless, and many of their number were beginning to refuse their duty to the king unless he would guarantee, in writing, their rights and privileges. The period of the interdict made matters much worse, so there came a point at which the barons and the king would have to enter into negotiations; and as negotiations require a mediator, the Archbishop of Canterbury seemed to be the man appropriate for the task. The exact extent of his contribution to Magna Carta (1215) is open to discussion, but its very first clause grants freedom to the English Church, and this may have been included and put at the head of the document by reason of his influence. But whatever peace ensued from King John's acceptance of the charter broke down very quickly, and a letter from Pope Innocent (written without exact knowledge of what was going on in England) made the situation worse. The Pope ordered Langton to restore order and to excommunicate anyone who continued to disturb either king or kingdom, and threatened both Langton and his bishops with suspension if they failed to make the Papal instructions public, a threat which was turned into reality by the bishop of Winchester, who suspended Langton just as the archbishop was leaving for Rome to attend the Fourth Lateran Council, on the grounds he had failed to excommunicate recent rebels against the king. Rome provided no comfort. Pope Innocent confirmed the suspension, and Langton was left in obscurity until a new Pope, Honorius III, allowed him to return to England in 1218.

He must have been restored to office because, once arrived, he began to exercise himself as archbishop, not an easy task, because John's successor, Henry III, was not yet of age and power lay in the hands of a triumvirate which included the bishop of Winchester, who had originally subjected Langton to suspension. But Langton crowned the king (Henry's second coronation) in 1220 and in July that year oversaw the translation of St Thomas Becket's relics to a new shrine in Canterbury, perhaps his greatest monument, and for the next few years, until 1227, resumed a major role in the politics of the royal Court and the implementation of the decrees of the Fourth Lateran Council in the whole of the kingdom. By 1128 he was in his early seventies and clearly failing. He died on 7 July and was buried in the south-west transept of the cathedral, in the chapel of St Michael, before the altar. His reputation has suffered over the years, partly from changing fashions in historical interest, partly because the enormous mass of his writings has still not received due scholarly attention. Frederick Powicke, who more than anyone else was responsible for a revival of interest in Langton the churchman rather than Langton the politician, summed up his impression as follows: 'I have tried to describe a great man, with a clear, sensible, penetrating, but not original mind, at work in a time more important, more critical, more full of opportunity, than any other period in the history of the Mediaeval Church'[5] – a judgement which, apart from its unhappy latent anglocentrism, may be allowed to stand as just and equitable.

We now enter upon a series of archbishops whose relations with King Henry III were not of the easiest. Two of them were saints, but not *Richard Grant* (1229–31), so called because he was *grand*, that is, 'of a large build', who produced one or two curious echoes of Stephen Langton. He too had studied and taught in Paris; his election as archbishop was also imposed on the monks of Canterbury who had tried to have one of their own appointed; and he too clashed with the king over royal taxation of ecclesiastics, on the grounds that secular authority had no right to extend that far. Grievances multiplied and Grant not only appealed to Rome but went there in person in spring 1231 to plead his case before the Pope. Whatever success attended this enterprise, however, was undermined by his sudden death on 3 August, about whose immediate aftermath Matthew Paris relates the following: 'While the dead man's body was waiting for burial, clad in full pontificals according to custom, [some of] the locals who had cast an envious eye over all these things came at night and opened the tomb, wanting to steal his ring and other episcopal insignia. But no force or ingenuity enabled them to do so; and since they had no forewarning that this would happen, they did not know how to accomplish their design. They retired in confusion and struck their chests in which their criminal hearts were lying hidden'.[6]

Edmund of Abingdon, sometimes known as Edmund Rich (1234–40), was a saint, canonised only six years after his death by Pope Innocent IV. In the hagiography written by Matthew Paris, we learn that he was brought up by his mother to be ascetic and devout, and that at the age of twelve – significant, perhaps, because it was at this age Jesus began to teach in the Temple – he made a vow of celibacy, wedding himself to the Virgin Mary by placing a ring on a finger of her statue in the local church, a ring which could not then be removed. Then after a period of study in Paris, and once he had gained his degree of Master of Arts, he began teaching in the university. While a student in Oxford, Edmund had a vision of Christ in the meadows just beyond the town. It was daytime at midsummer, and when Edmund's companions joined him, they saw a dazzling light but not the figure of Jesus in the light. To combat fleshly temptation, Edmund wore a hairshirt and a thick hair-cord about his body, and was abstemious in food and drink and sleep, remaining fully clothed and sleeping (when he did) upon the floor in front of his bed. After six years of further pronounced devotion, he suddenly had a vision of his dead mother, who had died not long before. This is an interesting incident, since it raises certain questions abut the nature of ghosts and people's reaction to them. The visitation happened while he was in the middle of lecturing to students on arithmetic. His mother, says Matthew Paris, 'appeared to him in sleep [*in sompnis*]', which can scarcely be understood literally, since he was clearly awake and engaged with other people. *Sompnus*, however, may also refer to a state of drowsiness or somnolence, so perhaps he was bored and not really concentrating on the lesson in hand. Even so, he cannot have been dreaming, which is what the word usually implies. *Sompnus* is used again at the end of the anecdote to explain that this was why Edmund changed the subject of his personal study from arithmetic to theology. His mother asked him about certain shapes he was using as visual aids, and he explained that they were diagrams illustrating the subject of his lecture. Nowhere is there any indication whether this conversation was internal or external. If the latter, could the other students see or hear the ghost, and what was their reaction? The point of this anecdote, as we shall see, does not require the recording of such details; but unless we are to dismiss the story as pious fiction – far too glib an excuse for shutting our eyes to something which does not accord with prevailing scientific-rationalist presumptions – these details need to be noticed and receive some kind of comment. Having had the diagrams pointed out to her, Edmund's mother then grabbed [*arripuit*] his right hand and painted [*depinxit*] three circles on it, and wrote inside the circles, 'Father, Son, Holy Spirit'. Then she told him to spend his time on these diagrams rather than the others: in other words, to study theology instead of arithmetic.

How substantial was this ghost? If she could seize his hand and write on it, she herself must have had substance, and so must the brush and colouring she used to paint the circles and write the words. We may also remark that she was perfectly recognisable to Edmund as his mother, which implies that her face and clothing and manner were those he remembered from when she was alive. He could also hear her clearly, and she addressed him as her 'dearest son', so there is no indication either that Edmund had any doubts about the nature of the apparition – whether it was an angel or an evil spirit in disguise is a question which does not seem to have occurred to him – or that he was in the least afraid of what he was experiencing. As for the nature of that experience, the language in which it is told is contradictory. *Sompnus* suggests a dreamlike state, but *arripuit* and *depinxit* are remarkably physical, and even if we propose that the apparition was entirely internal and that this physical vocabulary is used to express the vivid reality of the experience as it appeared to Edmund at the time, we should bear in mind that in doing so we are making certain assumptions to suit ourselves rather than drawing a definitive conclusion from sufficient evidence.

At some point after this, Edmund returned to Paris for higher study and was then appointed treasurer of Salisbury Cathedral in 1222. He was in his late forties and carried with him to his new post the ingrained habit of a lifetime: the austerity, the generous almsgiving, and the eloquence of a preacher and lecturer. Miracles, signs and wonders continued as well. He cured a student of a fistula by praying that it be transferred to him, which indeed it was; and on several occasions, when he wanted to preach the Fifth Crusade, he was able to ensure (by invoking the name of Christ) that it did not rain and so prevent people from coming to hear him. With such a reputation, Edmund should have been an obvious candidate for Canterbury. But, as usual, there had been others – three altogether – before the choice fell upon him and he was consecrated on 2 April 1234. He became archbishop just at the moment when there was a real threat of civil war between Henry III and some of his barons, who feared that in Henry they were seeing another John. War was averted, thanks to Edmund's skill in negotiation, but it was not long before Henry and the Church were embroiled in a dispute about the encroachment of royal courts upon ecclesiastical jurisdiction, almost as though Henry II and St Thomas Becket had never lived. Indeed, a protracted quarrel between Edmund and the monks of Christ Church revived eerie echoes of the earlier saint, underlined perhaps by Edmund's Thomasine willingness first to excommunicate some of the monks who had disobeyed him, and then to place the entire monastery under an interdict. Had his quarrel at this time been with Henry rather than with his own monks, Canterbury might have been on the verge of creating another martyr. But Edmund died abroad, in France, on his way to take part in a General Council summoned by Pope Gregory IX, a quiet death finding him in a small Augustinian priory on 16 November 1240.

After one saint, another. *Boniface of Savoy* (1241–70), says Matthew Paris, was, according to common talk, 'a man unknown [to the monks of Canterbury], inadequate in learning, character, and age for such a high office when compared with the preceding archbishops'. Henry III, however, insisted on his elevation and so the monks had little choice. Boniface's niece, after all, was Henry's wife, and the monks were still labouring under the excommunication imposed on them by St Edmund; so if they wanted the sentence lifted, and if they cared to come to terms with political reality, they would do as they were told and elect Henry's choice. Thus Boniface, who had never set foot in England before he arrived as its primate, became archbishop, although not until

25 April 1244, some three years after his election and about five months after his appointment had been confirmed by Pope Innocent IV.

Everything about Boniface seemed to happen in slow motion. Apart from the long delay between his election and confirmation, he was still a Carthusian novice in subdeacon's order until his arrival in England (when he was finally ordained by the bishop of Worcester), had to wait until January the following year to be consecrated archbishop in Lyon by the Pope, and was finally enthroned in Canterbury on 1 November 1249. His period in office is characterised by his long and frequent absences. Between 1244 and 1249, for example, he was resident at the Papal Court in Lyons where a sense of threat to the Church – the Pope was not at Lyons by choice but as a refugee from the Holy Roman Emperor – instilled in him a determination to defend her from any kind of attack. As far as the English were concerned, the glimpses they caught of their archbishop in between his sallies abroad suggested to their innate xenophobia that he was a negligent, aggressive foreigner with an unhealthy interest in money. This last impression was stimulated by Boniface's well-intentioned efforts to pay off debts run up by his predecessors and his own fairly extensive building programme, all of which meant that he had to be ruthless in exacting every last due from every one of his tenants. His reputation for violence came from one or two incidents during his early archiepiscopal visitations.

One in particular stemmed from a visitation in his own province. He had already visited St Paul's Cathedral in London, appearing there with a body of armed men in view of his unpopularity in the capital, an unpopularity which had manifested itself in brawls and disturbances. No one was there to greet him – an act of calculated discourtesy and contempt – except the Dean, who respectfully but firmly told Boniface he had no right to be there, since the bishop of London was the cathedral's legal Visitor. Next day, therefore, when Boniface went in similar style to the Priory of St Bartholomew, crowds gathered and shouted insults as he and his armed retinue passed through the streets. At first it looked as though the priory had learned a lesson from St Paul's; but Boniface soon realised that the prior and the canons were playing a game. They were receiving him as archbishop, but not as their Visitor. His patience snapped and he raced into the choir where the sub-prior made the situation clear, an explanation which resulted in Boniface's losing his temper completely. He punched the sub-prior several times in the chest, face and head, and called for a sword to finish the old man off.[7] Now, Matthew Paris is not an unbiased historian, so we must be careful how we interpret his information. We must also bear in mind the concept of 'face' and how important it was to maintain and assert one's status in relation to other people. One's authority depended on it. Had Boniface allowed his clergy to snub him, further liberties would have followed, and he would have found it nearly impossible to control insubordinate bishops and monks, effect desirable reforms, or even ensure that his revenues were collected efficiently. Lack of respect stimulated an angry response from saints as well as less virtuous individuals, as we find in many examples of hagiographical literature;[8] so Boniface's reaction to the deliberate rudeness of St Bartholomew's Priory is to be expected, even if its attendant histrionics are to be deplored. The details of these, however, are questionable. Adam Marsh, who was with the archbishop at the time, wrote that they had been much exaggerated, so we are caught between (to use modern parlance) the possible spin of Matthew Paris and that of Adam Marsh. What cannot be doubted, however, is that Boniface was subjected to a discourtesy quite intolerable for someone in his position, and that his reaction to it made his anger and embarrassment plain enough to restore a necessary measure of 'face'.

Such a man is unlikely to have been very accommodating to royal encroachments on and interference in ecclesiastical matters, and although Henry III had been keen enough to have Boniface appointed, they soon fell out over patronage, while Henry's constant demands for money exacerbated an increasingly tense situation. Nor did England's decline into civil war make any easier Boniface's task of holding the English Church together against a predatory state. Perhaps in part because of his own authoritarian tendencies, but much more because the state of England required it, Boniface frequently acted beyond his canonical authority, especially in his appointment or attempted appointment of bishops; and when he left England on archiepiscopal and family business in October 1262, disorder rushed in to fill the vacuum. Boniface did his best to cope, but the disorder was such that he was effectively an exile until May 1266 when the civil war had run its course and he was able to return to Canterbury. Pope Clement IV had undercut his authority by appointing a Papal Legate in 1265 to take charge of English affairs, and Boniface did not recover anything more than a semblance of 'face' until the Legate departed in July 1268. By this time, Boniface was a sick man. Just before he went abroad for the last time, the Archbishop of York managed one final insult by having his processional cross carried in front of him during a celebration of the Feast of Edward the Confessor in Westminster, a gesture of pre-eminence to which he was not entitled in the south of England.

Boniface died in July 1270, and as his death happened in Sainte Hélène, it meant he missed a great row between the Franciscans and Dominicans in Oxford, each order claiming to be more genuinely poor (and therefore by implication more virtuous) than the other. It was actually a quarrel ignited by a more general hostility between the two, one never adequately resolved, because both orders were essentially trying to do the same pastoral task and there were not enough potential novices for both in any given district. When news of Boniface's death reached England, yet again there was a dispute over who should succeed him until, on 11 October 1272, Pope Gregory IX appointed a Dominican theologian, *Robert Kilwardby* (1272–78), Provincial of the English chapter of the order, who seemed to be quite different from the fiery, aristocratic Savoyard Boniface. Kilwardby had studied at Paris and brought back with him an interest in teaching students. Many of his works preserve lectures on logic, grammar and ethics, or consist of reference books directed at his students in Oxford. As Archbishop of Canterbury, he maintained close contact with the university, especially Merton College whose Visitor he (and his successors) became. He continued Boniface's habit of visitations and exerting discipline over the clergy, but usually did so in a much gentler fashion, even though his intention to make sure the rules were obeyed to the letter was just as strict as that of his immediate predecessor. As far as secular politics were concerned, he opted for a quiet life, perhaps a judicious choice under the rule of as vicious and as bellicose a king as the megalomaniac Edward I. In March 1280, Pope Nicholas III created him cardinal, thereby in effect removing him from England for the time being, although as things turned out, the Pope's appointment removed him permanently, for he fell ill in September and died at Viterbo on 11 September.

After the Dominican, a Franciscan, *John Pecham* (1279–82), was in certain ways a companion-image of Kilwardby. Educated in a Paris which was dominated by the teaching of two illustrious Dominicans, Albertus Magnus who came there in 1240, and St Thomas Aquinas during his second regency, 1269–71, Pecham developed into a controversialist, somewhat more abrasive in many ways than Kilwardby had been, but, like Kilwardby, a dedicated teacher who produced quite a large body of written work – principally lectures, commentaries and sermons, as well as a book on perspective which rapidly became a standard university text in Paris and Prague. Perhaps it was his temperament, perhaps force of circumstances, which entangled him in controversy; but he was in Paris in 1269 when the mendicant and secular masters renewed a conflict about who was poorer than whom, a conflict which was not always restricted to words and sometimes resulted in peculiar non sequiturs, such as Pecham's argument that because Mary Magdalene was able to wash Christ's feet with her tears, it proved He did not wear shoes.[9] This controversy flared again in Oxford, as we have seen, and both Kilwardby and Pecham crossed swords (though not literally) in 1272 over this same theme of Apostolic poverty.

In 1275 he was elected prior of the English Franciscan province, and walked barefoot from Oxford to Padua to attend a general chapter of the order. It was a spectacular demonstration of strict adherence to the Franciscan spirit of complete poverty, and much admired at the time; but one cannot help feeling a little uneasy about it. Was this a piece of controversy by other means than the pen? Is there a touch of vanity about it? If we ask the legal question, *cui bono*, for whose benefit was this done, it is difficult to see any answer beyond Pecham's own reputation; and while it would be a grave mistake to import modern taste for restraint into an earlier, genuinely more florid period, Pecham's prolonged and very public gesture of humility grates, if ever so slightly, on one's sense of propriety. In 1276 he was invited to become a lecturer in theology at the Papal university in Rome, and this gave him a remarkable chance to become acquainted with the college of cardinals and the Papal Court, an acquaintance which worked to his advantage since he was appointed a cardinal himself and then became Pope Nicholas III's nominee for the vacant see of Canterbury at the beginning of 1279.

Despite Kilwardby's inheritance of an archbishopric which had had most of its debts repaid by Archbishop Boniface, the Dominican prelate had managed to introduce a degree of turmoil once again into Canterbury's finances, so that Pecham was faced at once by monetary problems which he never quite succeeded in solving. But he arrived with a religious programme which he set in motion straightaway, one which can be summed up in two words: discipline and efficiency. They were the keynotes of a programme of Church reform the Papacy had been encouraging for some considerable time, and included control of such abuses as pluralism, lack of celibacy and ignorance among clerics. The aim was to produce a clergy which would set an example of good Christian living to its flock, and be able to teach the Faith effectively through formal instruction and preaching. Admirable though these aims were, however, Pecham found, through his immediate extensive visitations, that his suffragans were less than helpful, being keener on making sure the archbishop did not violate or interfere with any of their privileges and spent his energies on resisting secular intransigence to those privileges than on assisting him in the performance of his proper duty. But Pecham pressed ahead regardless, and included the country's monasteries in his visitations, although here he blotted his good intentions by seizing the opportunity to put stumbling-blocks in the way of Dominican encouragement of the teaching of St Thomas Aquinas in Oxford. He was accused of stirring up rivalry between Franciscans and Dominicans, a charge he denied, but which cannot but carry some weight in view of his behaviour.

A bigger blot on his character, however, was caused by his attitude towards the Church in Wales. His view of the Welsh was simple. They were treacherous, sacrilegious, barbaric and lazy, and their desire to maintain themselves independent of England he regarded, in typical English fashion, as incomprehensible. So Edward I's assault upon Wales received the archbishop's support, financial as well as psychological, for in 1283 he persuaded his clergy to grant the king a subsidy to enable Edward to prosecute his war. All this renders his efforts the previous year to persuade the Welsh prince, Llewelyn ap Gruffyd, to betray his country in return for an English earldom an exercise in perfidy rather than a serious attempt to broker a peace; and it is noticeable that after the war was over in 1284 and the Welsh were defeated, Pecham hastened to visit all four Welsh dioceses in an effort (actually unsuccessful) to bring them under his control and thus add them to his province.

He died in December 1292. His final years had been marked by the expulsion of the Jews from England in 1290, an expulsion which was undoubtedly an act of state by Edward I, but one to which the archbishop raised no objection, partly because he almost certainly agreed with it, since as early as 1281 he had drawn King Edward's attention to the large numbers of Jews in London and elsewhere. His last years must also have been clouded by a realisation that Edward I was not a man to tread gently when it came to the liberties of the Church, and that even if he and Edward had managed to sustain a working relationship, the exigencies of the war against Scotland on which Edward had now embarked would mean further demands for money and therefore renewed chances of conflict between Canterbury and a monarch so self-centred and vainglorious that one wonders sometimes whether he was completely sane. But had Pecham's intended reform of the clergy, and of the monasteries in particular, been successful? No. The abuses continued, pluralism flourished, and the preaching orders were as much at loggerheads as ever. This last, of course, was partly his fault, and any attempt to summarise Pecham's character meets paradox after paradox. It would be churlish to doubt his sincere commitment to the service of Christ in the Franciscan way, and yet his conspicuously austere behaviour – the *Lanercost Chronicle* (p.144), for example, tells us that, as archbishop, he wanted to have his clothes and bedclothes made of cheap material, and that he would often light the lamps and candles in church himself (a somewhat theatrical gesture of humility) – smacks a little of opportunistic propagandising, as he loses no chance to controvert, by any means, the particular intellectual and disciplinary stance adopted by Dominicans. His wish to bring reformation in manners and morals to both secular clergy and religious was undermined by his all too worldly desire to bring the Welsh under King Edward's rule and his own; and his desire, as a Franciscan, to make his life a closer imitation of Christ's was spoiled by his eagerness to indulge in controversy and invective. Had he been a schoolboy, then, his end-of-term report might well have read, 'Able, but could do better'.

6

Royal
Self-Aggrandisement
Winchelsey to Arundel
(1293–1414)

It will be as well at this point to try to take stock of what kind of men had occupied the chair of St Augustine thus far. They were largely monks; well-educated, sometimes learned; many came from abroad (Italian) or of immigrant stock (Normans), although there had been a long period of just over 350 years when they had all been Anglo-Saxons. The habit of acclaiming them saints had lasted not quite sixty years, but the succeeding centuries had seen a few canonised in accordance with official Roman procedure. One or two had been promoted cardinal and Papal Legate, their status within the Church as a whole thus elevated and made significant, and the election of one or two others had been uncanonical. Most of them had built and beautified and founded new establishments; and most had sought, with considerable success over the centuries, to construct an English ecclesiastical unity held together by canon law and a coherent administration of that law. The English daughter of the Church had thus done well to survive her initial years and was continuing to survive both her self-inflicted faults and the waves of secular mayhem stirred up by a succession of turbulent kings.

Two preoccupations peculiar to England governed many of the actions taken by a majority of these archbishops: resistance to monarchs who persisted in seeing the English Church's money as cash diverted away from instead of into the royal exchequer, and who sought to impose their secular will upon the administration of ecclesiastical courts and the disbursement of ecclesiastical justice; and constant squabbles with the Archbishops of York over precedence. The first of these two perpetual considerations required the archbishops to be politicians. Some had the gift, others did not. The second gave rise to intermittent suspicion in Rome that the Archbishops of Canterbury were aiming to turn their archiepiscopate into a patriarchate of the west, suspicions probably not altogether without foundation from time to time. But many of the archbishops also demonstrate an adherence to the Papacy, in as much as the reforming efforts of the Pontiffs during the twelfth and thirteenth centuries received several archbishops' support, a support which helps illustrate the other general observation which can be made of most of them this far: that they were at bottom good Christian men aiming to do their duty by their flock and by the Church to the best of their several abilities.

Immersion in politics was not something any Archbishop of Canterbury could avoid, but *Robert Winchelsey* (1293–1331) plunged in further than anyone since St Thomas Becket. Like a number of his immediate predecessors, he had been educated in the schools of Paris and Oxford and spent several years in various ecclesiastical posts – rector, prebend, archdeacon – and as a teacher of theology, producing many scholarly works which gained general approbation, partly because he neatly threaded his way through contemporary controversies between Dominicans and Franciscans. When Archbishop Pecham died, Winchelsey was thus a figure whose election to Canterbury could go forward without the usual wrangling and dissension. Elected on 13 February 1293, he went to Rome to seek Papal confirmation of this election, only to find that Pope Nicholas IV had died in April 1292 and that the college of cardinals was unable to agree on a successor. It took them two years and three months to light upon Celestine V, who consecrated Winchelsey in September 1294 and then abdicated (the only Pope to do so) the following December. He was replaced by Boniface VIII, a formidable Pope who had no hesitation in asserting that a person's salvation depended on his or her subjection to the Roman Pontiff. It was a bold, not to say aggressive, claim which may help to explain why Winchelsey was prepared to resist Edward I in a manner reminiscent of that with which St Thomas Becket opposed King Henry.

The bones of contention were not new. Edward wanted to appoint his own nominees to vacant ecclesiastical positions, and Winchelsey objected. Certain royal chapels enjoyed privileges granted by the Crown, which limited the amount of control a bishop or archbishop could exert over them. Winchelsey objected. Yet more war – this time with France – meant that Edward needed money and raised large sums by plundering some Church funds, appropriating others, and imposing taxes beyond what the clergy regarded as acceptable. Winchelsey objected. All this took place in the first two years of his holding office, and it seems clear that Winchelsey was emboldened in his opposition to royal dictatorship by the knowledge that the Pope would undoubtedly support him against the Crown if matters reached that particular pass. Indeed, no one was left in any doubt, because in 1296 Pope Boniface published a Bull (*Clericos laicos*) which stated categorically that Papal consent was necessary before clergy could be taxed by secular rulers.

War with Scotland, followed by war with France, rendered the political situation immensely dangerous. Many of the clergy supported Winchelsey in his opposition to the exactions of the Crown; the king and his nobles, however, played upon the emotions of all concerned and tried to argue that the country was under attack and that it was therefore the duty of all the king's subjects, clerical and lay, to rally to its defence – a hollow piece of special pleading (since any danger to the realm had been caused by Edward's insane desire for war in the first place) which subsequent politicians have not hesitated to adapt and use for their own vain purposes. In 1297 matters reached the point of crisis. Edward threatened to make every cleric an outlaw if the Church continued to resist his will, and Winchelsey promised to excommunicate those who did not resist. Many clergy collapsed under the strain and paid the tax the king was intent on forcing from them; Christ Church was sequestered and Winchelsey's lands and possessions seized. But Winchelsey made it plain that he was prepared to die rather than concede, and so the political situation was on the verge of getting completely out of hand. The king did not have the support even of every noble at this juncture. Some kind of reconciliation between archbishop and king was necessary, and an agreement – largely mere words – was put together in July. Why was Winchelsey so adamant? It was not simply a matter of taxes. The Church could afford the money and many of the clergy had actually paid the exaction. What Winchelsey saw in Edward's depradation was an attempt to enslave the Church, to subject it to royal will institutionally as though it were a cross between a department of state and a milch cow – a blasphemous cast of mind which completely ignored the divine foundation of the Church as an autonomous body endowed with God's authority, the one and only guide of spiritual life, which exceeded the world of matter and of time and therefore, by its very nature, was more important to each individual than any temporal state or secular ruler.

The agreement, such as it was, broke down almost immediately. Further taxes were levied; King Edward left for France; Winchelsey supported by most of the clergy continued his opposition; and on 1 September the archbishop and Edward's regents confronted one another in Christ Church, the regents promising to take the matter to Rome for final resolution. What saved them all was a Scottish victory over the English at the battle of Stirling Bridge on 11 September. Now there was no denying that a threat existed for the English, and so both the archbishop and the regents worked out a compromise whereby the Church would pay a subsidy to the Crown, while the Crown would confirm the liberties of the Church promised by Magna Carta. But King Edward was not a man to thwart. He bided his time until he felt that his bellicosities against Scotland and France had been resolved, and then struck at Winchelsey. The occasion was the election of Pope Clement V in 1305. Since 1299 he had been Archbishop of Bordeaux, an English fiefdom, and before that he had served as one of Edward's clerks in Gascony. Personal experience of Edward had not, curiously enough, turned him against the king, and indeed he seemed content to act as Edward's creature when it came to English ecclesiastical affairs; and since it was Clement who cravenly acquiesced in the downfall of the Order of Knights Templar at the behest of the vicious Philippe IV of France, one must come to the reluctant conclusion that here was a Pope too weak and too frightened to resist the demands of bullying monarchs. So the consequences of his election for Winchelsey were more or less dire. In 1305 Clement released Edward from his obligation to observe the stipulations of Magna Carta and its additional clauses and then, in response to ridiculous accusations of peculation and exceeding his authority levied by Edward against Winchelsey, suspended the archbishop from office and summoned him to Avignon, where the Papacy was in exile. Winchelsey obeyed and left England for France, where he lived quietly until Edward I at long last died and his son, Edward II, succeeded to the throne.

The new king, however, so different in many ways from his father, resembled him in others. He permitted Winchelsey to return, but pursued much the same route of direct regal taxation of the Church, interference in her courts and appointment of royal nominees to ecclesiastical offices, as his father had done. He also made promises in 1311 to observe and maintain the liberties of the Church, and signally failed to keep them as early as 1312. So, by and large Winchelsey must have felt that father and son were little more than frying-pan and fire, and with the knowledge that the Papacy had fallen from a high point of strength under Boniface VIII into a slough of infirmity under Clement V, his death on 11 May 1313 is likely to have come

as something of a relief to himself no less than to Edward II. The
contrast between Winchelsey and Clement V speaks volumes. Faced
by a couple of tyrants, Clement caved in. Winchelsey, on the other
hand, stood firm and stared them down. He was clearly a very brave
man. Archbishops were not immune from assassination – the case of
St Thomas Becket had proved that – and if Henry I had been vicious,
Edward I was even more so. It also says much for Winchelsey that
there were several attempts after his death to have him canonised,
attempts which were ignored or pushed aside by Pope Clement. But
then, the Pope had already given ample proof of his pusillanimity, so
the refusals are scarcely surprising.

Edward and Clement then set about appointing a malleable archbishop, and in *Walter Reynolds* (1313–27), King Edward's Chancellor
and confidant, they thought they had found their man. The first
question we have to consider is whether or not he was illiterate.
Hostile chronicles describe him as (a) 'a layman and so badly-
educated [*illiteratus*], he had not the slightest idea how to decline
[*recite the Latin forms of*] his own name'; (b) 'a simple-minded cleric
and less than competently literate'; (c) 'a person practically illiterate
and, according to the opinion of cultured society, unworthy of any
honourable situation as much because of the way he lived as because
of his erudition'. *Illiteratus* is not an easy word to translate. It probably
means his Latin was very poor, not that he was unable to read or
write; but Robert Wright has suggested strongly that the evidence
of his personal library and his promotion of learning even before
he became archbishop, and a letter from Pope John XXII thanking
him for translating Papal letters from Latin into French, provide clear
indication that the chroniclers were traducing his memory.[1]

That said, Reynolds achieved his office against the wishes of the
monks of Canterbury, who elected someone else, and immediately
enjoyed a number of favours from both Clement V and Edward II,
who were determined not to encumber themselves with another
Winchelsey. Sure enough, Reynolds worked hard to induce the
English clergy to pay taxes when the king demanded them; but
growing dissidence in England against the rule of Edward II put
a stop to further collaboration on the archbishop's part, and when

rebellion flared in 1326, Reynolds hesitated for over five weeks until he was sure that Edward had lost, and came out of a discreet retirement to make his submission to Edward's victorious wife, Isabella, and to crown Edward III at Westminster in February 1327. But before the year ended, Reynolds was dead. Walter Hook's view of him is damning: 'he was not equal to the situation, whether we have regard to his talents, his learning, his piety, or his virtues', and even Robert Wright, who is more favourably disposed to him, is equivocal. 'Illiterate, stupid, simoniac, incompetent, indecisive: or a man who could moderate the tribulations of the English Church and realm? Both these view preserve a modicum of truth about Reynolds, and the full story will never be known'.[2] *Simon Mepham* (1328–33) was another ideal choice in the eyes of the Crown. The chronicler William Dene said he was 'completely ignorant of how people live and behave', so it is scarcely surprising that Queen Isabella and her lover, Roger Mortimer, were happy to have him elected. They must have been even happier when, in 1328, in the midst of near civil war, he was unable to keep his mouth shut regarding information with which he had been entrusted by the Crown's opponents, and blabbed it all to the king and Isabella. How they must have congratulated themselves on their choice of primate. But their contempt is obvious from they way they snubbed him by staying away from his enthronement in January 1329, and this set the tone for the rest of his archiepiscopate. In 1330, for example, Mepham alienated the monks of Canterbury by embroiling himself with them in an unnecessary dispute over the income accruing to the monastery from certain churches and chapels. Under Mepham's tactless intransigence the quarrel escalated to a point where the Pope became involved, and he himself was to be prosecuted by a canon of Salisbury. The canon was as detached from the real world as the archbishop, for when Mepham, on the advice of his lawyers, refused to appear in court, the canon thundered that 'he should submit to him under penalty of death', a piece of theatrical nonsense which got the case referred to Avignon. By this time Mepham was ill and had retired to the manor of Slindon, not far from Chichester. It was while he was there that two officers of the Papal Court, Thomas of Natendon and a Master

Mansel, arrived with a summons to appear before the commissioners appointed to hear the case against him brought by the monks of
St Augustine's. Violence broke out almost at once between Thomas's
retainers and the archbishop's men. Master Mansel broke his arm
and Thomas, whose horse bolted in the confusion, was eventually
fetched back to Slindon and kept prisoner for three days. It was an
outrageous way to treat Papal messengers, and it is impossible to
believe that Mepham knew nothing about any of it. So thought
Pope John XXII, and when the case was heard and went against the
archbishop, and Mepham refused to pay the resulting fine, the Pope
excommunicated him.

   This boundless lack of tact and refusal to compromise when clearly
in the wrong typify Mepham's character. It causes no surprise, therefore, to find that the Archbishop of York was prepared to play games
and try to have his processional cross carried in front of him on
formal occasions while he was in the see of Canterbury. This had
caused trouble between the metropolitans before, but this time the
provocation seems to have been entirely gratuitous. Mepham rose
to the bait and tried to gather support from his suffragans. Their
response was to ignore him. The bishop of Rochester, however,
advised him to obtain the king's permission to excommunicate
anyone who infringed the rights of Canterbury, although lawyers
warned him that if he did this and absented himself from Parliament,
the king would be within his rights to seize the archbishop's temporal
possessions. Rochester retorted sarcastically that an archbishop could
have no greater honour than to suffer for the Church, and Mepham,
upon whom a faint glimmer of common sense perhaps shone for a
brief instant, decided not to pursue the point further.

   It was not quite his last positive decision. Having made up his mind
to visit Exeter, where he found opposition from the bishop, instead
of retiring in the face of a large number of armed troops drawn up
before the cathedral to bar his entry, he decided to confront them
with eighty armed men of his own – in any other archbishop a sign of
preserving face and authority, in Mepham just another example of his
disconnection from reality – and it took government interference to
resolve the confrontation. Tellingly enough, it was Mepham who was

instructed to stand down, not his rebellious subordinate. This happened in 1330. Mepham lingered on in office until 12 October 1333 when he died, still excommunicate. We are told he was depressed. He had every reason to be.

Queen Isabella and Edward III had got the archbishop they wanted, but he had proved a liability rather than a pliable tool, so when it came to finding a successor, King Edward was a little more circumspect. His choice fell on *John Stratford* (1333–48), a lawyer with long training in governmental service and experience at the Papal Court. Edward appointed him Chancellor at the end of 1330, an office he resigned on becoming archbishop, although he took it up again twice during his archiepiscopate. A degree of luck, coupled with personal courage, enabled him to escape the consequences of opposing Isabella and Roger Mortimer during their ascendancy while King Edward was a minor, but once the king came into his own Stratford's career burgeoned and thus made him a clear candidate for Canterbury when Mepham died. Rather than accept immediately, however, Stratford temporised. He would submit himself, he said, entirely to the will of the Pope. Interestingly enough, Pope John had already made up his mind, because his Bull appointing Stratford to Canterbury arrived in England before King Edward's letters of commendation and request for the pallium had had a chance to arrive at the Papal Court. The reason seems fairly clear. In 1323 the bishopric of Winchester had become vacant and Stratford delivered King Edward II's letters recommending one Robert Baldock to the see. Pope John, however, preferred the messenger and appointed Stratford to the office instead. So the two men were already well acquainted, and the Pope had a high opinion of Stratford's abilities – hence his rapid promotion of the Chancellor.

One thing more than anything else about Stratford stands out. He was a diplomatist, spending much of his time in secular affairs and even, at one point, in January and February 1339, acting as a spy or an intelligence-gatherer in the Lowlands prior to Edward III's invasion of France the following year. For a few months while the king was out of England, Stratford held the Great Seal and was thus effectively regent, a task he carried out efficiently but with no subsequent thanks from the king, who later accused him of starving the English army of funds. From royal favour to royal hatred: parallels emerge (and were seen at the time) between Stratford and St Thomas Becket; and indeed Stratford was not loath to encourage them. He preached a sermon in his own defence in Canterbury on the feast of St Thomas, and two days later issued a pastoral letter defending the liberties of the English Church which, he said, had been trampled on by an unlawful tax on the clergy. The king riposted with a scurrilous pamphlet – Stratford dubbed it *libellus famosus*, 'a defamatory publication' – written by some anonymous hack,[3] charging the archbishop with maladministration of state affairs, malpractice, sedition and corruption, as well as personal arrogance and timidity – 'he was always puffed up when things were going well, and tearful when they were not, trembling with fear when the situation did not warrant it'. To this Stratford gave a measured answer and offered to defend himself in Parliament, but the only reply was another pamphlet traducing his character, 'Arrogance, the scar of [people's] hearts'.

It is notable that when Stratford did try to attend the parliament of April 1341, he was not permitted to enter the building. The king could not afford to have him put his case before the peers, and so force was used to keep him at arm's length. But neither Edward nor Edward's friends were stupid or ill-advised enough to provide Canterbury with another martyr, and so reconciliation of a kind took place in October, with Edward finding cause in 1343 and again in 1346 to repudiate his own nonsensical accusations against the archbishop, an acknowledgement of reality he should have made earlier. Stratford, then, is a good example of what St Thomas Becket might have been had he not taken so wholeheartedly to religion and thus set himself on the road to sainthood. He was a measured, effective administrator who did not seek out confrontation, but did not shirk it when it was thrust upon him. Haines says that 'had it not been for William Shakespeare... John Stratford would have been by far the best known of the sons of that Warwickshire town from which he took his name'.[4] Considering Shakespeare's reputation has been vastly overblown ever since the Victorians deified him and the twentieth century was silly enough to believe them, perhaps it would be more just to reverse that conclusion and say that John Stratford *ought* to be the town's most famous son.

God did not approve of Edward III. When Stratford died in 1348 the monks of Canterbury elected Thomas Bradwardine, a remarkable theologian and mathematician, as his successor. The king, however, disapproved of the way they made their choice, and forced them to elect John Ufford instead. But Ufford died before his consecration, so Edward was obliged to accept Bradwardine after all. *Thomas Bradwardine* (1349) was Archbishop of Canterbury for thirty-eight days. It was the time of the Black Death and plague took him off in August. He would probably not have been a success. When he was consecrated archbishop at Avignon by Pope Clement VI, the evening's banquet was interrupted by the entry of a clown on a jack-ass, who petitioned the Pope to make *him* Archbishop of Canterbury instead. But as Bradwardine scarcely survived beyond these festivities, Edward had to look for another primate, and was given *Simon Islep* (1349–66) by Pope Clement. Islep had not been a bishop before his consecration, a most unusual occurrence, but he had had plenty of experience in both ecclesiastical and secular administration and this stood him in good stead as he laboured to cope with the effects of the Black Death. The disease had killed large numbers of clergy, so that there was now a dearth which had to be met. Too frequently (although one can understand why it happened), men with too little learning and too few qualifications were being ordained and Islep was determined to raise the quality of the new priesthood. Hence his foundation in 1361 of a new college in Oxford, Canterbury Hall, which was supposed to take both monastic and secular students, an experiment which did not work, since four years later the college accepted secular students only. An indication of Islep's character may be found in one of the statutes which deals with the dress to be worn by the Warden and scholars. Islep emphasises simplicity and more than once sets an upper limit to the amount which can be sent on tunics and their fur trimming. He also tried to regulate the expensive custom of throwing feasts in college when anyone received his degree, by suggesting there should be a limit to the number of people who should be invited to any gathering and that newly graduated members give small sums of money to their friends rather than spend large amounts on a party. It is a concern for thrift he evinced in his will, too, where he directed that his funeral be private and conducted with as little expense as possible.

For so long a period in office, Islep's time was remarkably quiet in comparison with that of some of his predecessors. It is not that nothing happened – Islep was sent to France in 1353 to negotiate peace, for example, and was one of the Regency Council in 1355 when Edward III went there on the rampage again – but Islep seems to have been able to negotiate troubled waters without giving offence on the one hand, or allowing people to walk over him on the other. A measure of his emollient success may be gauged from the fact that he managed at long last to settle the running dispute over precedence between Canterbury and York, and to settle it in Canterbury's favour. The groundwork was done by the two prelates who then submitted themselves to the arbitration of the Pope and the king, and it is to the credit of both Islep and Thoresby of York that they worked out a compromise which the arbitrators could then formally propose for their acceptance.

Islep's final years were not altogether happy. He suffered a stroke in January 1363 and lingered, his mind unimpaired but his body paralysed, until April 1366 when he died in one of his manors at midnight between the 25th and 26th of the month. Of all the recent Archbishops of Canterbury, he is the one to whom the adjective 'likeable' could most properly be given. *Simon Langham* (1366–68), however, seems to have been of similar quality. He was a Benedictine monk, the last monk but one to be an Archbishop of Canterbury, becoming abbot of Westminster in April 1349 at the height of the Black Death. He succeeded to the rule of a monastery weighed down by debt and rife with indiscipline, and set about restoring the monks to their proper obedience. Langham's care for monastic discipline suggests a parallel with Islep's concern for simplicity. For example, he enjoined that the monks should always wear their habit, and that they should not indulge themselves with coloured cloaks, costly saddles and spurs, or fancy gloves and boots. In a word, they were to wear monastic, not secular dress. (One is reminded of Pope John Paul II's injunction to clergy and religious at the beginning of his pontificate not to wear secular attire, an instruction largely ignored in defiance of the obedience owed to the Pope in religious matters). Langham was, if only for the moment, better regarded).

It is notable that his experience in restoring Westminster's fortunes and bringing the community back under proper control was repeated when he was archbishop. For in 1367 he curbed the religious dissent being fuelled by a radical and heretical preacher, John Ball, by ordering the man to cease preaching, and in 1368 intervened in a bitter theological quarrel in Oxford by producing his own conclusions, and addressing a letter to the university requiring that defence of heretical propositions in the schools should cease; and his talent for financial administration can be seen in his secular appointments – royal treasurer in 1360 and Chancellor between 1363 and 1367 – and in the enormous benefactions he was able to make to Westminster once he had its finances under control. But his period as archbishop was limited. In 1368 Pope Urban V created him cardinal and Langham accepted without reference to King Edward, probably because he calculated that such an elevation, which would require his presence at Avignon, would benefit the king, who would then have an English representative in the midst of a hostile French-dominated Papal Court. Edward, however, interpreted Langham's acceptance differently and seized the chance to confiscate to his own use the archbishop's temporalities (that is, his secular possessions), on the grounds that by accepting a cardinal's hat the archbishop had left the Canterbury see vacant. It is perhaps typical of these royal Edwards that they were quite unable to appreciate the qualities of good and loyal men when these were self-evident. But Urban's gain was Edward's loss, and although Langham still managed to serve England's interests from time to time in the diplomatic dancing between Edward and the French, when the archbishopric fell vacant again in 1374 at the death of William Whittlesey, no one in England thought to restore Langham to office, even though he had expressed interest in returning. Cavalier ingratitude thus coloured his final years, lightened too late in 1376 by royal and Papal permission for him to go back and spend his last days in Westminster. He never did. Like Islep, he suffered a stroke; but this was much more serious than the one which had afflicted Islep, and within two days Langham was dead.

His place as archbishop had been filled by Islep's nephew, *William Whittlesey* (1368–74). For most of his time in office he was an invalid, but his previous career had not been without a certain brilliance. He was a doctor of both canon and civil law, had served as Master of Peterhouse in Cambridge, taught in Oxford, been bishop of Rochester and then of Worcester; so one can see in him a type which would become familiar later on – a scholar and a man so immensely discreet that he practically faded to nothing in the eyes of the powerful. *Simon Sudbury* (1375–81), however, was somewhat different. He came to official attention in 1345–46 when he became entangled in a dispute between the abbot of Bury St Edmunds and the bishop of Norwich. Letters were issued for his arrest and he fled to Avignon, where he attracted the favourable notice of Pope Clement VI and thus accumulated a string of English benefices. Clement's successor, Innocent VI, gave him a chance to be reconciled with the English king by sending him to London on a diplomatic mission, and Edward III was sufficiently impressed to use him as a go-between in other royal business. Hence, when Pope Innocent deprived Simon Langham of the chance of becoming bishop of London in 1361, Sudbury filled the vacancy and made such a good impression on everyone that, while Whittlesey declined and retired, Sudbury effectively managed the English Church. If Whittlesey had provided one pattern of a certain type of Archbishop of Canterbury, Sudbury offered another. His policy was simple. The Church should be persuaded by any means available, from cajoling to threats, to pay whatever money the king might demand of her. It is a policy which reveals how he thought of himself and his office – subservient to the English Crown – and when William Courtenay, who replaced him as bishop of London on his elevation to Canterbury, tried to object and defend the clergy's rights, Sudbury did his best to circumvent him.

The circumvention may have been carried out with a certain charm. One of his officials noted that he was 'magnanimous and does not make himself very difficult', but against this we must balance an anecdote dating from 1370, which shows him in a different light. Large numbers of pilgrims were making their way to the shrine of St Thomas Becket in Canterbury, and several stopped him as he was taking part in a religious procession. They simply wanted his blessing and a few words of encouragement, but what he gave them was a series of sour observations on their motives for going on pilgrimage. The plenary indulgence granted at this time, he said, was what they were really interested in. Unless their repentance for their sins was genuine, however, the indulgence would be worthless; and he made it clear to them that he thought there was little or nothing genuine in their intentions. Technically, he was right about the relationship between penitence and the indulgence, but this was not the way to say it, and his openly expressed doubts about their sincerity were merely offensive. The mood of the pilgrims turned hostile and one man ventured to tell Sudbury that he would die an ignominious death – a prophecy, not a threat – to which the rest of the crowd shouted, 'Amen, Amen!'

Of Sudbury one can probably say that he was a better king's man than he was a defender of the Faith. In spite of a direct command from Pope Gregory XI to imprison John Wyclif, *persona non grata* with Rome because of several heretical notions he had published and preached, Sudbury failed to do so, even though he had examined Wyclif personally at Lambeth in May 1378. This, then, was a piece of disobedience which allowed Wyclif to remain at large and spread his heresy. On the other hand, appointed as Chancellor in 1380, he imposed the poll-tax on the king's subjects because money was required and the state of the realm unsettled. But this final acquiescence to the needs of the Crown proved his undoing. The south-east of England broke into open rebellion against the new and inequitable tax, forcing the king and archbishop to take refuge in the Tower of London. There Sudbury urged young Richard II to stand firm and yield not a jot to the rebels, a stance one can praise as courageous opposition to civil strife or foolhardy recalcitrance, according to one's view of his character. Richard was more flexible, and young enough to be impressionable, so his decision to face the rioters combined youthful bravado and a willingness to bend to the moment. With the king gone, however, the Tower was less impregnable and a mob soon broke in, tied Sudbury's hands, marched him to Tower Hill, and removed his head. The executioner was not a professional. It took eight strokes before the head finally rolled from the body.

What England needed at this juncture, when the country was in an uproar and the Church in turmoil (having elected Urban VI, some cardinals decided they had made a mistake and elected the antipope Clement VII in his place, thereby splitting Christendom into two opposing camps) was an Archbishop of Canterbury who would steer the English Church through these treacherous shallows and bring her safely to shelter until both the English and the wider European storms had finally blown out. What England got was *William Courtenay* (1381–96). Courtenay and Sudbury, as I have mentioned, had crossed swords while Courtenay was bishop of London, typically enough over a question of Sudbury's pliancy to the royal will. It might be thought, therefore, that Courtenay would be less of a courtier and more of an archbishop, a notion confirmed by his defiance of Edward III in 1373 over a request for clerical taxation. Refusing to pay the king could be done with some degree of impunity only if one were of elevated social status, and Courtenay was certainly that – a younger son of the earl of Devon, promoted bishop of Hereford in 1369 below the canonical age with the permission of Pope Urban V. At quite a young age, then (he was thirty-two when he refused King Edward), he made his mark as a defender of clerical liberties. This willingness to stand up to secular authority, however highly placed, can be seen again in 1377 and 1385 in quite serious clashes with Richard II's uncle, John of Gaunt, and then with Richard himself.

The first of these arose over the person of John Wyclif. The heretic had the prince's support, and when he was summoned to a confer- ence at St Paul's in February 1377, Gaunt came with him and tried to impose himself on the court by demanding a comfortable seat for his protégé. Since Wyclif was effectively under examination for heresy, this was a nonsensical request. Chairs were a mark of status both then and much later – one thinks of the quarrels they precipitated in the Court of Louis XIV, for example – and naturally Courtenay objected that a cleric on trial should be allowed to sit in the presence of his judge who was a bishop. Gaunt lost his temper and made a number of threats, including one to haul Courtenay out of the church by his hair; but Courtenay stood firm and Gaunt decided to retreat. The second incident, according to the chronicler Adam Usk, took place when Courtenay and the king were on the Thames (presumably in the royal barge), arguing about the way clerical taxation was being imposed. King Richard, Usk records, attacked the archbishop – the *Westminster Chronicle* is more specific and says that Richard tried to run Canterbury through with his sword – and so Courtenay was obliged to flee to Devon in disguise.[4] In fact, in spite of Usk, the argument was much more personal. Courtenay was criticising the king for his apparent willingness to have Gaunt put to death, so no wonder Richard became incensed. The archbishop had touched a very raw nerve.

Physical and moral courage, then, are clearly two of Courtenay's most notable characteristics. So were a staunch adherence to the Faith, and a willingness to be flexible in matters which did not involve fundamental principles. Thus, he took his position as archbishop seriously and, unlike Sudbury, was prepared to root out Wycliffite and Lollard heretics wherever he might find them – first at Oxford, then at Peterborough and Leicester. But he could also be understanding. When, for example, he visited the canons of St Augustine's convent in Bristol and reprimanded them for the dirtiness of their attire, and they explained they could not keep their habit clean because it was white and the black leather boots they were obliged to wear kept soiling their clothes with mud and grease, Courtenay gave them a dispensation to wear black or brown stockings while they were within the precincts of the convent.

Courtenay died on 31 July 1396. He was, in an age of volatility, when people of noble and royal birth in particular were able to vent their emotions in ways detrimental or even fatal to those beneath them, a man of self-restraint, and it is perhaps an interesting comment on his character that when Pope Urban VI offered him a cardinal's hat in 1378, he refused it. Acceptance would have elevated his status immensely, taken him away from the bear-pit of the English Court, and still allowed him to exercise influence abroad on England's behalf. The example of Simon Langham must have come to mind. But he stuck to his English post, braved the storm, and did his country a great favour in silencing the Oxford Wycliffites. As Joseph Dahmus puts it, 'almost any other policy would have left a disgruntled group of secular intellectuals encouraging the growth of Lollardy from exile';[6] and the dire consequences of secular intellectuals on the loose are provided by the histories of many a subsequent society.

In the case of his successor, *Thomas Arundel* (1396–97, 1399–1414), another nobleman, the innate courage born of confidence in class can be seen again. Arundel had to deal with three autocratic kings, Richard II, Henry IV and Henry V, and he did not hesitate to resist them or upbraid them for their faults. In 1386, while bishop of Ely, he argued with Richard in Parliament, reminding the ridiculously egocentric king that if the reigning monarch violated the statutes of the realm and alienated himself from his people, he could be deposed and replaced – a none too subtle reminder of what had happened to Edward II. For the moment, Richard caved in and even sought to placate the opposition by giving Arundel charge of the Great Seal; but it was not long before Richard was able to strike back, and in April 1388 he was effectively sent into internal exile as Archbishop of York. But Richard II's reign saw noble and royal volatility reach new, irresponsible heights and so, although Arundel became Archbishop of Canterbury in 1396, he scarcely had time to occupy his seat before Sir John Bussy (clearly acting as the king's lackey), accused him of treason and asked the king to put him under arrest. The treason to which he referred dated back to 1386 when Arundel's brother, the earl of Arundel, and other English nobles had been caught up in a feud with the king's favourites, an episode which had rankled in Richard's psyche and now, in 1397, caused him to aim a blow at the Arundel family. One phrase used by Bussy strikes a peculiar note. 'This Archbishop', he said to Richard, 'is a man of the most crafty and merciless temperament'.[7] Had he been speaking to Arundel about Richard, he would have been perfectly accurate. The result of Bussy's manoeuvre was a further exile for the archbishop, this time overseas. The temporalities of Canterbury were forfeit to the

Crown, and Courtenay was in effect deprived of the archbishopric, a deprivation confirmed by Pope Boniface IX in November that same year.[8] Arundel's replacement, *Roger Walden* (1397–99), was a competent royal hack. He had had a good deal of legal experience, especially in the Channel Islands of which he became Warden in *c.*1383, but suddenly leaped to office in the Church in 1387, combining a number of prebendaries in England with administrative and military duties in Calais until *c.*1393, after which he acted as royal secretary and treasurer until Arundel's enforced exile in 1397 precipitated him into the office of Archbishop of Canterbury. It was a ridiculous appointment, not because Walden was incompetent, but because his expertise and experience were almost entirely secular, and he was clearly unfitted for the prime ecclesiastical seat in England. The Pope acceded to King Richard's request for his appointment, but Boniface had far more important problems to face – a divided Church, an empty treasury, and the election of an antipope – so the parochial machinations of the English Court were unlikely to occupy much of his attention.

In 1399, however, everything changed and Arundel returned to England with Henry Bolingbroke, Earl of Derby, who lost no time in deposing King Richard and having himself crowned in Richard's place, while Arundel was restored to his archbishopric. Pope Boniface must surely have wondered at this point whether the English Court was quite sane.[9] Almost certainly Arundel had colluded in the deposition, but by 1404 relations between himself and Henry IV had grown distinctly cool. In that year, the House of Commons proposed alienating the temporalities of the English Church for a period of twelve months so that the king could benefit from them, and Arundel had objected forcibly. The wording of the Commons' motion made it clear that the members were moved more by anticlericalism than the national good, and Arundel did not fail to point this out. Walter Hook records a particular exchange:

An altercation ensued between the archbishop and Sir John Cheney, who declared himself an infidel as to the efficacy of prayer, and maintained that the lands of the clergy would be far more beneficial to

the public than their prayers. The archbishop protested against such
profaneness; and, turning to Cheney, he said, 'As for you, sir, who think
proper to speak with scorn of the functions of the clergy, I promise
you, that you will find an invasion of the rights and possessions of the
Church no very easy matter'.[10]

It was no way to win friends and influence people, and the potential
danger to anyone defying Henry IV or causing him to suspect his
disloyalty can be seen from the fate of Richard Scrope, Archbishop
of York, who in the same year raised an army of insurrection against
the king and was executed for it. Admittedly, Arundel's opposition
had not been of the same kind, but Scrope's case illustrated that no
ecclesiastical status, however exalted, was sufficient to keep a man
immune from a monarch's exercise of ultimate force against the
person. Yet he had ridden all day and all night from London to York
in order to confront the king and warn him not to carry out his
intention of executing Scrope, an action which speaks of his courage and personal commitment to the obligations of his office. One
cannot help thinking that at this juncture Arundel had been touched
by the ghost of St Thomas Becket. It was the same when he dealt
with Prince Henry, later Henry V. Arundel was out and in and out
of office as Chancellor between 1409 and 1413, remaining out the
day young Henry succeeded to the throne, and dying the next year
in something like obscurity.

Adam Usk, who had several reasons to be grateful to Arundel
for ecclesiastical preferment, called him 'the steadfastness, the torch
and wisdom of the people, the lamp and delight of the clergy and
of the Church, and an unsuppressable pillar of the Christian faith'.[11]
His stout defence of the Church and opposition to royal high-
handedness would have been sufficient to confirm this impression,
but to these we must also add his character as a prelate and a pastor.
England was plagued by the Lollard heresy derived from certain
teachings of John Wyclif. It complained about the subordination of
the English Church to Rome, clerical celibacy, transubstantiation of
the Host during Mass, prayers for the dead, pilgrimages, confession,
and the use of art to decorate and beautify churches. It was a fairly

general rejection of the Catholic Faith and the Church of Rome, so one can scarcely be surprised that Arundel bent many an effort into suppressing it, especially through his visitation of Oxford. As usual, the university required firm measures to curb its appetite for unorthodox pursuits. In fact, Lollardy was an expression of the prevailing anticlericalism of English society during the late fourteenth century, and Arundel's greatest service to the Church was to reiterate confidence in her ability to ride out this trend and others like it, until the heretical and antinomian winds had died down.

Arundel's personal faith centred upon one of the targets of the Lollards, devotion to the Real Presence, which he encouraged and defended against the discourtesy of certain courtiers who turned their backs on the Host when it was carried in public processions. He also gave a sympathetic hearing to the mystic Margery Kempe in 1413, as she acknowledged (writing of herself in the third person):

> When she came into his presence, she saluted him as she could, praying him of his gracious lordship to grant her authority of choosing her own confessor and to receive communion every Sunday... And he granted it her full benignly, all her desire, without any silver or gold; nor would he let his clerks take anything for writing nor for sealing of the [necessary] letter... And she showed this worshipful lord her manner of living, and such grace as God wrought in her mind and in her soul, to know what he would say thereto, if he found any fault either in her contemplation or in her weeping. And she told him also the cause of her weeping and the manner of conversation that our Lord conversed to her soul. And he found no fault therein, but approved her manner of living.[12]

Margery Kempe did not escape the sneers and brickbats of contemporary society for her unusual mode of living the spiritual life, and was more than once threatened with burning as a Lollard heretic. But it is clear she was actually a woman of orthodox beliefs, with a peculiar devotion to the eucharist, and her essential goodness shines through the pages of her autobiography. It looks as though she and Arundel recognised goodness in each other, and if we can accept her judgement of him, the epitaph pronounced by Arundel's contemporary, Thomas Walsingham, rings memorably true – that he was 'the most distinguished pillar of the English Church and its unconquered champion'.[13]

7

Spiralling to Disaster
Chichele to Cranmer
(1414–1556)

The autocratic and brutal nature of many of England's fourteenth-century monarchs seems to have brought out the best in several of their Archbishops of Canterbury, a completely uneven *quid pro quo* which left the country spiritually better served than it had any right to expect. Aggressive wars against France were a constant drain on finances, the Black Death had had both a dire and an unsettling effect on the population, heresies burgeoned, and internal wars contributed to a social maelstrom in which the archbishops found it impossible not to be engaged as important players. Thomas Arundel, however, had initiated the new century with a Church remarkably well able, under the circumstances, to tend the needs of the people, since one

of his prime concerns had been the quality of the clergy, and presenting a disciplined front to royal predators. It was an extremely useful
legacy which his fifteenth-century successors should have been able
to preserve.

Henry Chichele (1414–43) enjoyed the longest period in office since
Boniface of Savoy in the thirteenth century and St Dunstan in the
tenth. Educated at Winchester and spending much of his professional
life as an ecclesiastical lawyer, he began a diplomatic career in 1404
when he was about forty-two and continued it after he became
archbishop. The most significant events of his time in office were
the continued rampages of the English Crown in France – this time
victorious under Henry V – the challenge of Lollardy, and (a positive
development) the reunification of the Church under a single Pope,
Martin V. But the most noteworthy thing about Chichele's participation in or reaction to these events is his apparent identification with
the aims and motives of the Crown. He frequently lent the king
substantial sums of money and played a key role in negotiations with
the Roman Curia and France, as well as being a notable member of
the Regency Council which governed England during Henry VI's
minority. Legalistically minded and efficient, Chichele ran the Church
as though it were a corporation, making sure, as far as he could,
through frequent visitations, that clerical discipline was maintained,
especially in the business of clergy paying taxes, and in countering
those remnants of Lollardy left over from Arundel's time.

In 1414, Henry V had made heresy a felony, and so trials of heretics
took place in Convocation and bishops' courts against a background
of secular co-operation where necessary. 'On the whole', says E.F.
Jacob, 'given the contemporary climate of opinion, the procedure
in Convocation under Chichele was relatively merciful'. This, he
thinks, is because Chichele tried, where he could, to have the heretic change his opinion by educating him out of his errors rather
than by enforcing orthodoxy upon him through the judicial process,
an instinct which he attributes to Chichele's basic desire to have
the Church staffed by university-trained clerics who could combat
theological divergences by intellectual means. Certainly the archbishop was deeply concerned to improve the standard of learning

among the clergy, but to say, as Jacob does, that this was because 'he had confidence in the good sense of most academics' is both to misread his motives in encouraging clerical education, and to attribute to academics the one gift most of them conspicuously lack.[1] Chichele's frequent benefactions and foundations did certainly advance the causes of piety and learning, but one cannot help but notice that many were concerned with prayers for Henry V, and that he was eager to incorporate into the Sarum ritual the cults of saints especially associated with the king's military victories; while his provision for education was motivated by a concern for the welfare of the state as much as that of the Church. Thus, his foundation of All Souls College in Oxford in 1438 was intended to provide a chantry for the souls of Henry V and those who had fallen during his French war, and as a place of learning which would encourage education for the advancement of both Church and commonwealth, preparing students for careers in ecclesiastical administration and royal service. Chichele turns out, in fact, to be a good royal administrator, closer to the king than the Pope, with a view of the English Church which saw her obedient but not subservient to Rome, and if not altogether a creature of the Crown, one of its superior servants. In this regard, the preface to a return of rents for the city of Canterbury from 1420 contains a significant word: 'Returns of the Church of Christ in Canterbury... and of the *patriarchatus* of the most reverend father in Christ, and of the Lord Henry Chichele, Archbishop of Canterbury'. *Patriarchatus* may mean 'archbishopric', but it may also mean 'patriarchate', and if the prior-treasurer's clerk knew what he was writing, or was simply repeating something he had heard, it is possible that here we have a small insight into Chichele's view of the English Church, which had filtered down to his subordinates.[2]

If so, it was not a view peculiar to Chichele, of course – we have met it before more than once – but it was scarcely one which could withstand a hostile royal onslaught, and it was therefore fortunate that Chichele and Henry V saw eye to eye. But they did so because Chichele, no doubt genuinely, identified the fortunes of the Church with the aims of the monarch, a derogation of duty which St Thomas Becket would have found unthinkable, and one which was to have dire consequences in the future. In 1443 Chichele was about eighty-one and wanted to retire. He addressed a letter to Pope Eugenius IV, but was dead before the Pope's reply could arrive. *John Stafford* (1443–52), whom both Chichele and Henry VI suggested as a replacement, was a clerical lawyer, diplomatist, and administrator in the same mould as Chichele, so it is not surprising his career ended with an elevation to Canterbury. His period as archbishop was worthy enough but dull, apart from a brief few weeks in 1450 when he dealt with the ringleaders of Jack Cade's rebellion on behalf of the government. Some faint spark of interest in him may be struck by the fact that he was born illegitimate, and by the gossip (which may or may not have been true) that he had several children by a nun during the mid-1420s. He died on 25 May 1452 and was buried in Canterbury under a flat marble stone. In his case, 'flat' seems to be the *mot juste*.

John Kemp (1452–54), another cleric-lawyer-diplomatist, is most notable in his early years for his constant intriguing to achieve personal advancement in the Church. Fortunately for him, he enjoyed the good will of Henry V and quickly rose in secular offices because of it. But having failed to get the see of Winchester in 1419, he managed Chichester in October 1421 and, having already been in correspondence with influential members of the Papal Curia to get himself promoted bishop of London, triumphed by being nominated to that position in November the same year. His rise had been so rapid that even though he had been bishop of Rochester, Chichester and London, it was only in London he stayed long enough to be enthroned. Even so, he enjoyed London for only three and a half years before becoming Archbishop of York in July 1425 – a compromise candidate as it happens, and one who saw little of his northern see because he was so heavily engaged in the intricacies of a febrile secular government in which he became Chancellor in 1426. As such, he bore the burdens of working out yet another peace treaty with France, mediating between factions in Henry VI's Council, and pressing the Church for yet more extra sums of money. No wonder, therefore, that by the beginning of 1431 he had had enough and was using connections at the Papal Court to get himself called to

Rome. But as it happened, ill health overtook this manoeuvre, and in February 1433 he resigned the Great Seal.

A few months in Yorkshire, however, proved quite sufficient to send him back to London. He had missed being sent as an envoy to the Council of Basel at which a long-standing dispute about ultimate authority in the Church – did it lie with the Pope or with a Council? – was resolved in favour of the Papacy. But Kemp was soon at the centre of English things again, negotiating with French envoys, helping to raise the siege of Roxburgh Castle which was under threat from James I of Scotland, scuttling back and forth over the Channel to look for ways to ease the strained relations between the English king and the duke of Burgundy – mainly by treating with the duchess, with whom Henry VI was prepared to be on speaking terms. His efforts were rewarded with a cardinal's hat in December 1439, which he accepted even though Archbishop Chichele fought against it. Jealousy may explain his opposition perfectly well. Even with this enhanced status, though – perhaps even, at least in part, because of it – Kemp was passed over for Canterbury when Chichele died and conspicuously stayed in his diocese for sixteen months, an unprecedented length of time for him to spend there, in what can only be called an extended sulk. Absence from the political centre meant that in spite of his being needed in 1445 to add weight to negotiations connected with the marriage of Henry VI to Margaret of Anjou, he was not a key component in the maelstrom which whirled round Henry's head until 1450, when the principal officers of state were dismissed and Kemp was recalled as Chancellor.

He dealt vigorously with Jack Cade's rebellion, rode out the inevitable English storm caused by the news in 1451 that every English possession in France save Calais had been lost, and faced down an attempted *coup d'état* by the duke of York in 1452. His success in surviving these various potential catastrophes meant that when John Stafford died, Kemp's long-desired elevation to Canterbury took place at last, in spite of clear evidence that his health was now rather poor. King and archbishop degenerated together, the one quickly, the other slowly. Henry's mental collapse in August 1452, attended by some kind of crippling physical disablement, lasted until Christmas

1454. The vicious jockeying for power among the nobility during the king's illness meant that Kemp's last months were a misery, his position as Chancellor requiring him, under these circumstances, to attend to the state rather than the Church, and by the time he died in March 1454, the duke of York had seized the occasion to exert himself on his own behalf, ignoring the stricken king and, indeed, the rights of Henry's son Edward, born the previous year.

Can we say Kemp was a brave man? Courage both physical and psychological was certainly required of men in high places at this time, to face the dangers of rebellions or hostile crowds, and to negotiate the violent caprices of monarchs and nobles seeking important office and therefore looking for ways to cripple an opponent or rival. Kemp showed enough to see him through, but perhaps no more. His status as cardinal raised him to an equality with the greatest of princes and thus offered a good, but not an entire measure of protection against physical assault. But the treachery of a failing Court and the resurgence of social unrest meant that he could never afford to relax his vigilance. He neglected the diocese of York to fulfil the demands of his temporal posts, and did little enough for his diocese of Canterbury. When Henry VI recovered from his illness and was told that Kemp had died, he paid him a compliment: 'one of the wisest lords in all this land', he called him. But then, Kemp had never sided with others against him, so the verbal gesture may have been more polite than heartfelt. Kemp had been all his life a useful and talented servant of the English Crown. He had been a good deal less for the English Church.

He was succeeded by *Thomas Bourchier* (1454–86), a grandee following a worthy, who had the distinction of crowning three kings – Edward IV, Richard III and Henry VII – and of failing to save the life of a fourth, Edward V. His noble family, royal connections and aristocratic friends meant that his career was assured from the start. He became bishop of Worcester in 1434 by the time he was twenty-three (well below the proper canonical age), after protracted negotiations with Pope Eugenius IV, then Chancellor of Oxford and bishop of Ely, and then Archbishop of Canterbury and Chancellor of England, this last a double appointment which more or less guaranteed that its holder would spend more time on secular than ecclesiastical matters. The wavering fortunes of Henry VI meant that in order to be successful, Bourchier would have to be a diplomatist of unusual talents, as indeed he proved during a particularly volatile period, 1455–58, at the end of which he managed to secure an apparent amity between the Lancastrians in possession of the crown and the Yorkists in pursuit of it. By 1460, however, after being persuaded partly by his own common sense and partly by the partisan arguments of the Papal Legate that the political situation in England was dire and needed amendment, he began to incline to the claims of the duke of York to protect (but not supplant) the ailing Henry VI. But when the duke was killed in battle, Bourchier agreed that, in the event of the king's death, the duke's son, Edward, should be king; and in 1461, in spite of the fact that Henry was still alive, Bourchier was happy enough to recognise Edward IV.

This support did not go unrewarded. Bourchier was put forward to be a cardinal in 1465, although it took eighteen months for his nomination to be approved by Pope Paul II and nearly six more years before the red hat arrived in England. But the elevation, effective from 1467 when he was named cardinal in an official Papal letter, meant that he was dependent on royal approval before he could accept it and also retain his position as Archbishop of Canterbury – without such approval he would automatically cease to be Archbishop – and although Edward IV undoubtedly gave his consent, the reversal of his political fortunes between October 1470 and April 1471, when Henry VI briefly regained the crown, meant that Bourchier had to wait until Edward's final victory (secured by Henry's murder in May 1471) before he could exercise his full powers as the king's servant during the rest of the decade.

As archbishop, Bourchier was not entirely inadequate. Soon after he was enthroned, he held a diocesan visitation and lamented the gross irregularities he found both in behaviour and psychology among many of the clergy. The younger clerics especially put aside clerical dress and wore doublet, short cloak and long shoes with fashionably curled toes, and sported a sword and a dagger.[3] They also drank, fornicated, and neglected their pastoral duties. All this

Bourchier wished to amend, but his constant absences from York and then from Canterbury meant that, in effect, he did little more than fulminate. In one instance of heresy, however, he did stir himself sufficiently to achieve success. Reginald Pecock, Bishop of Chichester, was accused of heresy in 1457 and, after Bourchier had examined him and listened to the detailed report of a commission he had established to investigate Pecock's writings, he came to the conclusion that the charges were accurate. He therefore delivered his judgement in the form of a choice.

> Seeing you are convicted of not only holding what is contrary to the saying of all [the Church] Doctors, but, moreover, to be a contradicter of them; it behoves us, according to the doctrine of the said Doctor Jerome, to cut you off from the body of the universal Church, as rotten flesh, and to drive you from the fold as a scabbed sheep, that you may not have it in your power to corrupt or infect the whole flock. Choose, therefore, for yourself one of these things; whether you had rather recede from your errors, and make a public abjuration, and so, for the future, agree with the rest of Christ's faithful ones in your opinions; or whether you will incur the penalty of the canons, and not only suffer the reproach of degradation, but also, moreover, be delivered over to the power of the secular arm, that, because you have attempted by force to plunder the treasury of faith, you may become, according to the saying of the prophet, as well the fuel of the fire, as the food of the burning. Of these two choose one for yourself, for this is the immediate division in the coercion of heretics.[4]

Not unsurprisingly, Pecock chose to abjure, but refused to resign his see; whereupon Bourchier imprisoned him in Canterbury, issuing the following instructions:

> He shall have a secret closed chamber (having a chimney), and con-
> venience within the abbey, where he may have sight of some altar
> to hear Mass, and that he pass not the said chamber. To have but one
> person that is sad [*grave*] and well disposed to make his bed, and to
> make him fire, as it shall need. That he have no books to look on, but

only a portuous [*breviary*], a Mass-book, a psalter, a legend, and a Bible. That he have nothing to write with; no stuff to write upon. That he have competent fuel according to his age, and [as] his necessity shall require. That he be served daily of meat and drink, as a brother of the abbey is served when he is excused from the freytour [*from dining in hall*] and somewhat better after [the first quarter], as his disposition and reasonable appetite shall desire, conveniently after the good discretion of the said abbot.

Life under Bourchier, however, was not all gloom and rigour. In 1468, for example, he diverted the people of Canterbury with two camels and four dromedaries, and a sensational visit from the Marionite Patriarch, Peter II, who had been driven out of Syria by the Turks. But these were sparing levities in the middle of a deepening crisis. In 1483 Edward IV died and the young king, Edward V, asked Bourchier to see to his safety and that of the treasure-house in the Tower of London. So the king was sequestered in the Tower and his younger brother delivered there with him from sanctuary in Westminster at Bourchier's persuasive insistence. Whether Bourchier realised he was thereby encouraging a murderous usurpation of the throne by their uncle, Richard of Gloucester, or whether he genuinely believed that the Tower would be the safest place for the two boys is open to debate. A chronicler of the time, Dominic Mancini, absolves Bourchier of this potential blot on his reputation, that of know-ingly co-operating in the machinations which led to the deaths of Edward V and his brother – 'The cardinal had no suspicion whatever of treachery' – and it is quite true that Bourchier was absent from Richard III's coronation banquet. Nevertheless, the apology does not quite ring true. Bourchier was an old man, of course. Perhaps he did not care, or perhaps the obvious escaped him. But in view of his long experience at the centre of a political system which for decades had thrived on violence and the riotous overthrow of the existing monarch, it is hard to believe he was unaware of the implications of what he was encouraging. Whatever his mind at the time, he managed to crown Gloucester as king and then go into retirement (or 'hiding', as one might prefer to call it) until the battle of Bosworth was over, and Henry Tudor emerged victorious and was crowned in due time by Bourchier who ended a complaisant career by marrying him to Elizabeth of York in January 1486.

This brings us to *John Morton* (1486–1500), notorious for his 'fork'. The archbishop used to say, 'If the persons applied to for benevolence live frugally, tell them that their parsimony must have enriched them, and that the king will therefore expect from them a liberal donation; if their method of living on the contrary be extravagant, tell them that they can afford to give largely, since the proof of their opulence is evident from their expenditure'. Morton never said it, of course. Like so many famous dicta, it was invented much later, in Morton's case, by Francis Bacon. But does it tell us anything about his supposed ingenuity or deviousness? Like several of his immediate predecessors, Morton was educated at Oxford and then entered legal service, becoming closely identified with the House of Lancaster when he became Chancellor to Henry VI's son in 1456. The changing fortunes of that House, however, meant that with the advent of Edward IV he fared badly – to the extent of being imprisoned in the Tower of London, although he managed to escape thence and join the Lancastrian remnant in Flanders. Unfortunately, the chroniclers do not tell us how Morton accomplished the remarkable feat of escaping from what should have been a well-secured fortress. He was not yet the important figure he became later, but nor was he a nobody. The conditions of his imprisonment will therefore have lain somewhere between comfort and more or less restricted movement within the Tower along with a constrained, unpleasant durance; so one presumes that bribery rather than derring-do effected his liberty. But once the House of York seemed to be settled firmly upon the throne after 1471, Morton attached himself to the realities of political power and was rewarded with a series of posts and responsibilities of ever-increasing significance – Master of the Rolls, diplomatist in France and Burgundy on behalf of the English Crown, and finally, in 1478, bishop of Ely. Preferment was accompanied by benefices which made him rich, ten altogether between 1472 and 1479, thereby turning him into a pluralist on a fairly grand scale. That he deserved his recognition by King Edward can be seen from his work in Chancery, where he laboured hard to bring order into the confusion of public records caused by so many years of civil strife and political disorder. 'Methodical' is thus a description which suits Morton well.

His political touch, however, was not so sure. During the short protectorate of Richard, Duke of Gloucester, he was arrested along with others in the course of a meeting of the Council on 13 June 1483. Richard complained that the queen and the late king's mistress, Jane Shore, had inflicted physical harm on him by hostile magic. St Thomas More, who seems to have been told about this episode by Morton himself, supplies two different versions of Richard's words, one English, the other Latin. The English version reads simply that the two women 'have by their sorcery and witchcraft wasted my body'. The Latin is much more explicit. 'You will see, he said, that this criminal female [the queen] along with Mistress Shore and other magical tricksters, has cast the evil eye upon my body and deprived it of physical strength by means of acts of poisonous magic'.[5] Morton's arrest at this time seems to have occurred merely because he was in the wrong place at the wrong time, and a petition for his release from the university of Oxford, where he was detained, secured his relaxation into the custody of the duke of Buckingham. This provision was to have dire consequences. Morton soon gained great influence over the duke, who took little time before planning a coup against Richard, and while it is clear that Buckingham was both vain and ambitious, it can scarcely be denied that Morton worked upon these traits to further intentions of his own. The death of Edward V and his young brother provided a pretext to rise against their protector, now king, and however much Buckingham personally desired to avenge the boys' deaths and displace the man widely regarded as their murderer, the hand directing his movements was that of Morton.

The coup failed and Morton fled the country, going once again to Flanders where Henry Tudor now represented the Lancastrian cause. During the dying months of Richard III's reign, a lure was set for him – a pardon for his role in Buckingham's conspiracy, if he would return to England – but he was acute enough to ignore it and went to Rome instead. There he pleaded the Lancastrian (now the Tudor) cause to Innocent VIII, winning over the Pope to Henry

Tudor's claim and subsequent occupation of the English throne. It was a diplomatic success for which Henry should have been grateful, and was. So in 1486, at Henry VII's request, Morton was translated from Ely to Canterbury and the following year became Chancellor. As always, civil war had proved expensive, and King Henry was determined to recoup the costs to the Crown. Consequently, for the first twelve years of his reign, taxation was heavy and Morton, as Chancellor, bore the brunt of people's complaints. He bore them with fortitude. The efficiency which had characterised his period in office up to this point continued for the rest of his active life, and it was largely because of this efficiency that the king was able to put down potential and actual rebellion at home with relative ease, consolidate peace, rationalise the court system, and encourage exploration by John Cabot and his sons. Little wonder, then, that in 1493 Morton was created a cardinal with Henry's willing consent.

As archbishop, Morton proved equally managerial. He had scarcely arrived in Canterbury before he issued a pastoral letter condemning the prevailing fashion for clergy to wear lay dress – so Bourchier's similar letter had had little effect – and then undertook extensive visitations of various dioceses and monasteries. His inspection of the Abbey of St Albans was particularly disconcerting for all concerned. The conduct of several of the monks and of the abbot himself was deplorable, and Morton directed that proper discipline be resumed at once, with the promise of a second visitation at the end of two months. No doubt it was experiences such as these which led him to initiate an Act of Parliament to punish any clergy or religious found to have broken or be breaking their vows of chastity. But the visitations were not entirely motivated by what appears to have been his perfectly genuine desire to see amendment of the clergy. They raised sums of money for the Crown – 'benevolences' in the management-speak of the day – and also helped to underline, if underlining were needful, the primacy of Canterbury in England's ecclesiastical establishment. For, statesman though he was, Morton never forgot that his power rested ultimately on his being a Churchman rather than a politician. Henry VII could have dismissed him as Chancellor in an instant, and he would still have been Archbishop of Canterbury and a cardinal of the Church. Hence he took care to maintain the rights and privileges pertaining to his caste, to retain and exercise control over religious houses claiming the privilege of being exempt from his governance, and to preserve the prerogatives of the church of Canterbury against anyone who might seek to alienate them.

What of Morton personally? He was a supporter of learning with a particular interest in the practical arts of law and rhetoric, and it is undoubtedly no accident that the first book of St Thomas More's *Utopia* consists of a supposed conversation at Morton's dinner-table. More, of course, held him in high esteem, as we know, and he waxes almost lyrical in the English version of his *History of King Richard III*. 'The bishop was a man of great natural wit [intelligence], very well learned, and honourable in behaviour, lacking no wise [in no manner] ways to win favour'. This last phrase means he attracted other people's good opinion because they liked what they saw in him. It is interesting, therefore, to read Sir George Buck's *History of Richard III*, published in 1646, since it was written by a man sentimentally attached to the House of York, who interpreted Morton's character in a quite different way. The comments are scattered, but Morton is described in these various places as 'crafty, wicked, false, disloyal, factious, and seditious', as a 'secret treacherous instrument' who 'infected [Buckingham's] ears' and 'poisoned his heart' with 'subtle and malicious persuasions and arts'.[6] That Morton manipulated Buckingham is clear. For what motives exactly is not so clear. But if he was not altogether the fatherly patron suggested by St Thomas More, he was also not the stage villain portrayed by Buck. Rather, he was another clerical statesman in the mould which had become common under the Plantagenets, more politically aware than some and more efficient, though perhaps less genuinely religious as well. His kind, had he been able to see into the future, was doomed. With the advent of the Tudors, a new and quite ruthless secular government was born, under which the old order and its ministers would be swept aside.

But not immediately. Morton died on 15 February 1500, and *Henry Deane* (1501–03) stepped briefly on to the Canterbury stage. Deane was an Augustinian monk, the last religious to occupy the primate's seat, and had gained a remarkably useful amount of experience in Ireland, of which he was Chancellor in 1494, and deputy governor and justiciar in 1486, and in Wales where he was bishop of Bangor in 1495. Stories are told of him, that he personally led an armed raid to the Isle of Seals north of Anglesey to establish the bishopric's rights to fish caught in the island's fisheries, and that he had done much the same to compel certain Irish settlers to pay rent to him as bishop of Bangor. Both stories could be true, of course, or simply *ben trovati* as illustrations of a forthright personality who would stand for no nonsense where the rights of the Church were concerned. In 1499 he was translated to Salisbury where he would probably have stayed, because the choice for Canterbury upon Morton's death was the bishop of Winchester. He, however, died and thus Deane found himself elevated. His brief period in office was occupied by a royal betrothal, that of James IV of Scotland to Margaret Tudor, and a royal marriage, that of Katharine of Aragon to Margaret's brother, Arthur.

So much delicate negotiation and so much splendour appear to have sapped his strength, for on 15 February 1503 he died, leaving £500 in his will to pay the expenses of what he clearly hoped would be a lavish funeral, and *William Warham* (1503–32), who had the unenviable task of coping with Henry VIII's monumental egocentricity, was translated from London to Canterbury to begin more than twenty-eight years in office there. Warham had had the usual career – education at Oxford, legal posts in London, and a decade of various diplomatic missions abroad – and, having proved himself efficient and trustworthy in the Tudor cause, he was suddenly elevated to be bishop of London in 1501, and thence to Canterbury and Chancellor. The official world he inherited from his predecessors, however, was about to pass away. On 24 June 1509 he crowned Henry VIII and Katharine of Aragon, and thereby, quite unknowingly, consecrated as king a man who was little better than a cultivated thug. A signal of troubles to come flashed into view in 1511 with the case of Richard Hunne.[7] Early the previous December, Hunne was found dead in the bishop of London's prison. Anticlerical elements in London said he had been murdered and that his death had been made to look like suicide. Hunne, a merchant tailor, had refused to pay his local priest the customary fee on the death of one of his children – in this case, the sheet in which the child's body had been wrapped – and so the priest sued him for it. The demand and the refusal embodied a far more serious question: which was to have sovereignty over the other, canon law under which the priest was demanding his fee, or English common law, one of whose technical points Hunne was using to justify his refusal? In May 1512 the case was heard by Warham and judgement was given in the priest's favour. Hunne struck back with a further court-case based on an English statute known as Praemunire which stated, among other things, that church courts could not be used instead of common law courts to settle a dispute when the latter provided a remedy. Hunne had a history of anticlerical actions, and an outburst of heresy trials in 1511 made it somewhat more likely that if he persisted in defying the Church he might sooner or later fall foul of a charge of heresy. So when he was arrested, locked up, and then found dead, it did not take long for his death to turn into a *cause célèbre*.

At this point, the bishop of London made a grave mistake. He asked the king to have the matter considered by the Privy Council. What was he thinking? The natural thing to do would have been to appeal the case to Rome, but under the peculiar circumstances of the day, the English authorities might well have interpreted such an appeal as contrary to the Statute of Praemunire. Hence the bishop's letter to the king. But asking the monarch to step in and adjudicate in a matter which, originally at any rate, concerned a Church dispute was most unwise since it suggested to everyone that the monarch could extend his control of the Church further than it had gone before. Cardinal Wolsey and St Thomas More were both dragged into the business – now not only a murder trial in which the bishop of London's Chancellor and two others had been indicted, but also a heresy trial which resulted in Hunne's body being burned at Smithfield, the common execution spot in London. The London crowd, now more eagerly anticlerical than ever, had further oil poured on its flames by a public disagreement in the Convocation of Canterbury between the abbot of Winchcombe who complained that clerical privilege had been violated by the murder-trial, and one of King Henry's chaplains, Henry Standish, who steadfastly opposed Warham and was rewarded for his loyalty to the Crown by being appointed bishop of St Asaph three years later. Finally, in autumn 1515, the case came before the king and Wolsey, and it was there that Warham received the signal that his time as archbishop was liable to be difficult; for in reply to Warham's reminder that St Thomas Becket had died in defence of the liberties of the Church, Henry uttered words which revealed as clearly as anyone might have wished his self-identification as a Byzantine Emperor. 'We are, by the sufferance of God, King of England, and kings of England in times past never had any superior but God. Know therefore that we will maintain the rights of the Crown in this matter like our progenitors'. It was a reading of history to suit himself, but Henry was certainly voicing claims which the English Church had had to resist over several centuries, and if Warham was going to invoke the shade of St Thomas Becket, it would be apt only if, like St Thomas, he was prepared for personal martyrdom.

He was not, of course. The testing time came in 1531. Henry had been seeking an annulment of his marriage to Queen Katharine, an annulment which only the Pope could grant. Clement VII sent a legate, Cardinal Campeggio, to preside over a special court in England alongside the English legate, Cardinal Wolsey, and for this hearing Warham was appointed one of Queen Katharine's counsel. Not that he did much for her, merely repeating the well-known phrase, adapted from *Proverbs* 16.14, that the anger of a king is death. As surely as Henry's earlier boast had revealed his inmost thoughts, so did this glib timidity reveal those of Warham. During the annulment hearing it was St John Fisher who fought most valiantly for Katharine and, unsurprisingly, it was Fisher who later exhibited the courage of a martyr, dying by the axe under Henry's vengeful egoism. The results of the hearing are notorious. Henry's case was referred to Rome and Henry set about making himself master of the English Church in fact as well as in theory. In 1531 the Statute of Praemunire was used to intimidate the whole English clergy on the grounds that they had recognised Wolsey's legatine authority without permission and were therefore to be fined for their fault. Acts were then laid before a complaisant Parliament, which overtly amounted to setting the English monarch supreme over the English Church, a programme of self-aggrandisement which would see Henry independent of Rome and, in the words of the relevant Act, 'Protector and only Supreme Head of the English Church'.

Faced by such an obvious assault upon Papal authority – which, as a Catholic, Warham must have believed was conferred by God Himself on St Peter and St Peter's successors – Warham failed the test of martyrdom. Others were to die resisting Henry's blasphemous claim – St John Fisher, St Thomas More, several monks from the London Charterhouse – but not the English primate. All he could think of doing was to propose that a phrase be added to the king's proposed new title, 'as far as the law of Christ allows', a meaningless phrase, as Warham and every other bishop must have known, because the law of Christ in their eyes allowed nothing of the kind.

It was a crucial moment in the history of the native Church. English kings had had similar pretensions before and had been resisted by some of their archbishops. But 1532 was the year which required a martyr and Warham was found wanting. Indeed, when the king told Convocation to submit to his will, most of the bishops equivocated either by absenting themselves or adding reservations. Two refused altogether, but three caved in and gave unequivocal consent: and of these three, Warham was one. His fine words about St Thomas Becket, which he had uttered before the king in 1515 and wrote again now in 1532, turned out to be so much wind. One can make excuses for him, of course. In 1532 he was about eighty years old. He may well have been fearful of the political consequences of resisting the king, who was riding a wave of overt and intense anticlericalism, not to mention the xenophobia for which the English were notorious and which the Hunne affair had whipped into a fury. His personal safety was by no means assured if he crossed the king. Neither status nor age mattered to Henry. He executed Fisher, who was a cardinal at the time of his death, and butchered the eighty-year-old countess of Salisbury as part of a general clear-out of prisoners in the Tower. But, when every allowance had been made, the fact remains that when the Church in England, of which he was primate and for which he therefore bore ultimate responsibility, came under sustained royal attack, Warham crumbled and let the secular state have its way. But it was a failure of nerve and dereliction of moral duty which would be repeated in later times.

Still, it would be unfair not to include information which points to attractive features in Warham's character. On 1 October 1532, Erasmus wrote to Charles Blount, expressing sorrow at Warham's death:

> I wrote this lamenting, grieving, and completely at odds with myself, because I had heard that that undoubted, incomparable hero, William Warham, Archbishop of Canterbury, had exchanged life for death… I weep for my life, not his. He was truly a holy anchor to me… Undoubtedly neither old age nor disease has taken him from us, but a chance unfortunate not just for him but for learning, for religion, for the kingdom, and for the Church, so great was the man's devotion, so great his practical understanding in giving counsel, so great his kindness in helping everyone.[8]

The last words were probably heartfelt, since Warham had assisted Erasmus with a generous income from his own purse during the Dutchman's stay in England. Generosity apart, however, if the truth be told, there is not much else to say about Warham's virtues. He was frugal in his personal life, but lavish when his public office required it. He was eager for clerical reform, but took his desire no further into practice than several of his immediate predecessors. Hook, whose chapter on Warham in his *Lives of the Archbishops of Canterbury* is both long and full, makes a damning observation: 'In perverting a high and important office into a station in which he might enjoy his *otium cum dignitate* [leisure with public esteem], he yielded to the influence of the age in which he lived'.[9] This can perhaps be re-expressed in the well-known modern jibe, that 'he was like a cushion and always bore the imprint of the last person to sit on him'. Thus, when he proposed certain reforms of the clergy in 1518, he summoned a meeting in Lambeth, leaving Wolsey, as Archbishop of York, to call a similar meeting in the north. But he had forgotten that Wolsey was a Papal Legate and that he would see Warham's initiative as an encroachment on his superior authority – points he made very forcibly in a letter to Warham, which positively sparks and crackles with indignation. So Warham surrendered and the synod was rearranged in Wolsey's name and by his authority.

Warham died in the early hours of 22 August 1532. He may have welcomed death. He was old and sick and had witnessed an attack on his Church unparalleled in its ferocity. Even Henry II or John had not gone as far as Henry Tudor, and there was to be more destruction yet. That, however, would be witnessed by *Thomas Cranmer* (1533–56), an archbishop who embodied the new subservience to secular power. Unlike so many of his predecessors, he had been educated at Cambridge, where he took an unusually long time to acquire his bachelor's degree. He married – we know more or less nothing reliable about his wife except that her name was Joan and that she died in childbirth along with her baby – but after his wife's death he took holy orders and was then readmitted a Fellow of his old college, Jesus, a mark of personal favour to him, for which he was singularly ungrateful later on in his days of authority. By 1527 he had made sufficient impression to be included in a diplomatic mission to Spain, but thereafter retired again to Cambridge and buried himself in the university. A chance meeting in 1529 with two other Cambridge men, Stephen Gardiner and Edward Foxe, who were working on the annulment of King Henry's marriage to Katharine of Aragon, led to his suggesting that the king canvass theological opinion from universities throughout Europe, a suggestion which was taken up and brought him to Henry's notice, a notice made the more favourable by Cranmer's current friendship with the Boleyn family.

From the start, Cranmer had been of the opinion that the king's marriage could and should be annulled, and for the next four years he was employed as a key figure in Henry's team of researchers, producing books and documents relating not only to the annulment but also, by extension, to the nature of Papal authority; and it was this body of written and published work which stimulated the king's egocentric desire to become both Pope and monarch within his kingdom, and fed his eagerly receptive brain with arguments he could use to justify his break from Rome. But the years of research also had an effect on Cranmer himself, for it is clear that by 1532 he had come to the conclusion that he would reject Papal authority when it was inconvenient to his own career or personal wishes. He had met a reformer from Basel the previous year, Simon Grynaeus, who was struck by Cranmer's sympathy with the evangelical reforming movement – one which would loosely be termed 'Lutheran' or 'Protestant' – and in 1532 Cranmer openly displayed his personal break with the Catholic Church while posted as ambassador to the Holy Roman Emperor by marrying again, something he had no right to do, since he was a priest and was therefore subject to the discipline of celibacy. Breaking this vow, it seems, was of secondary importance to his taking advantage of being in the Lutheran city of Nuremberg where clerical marriage was acceptable. It was while he was in Italy in attendance on the Emperor that he learned he was to be the next Archbishop of Canterbury. Henry Tudor recognised a pliant opportunist when he saw one and confidently assumed that his new archbishop would put an end to the marriage with Katharine, a confidence which, it turned out, was not mistaken.

Concealing the fact that he himself was married, Cranmer returned to England and, on 30 March 1533, was consecrated archbishop. His conduct on this occasion was contemptible. Knowing that he was personally committed to the reforming cause and that he had thereby reneged on his obedience to the Pope, he nevertheless swore an oath of loyalty to the Papacy before going on to make a solemn declaration that this oath would not override his loyalty to the king or hinder 'reformation of the Christian religion, the government of the English Church, or the prerogative of the Crown, or the well-being of the same commonwealth', a protestation which was followed by two further oaths of loyalty to Rome. As his biographer Diarmaid MacCulloch acidly observes, 'In a procedure which can reflect no credit on him at all, Cranmer had formally benefited from Papal Bulls while equally formally rejecting their authority'.[10] But since Cranmer had already broken his vow of celibacy in order to marry, and then concealed his marriage in order to take advantage of the promotion offered him by Henry, it is clear we are dealing with someone to whom the sacredness of a vow meant little and the advancement of his career a great deal. The phrase 'ruthless chancer' springs to mind.[11]

The rest of his period in office under Henry VIII displays a servility to the royal will which emerges in his ready annulment of the king's marriage to Katharine of Aragon; his marrying Henry to Anne Boleyn; his use of the case of a famous self-proclaimed mystic, Elizabeth Barton, who had prophesied doom to Henry if he repudiated Katharine, to sweep away her clerical support-ers, largely traditionalists, and fill their place with clients of his own; and his co-operation with Henry in the destruction of Anne Boleyn, to whose family he had once been close. In 1536 Henry entered on his destruction of England's monasteries and chantries, beginning with the small and ending with the large, committing to the hammer and the fire not only a religious way of life, but also the great accumulated wealth of English artistic and archi-tectural heritage, the most widespread and devastating destruction England's cultural life had ever seen or would ever see again. So it scarcely comes as a surprise to find that in February that year Cranmer was publicly preaching at St Paul's Cross in London – the usual platform for government propaganda – that the Pope was Antichrist, and then later, during Lent, that the monasteries and chantries should be destroyed: and so the sorry tale of partnership and complaisance goes on.

It is clear, of course, that we must now begin to talk of the Church as the Church *of*, not the Church *in* England, since Cranmer, constantly in touch with European radicals throughout the 1530s, had shifted his own opinions and beliefs beyond orthodox Catholic teaching and was busy co-operating with Henry in dismantling certain of those key structures which made the Church Catholic in favour of others which would, under Edward VI, make it unmistakably Protestant. He was assisted by Thomas Cromwell, a man whose gifts of politi-cal tactics enabled both Cranmer and Henry to weather factional resistance to their schemes, Cranmer doing so in his usual fashion by submitting to Henry's declared intentions against the dictates of his own conscience. Thus, passage of the Act of Six Articles by Parliament in 1539 placed on the statute book a highly conservative piece of legislation intended to act as some kind of reassurance to the Catholic powers of Europe. Cranmer vigorously opposed it, perhaps especially because the articles reaffirmed the Catholic requirement for priests to be celibate; but Henry insisted on his Act, Cranmer gave way, and Mrs Cranmer was obliged to flee the country. In typical fashion, too, when Cromwell, his erstwhile ally, was indicted for treason in 1540, Cranmer wrote the king a letter in his defence, but then calmly voted with the rest of the Lords to have Cromwell put on trial. These oppositions of his look principled, even brave, but in fact they were merely playacting. The king knew perfectly well that Cranmer would always do as he was told, and Cranmer knew it, too. Both men needed each other – who else would so complaisantly divorce the king's wives or acquiesce in their executions? Who else could sustain the archbishop in his office in the teeth of conservative opposition? – and thus their alliance lasted, unholy to the end when Henry died holding Cranmer's hand and Cranmer offered Henry no more consolation at the moment of death than a few pious platitudes, thereby causing Henry to die without any of the Catholic sacraments in which the king professed he still believed.

The accession of Edward VI furnished Cranmer with an opportunity to ensure that the English Church was now overtly Protestant, and if there is one consistent thread running through all Cranmer's various inconsistencies, it is his determination to force through a reform of the English Church in accordance with evangelical prescription. New churches require new liturgies, and Cranmer's prayer books of 1549 and 1552 stand as a monument to his command of the English language. If there is one thing we can say in Cranmer's favour, it is that he had an unmatched ear for the musicality of English. No prayers written in that language have surpassed his, and the replacement of the *Book of Common Prayer* (still largely his in spite of revision) in the twentieth century was an act of vandalism quite the equivalent of those perpetrated by Henry VIII.

Cranmer's enjoyment of government support during Edward's short reign, however, did not go untroubled by opposition. Stephen

Gardiner, Bishop of Winchester, attacked him from, so to speak, the Catholic wing and John Hooper, Bishop of Gloucester, from the more radically Protestant, not to mention the Scots Calvinist, John Knox, who objected to Cranmer's retaining the practice of kneeling to receive holy communion. But Cranmer won the day, largely because he relied on Parliament as an instrument to force through and impose religious change – an interesting, but perhaps not unexpected development. A cleric who subordinates both the Church and its teaching to the power of a secular monarch will have no difficulty in relying upon a committee composed principally of laymen to act as a substitute monarch or as an additional witness to the monarch's will. The English Church had faced the possibility of this arrangement before, of course – it was the kind of settlement Henry II would have welcomed, for example – but Cranmer now made it the overt mechanism by which the English Church operated and, more than any other of his or Henry VIII's changes, this can be counted his most revolutionary act and his permanent legacy to the English people.

Cranmer's death during the reign of Queen Mary, who made a concerted effort to restore England to the Catholic communion, has made him famous. Some of the details are affecting (but perhaps not altogether reliable, since they come from a splatter of pamphlets and other documents intended to represent Cranmer either as a martyr or as a Machiavelli trapped by his own deceits and tergiversations)[12] and no one can fail to have pity for someone condemned to the dreadful death of being burned alive. His execution caused little stir in Oxford (where it took place) at the time, however, and could scarcely have come as a surprise either to him or to anyone else. When Edward VI died, there was a failed *coup d'état* which sought to supplant Mary Tudor with Jane Grey, an attempt which Cranmer openly supported and to whose cause he contributed twenty of his own armed retainers. It was an act of treason for which the ringleader, the duke of Northumberland, would pay with his life. A Catholic establishment could hardly allow an overtly Protestant archbishop to continue in office, so his arrest and replacement were bound to happen, a change of fortune which he must have realised would almost certainly result in his own death unless he could circumvent it. But there is no need to assume that the various submissions to Papal authority he signed were necessarily dictated by a conscious, cunning attempt to avoid the torments of burning. Someone in his position must find it extremely hard, if not impossible, to maintain his rationality uninfluenced by his emotions, and the same can be said anent his subsequent recantation of heresy, and the recantation of his recantation. Few people are made of the stuff of martyrs, and Cranmer was not one of them. He should not be criticised for it. What he can and should be criticised for is his abandonment of the Church and its teachings to the decisions of secular authority. It is one thing to subordinate oneself to a king or a parliament, quite another to subject one's faith and one's Church to them, thereby more or less ensuring that should the need arise to defy the secular power and defend the Faith and the guardian of that Faith from the temptation or pressure to compromise with the prevailing secular ethos of the moment, defiance would require an act of quite exceptional personal courage, and defence a willingness on the part of every Church officer, small and great, to be subject to persecution by a political establishment which has been allowed to believe that it, and not the Church, is the ultimate repository of truth.

8

Vicars of Bray
Pole to Laud
(1558–1645)

Thomas Mayer, borrowing from Nietzsche, characterised *Reginald Pole* (1556–58) as 'a fighter against his time'. Philip Hughes, taking into account testimonies from contemporary historians, provides a brief portrait of him in 1553:

> Pole, at fifty-three, was a kindly, gentle, dryly humorous scholar, with a vast experience of the sorrows of life in high places, and great patience bred thereby; with an unshakable confidence in the providence of God as a factor in everyday life; a man of habitual prayer, who passionately desired, and had worked hard for, the reform of the festering ecclesiastical system; a man utterly unworldly and – to a fault, it may

be – revolted by the use of worldly means to attain ends that were
spiritual; a great nobleman, passionately English, something of a saint,
and the Renaissance at its best; a spirit always rare, by the nature of
things, but nowhere more rare than in the England ravaged by such
men as had ruled through the last twenty years.[1]

Pole's passion for his country may have been that of the exile, because
he spent most of his life abroad. He was educated at Oxford and
then Padua where he met a wide variety of both lay scholars and
ecclesiastics, one of whom later became Pope Paul IV. Between 1527
and 1531 he was preoccupied, at Henry VIII's request, with the question of the annulment of Henry's marriage to Katharine of Aragon,
but by early 1532 he was back in Padua, having failed to attain any
important office of state in England. Once there, he turned from
philosophy to the study of theology and began to acquire a reputation as a man of international consequence – so much so that the
Imperial ambassador quite seriously suggested him as a husband for
Henry VIII's daughter, Mary. Pole was not a priest – he would not
be ordained, in fact, until 1556, three months after his appointment
as Archbishop of Canterbury – and his Plantagenet blood, inherited
from his mother, the Countess of Salisbury, actually gave him a better
claim to the English throne than that of the upstart Tudors. Marriage
to Mary would have effectively made him king. But the proposal
petered out, and Pole remained sequestered in his scholarship and
what seems to have been a genuine religious conversion, until he
was called to Rome in 1536.

These years produced a book, *A Defence of the Unity of the Church*,
which took its rise from some of the problems inherent in Henry
VIII's quest for an annulment of his marriage. It is divided into four
parts. In the first, Pole attacks the notion of royal supremacy over
the Church and argues that the priestly office is greater than the
monarchical. But, in order to avoid the charge that he is attacking
the king directly, he writes of Henry as a sick man in need of a
physician, and offers to supply that role himself. 'Can I really pretend
I am so acquainted with your disease of mind that I dare not even
put a name to it, especially since everyone else, moved to anger by

the atrocity of your deeds, thinks about the matter in just this way and talks [about it] all over the place, [saying] that now you are no longer sick but have plainly taken your last gasp, and at this very moment breathed your last?' Spiritually moribund, Henry therefore needs whatever help he can get. In the second part, Pole defends Papal supremacy, and then in the third returns to Henry's particular troubles brought on, says Pole, by marriage to Anne Boleyn whom he characterises as a whore. Finally, in the fourth part, he offers the king his medicine – repentance (which, of course, implies not only a recognition of fault, but a sincere desire to put right what is wrong and not to repeat the offence).

The book irritated Thomas Cromwell, for fairly obvious reasons, and once it was off his hands Pole had to deal with the effects of English reaction to it, which included several assassination attempts on himself, originating with the English ambassador to the Court of Hungary. In December 1536 Paul III created him cardinal and Papal Legate, and for the next five years Pole moved about, from Paris to Cambrai to Liège to Rome and then Toledo, continually dogged by English hostility to him, while he himself encouraged such rebellions as there might be against Henry's increasingly despotic rule. On 27 May 1541 he lost his mother. Her butchery was Henry's final answer to Pole's book. She was never brought to trial on any charge. A complaisant Parliament condemned her at Henry's bidding. When Pole heard of her death, he wrote to Cardinal Juan Alvarez of Toledo that neither Christ nor the Apostles or martyrs or virgins would regard her death as shameful, and that he himself deemed it an honour to be the son of a martyr. He had good cause to call her such. His mother was nearly seventy and climbed the scaffold and knelt down calmly at the block. But her executioner was an inexperienced youth, a substitute for the official headsman who was unavailable at the time, and when he failed to remove her head with the first blow of the axe, he hacked away at her head and neck and shoulders until his carnage succeeded and the old lady finally died. Reparation was made, and her son's opinion justified, however, in December 1886 when she was beatified by Pope Leo XIII.

In October 1542 Cardinal Pole was appointed to attend the Council of Trent, the great reforming Council which at long last began to provide answers to the cries for ecclesiastical reform heard from within the Church for the past 200 years. Pole's part in this was not the most prominent, and he retired from its sessions in 1546 because of ill health. It was not until 1548, with the advent of Edward VI's government, that Pole felt able to contact his native land; but a Catholic-inspired rebellion against Edward's Protector, the duke of Somerset, effectively put an end to any possible rapprochement, and before the cardinal knew it, Paul III had died and Pole had become a favourite to succeed him. The college of cardinals, in fact, gave him twenty-four of the twenty-eight votes required to make him Pope, and Cardinal Farnese actually proposed forgetting the other four and declaring Pole Pope by acclamation, a proposal which stumbled largely on Pole's refusal to canvass votes, and on French opposition to his candidacy. He gained two more votes at another ballot, but there his cause stuck, and so reluctantly the cardinals looked elsewhere and elected an Italian who took the name Julius III.

It is perhaps typical of Pole that he should have been too high-minded to sully the Papal election with political behaviour and that once wedded to this moral stance he was too stubborn to change it. He was to exhibit the same exasperating combination of virtues when, in 1554, he was appointed Papal Legate to England and offered the chance to undo much of Henry VIII's and Edward VI's work, and reconcile England to the Papacy. England, he wrote to Queen Mary, must return to her obedience first, before reconciliation could take place, and monastic property looted by the state in the persons of its monarch, nobles and gentry must be restored to the Church as well. Politically, too, Pole made another mistake in letting it be known that he opposed the suggested marriage between Queen Mary and King Philip of Spain, since his objection immediately angered the Holy Roman Emperor, Philip's father. But these points were not sufficient to block altogether his return to England, or indeed to prevent his appointment as Archbishop of Canterbury on 11 December 1555, although they did mean he was obliged to reconcile the country with

Rome before he had achieved his declared goal of seeing monastic property surrendered.

The spirit of Trent was clearly active in Pole, even though he himself would have taken a somewhat different line from some of its eventual decrees. He had no doubt that the English Church needed reform and equally little doubt that most of its troubles were due to the English clergy themselves, a conviction which seemed amply to be borne out when he tried to implement reforms through specially convened synods and found himself greeted by resentment and delay. That his attempts to re-establish the Church in England on a surer, more virtuous basis came to little can be attributed partly to the very short time he had in office, partly to exterior difficulties caused largely by Pope Paul IV who had opposed Pole's candidacy in the Papal conclave of 1549 and was still hostile to him, and partly because his situation in England after Queen Mary's marriage to Philip of Spain made him appear to be a Spanish agent whenever he ventured into foreign diplomacy. Since in fact he was not, this misrepresentation caused him endless problems. More serious, however, was Paul IV's determination to prevent Pole from ever being elected to the throne of St Peter. Withdrawing Pole's legatine powers in 1557 was an early mark of his disfavour. Trying to smear him as a heretic – the tactic Paul had originally tried at the Papal conclave – was much more hurtful and damaging. That King Philip continued to support him, therefore, says much about Pole's character and its effect on those who came into frequent contact with him. Ruy Gómez de Silva, for example, writing from England on 15 April 1555, assured his correspondent, 'You may believe that he [Pole] is a good man, without fault as far as one can judge from outside';[2] and we get a touch of Pole's natural temperament in his reply to extravagant praises heaped on him when he arrived in Canterbury in 1557. 'Thou art Pole', exclaimed Archdeacon Harpsfield, 'and thou art to us as the polar star, opening to us the kingdom of Heaven; all nature hath been pining for thee, the sky, the waters, the earth, and those very walls' – pointing to the archiepiscopal palace, in fact now ruined after a serious fire in 1554 – 'and now by thy return all things are happy, smiling in tranquillity and peace'. The cardinal had

had enough. 'While you were praising God', he said, 'I heard you with pleasure. My own praises I have no wish to hear'.

He died the day after Queen Mary, in the new apartments he had built in Lambeth Palace. His will contained a reference to the Pope who had hated him for so long and had tried to undermine him at every turn.

> First, through the grace of God in the sincerity [purity] of whose faith I was taught by my elders and accepted from the holy Roman Church, integral and undoubted mistress of all churches, with all humility I commend my soul to omnipotent God... in whose one holy and Catholic Church and in obedience to the Roman pontiff... I have always lived and wish to die. From our most holy father and lord Pope Paul IV, who before his pontificate I always loved like a father and whose honour after God I have always faithfully served during his pontificate, just as in all my actions and legations which I have undertaken for the apostolic see I am conscious that I have never sought anything but God's honour and the dignity and utility of his Church... I ask benediction with all reverence, wishing him peace, safety, and all true consolation.[3]

Matthew Parker (1559–75) was of the opinion that 'the thing which will weigh against Pole, to the eternal memory and infamy of his savage time in office, will be that Cranmer was burned to death'.[4] This is, perhaps, typical of the way in which history is written by the victors, because in fact Pole played very little part in Cranmer's trial and execution. But Parker was to preside over the triumph of Protestantism in England, and while Mary Tudor has gone down to legend as 'Bloody Mary' for her execution of a large number of Protestants, her half-sister, who executed a large number of Catholics, both priests and laity, and allowed the infamous Richard Topcliffe to set up a private torture-chamber in his own house, has escaped the sobriquet 'Bloody Bess'. The immense complexities of the religious settlement during Elizabeth Tudor's reign cannot be rehearsed here but can be reduced to a single essential sentence. The political establishment was determined to impose on the English people,

Left: 1 St Gregory, also known as 'The Great', Pope from 3 September 590 to 12 March 604. He came from a wealthy patrician family and turned one of the family homes into a monastery where St Augustine and many of the companions he later took to England received their training.

Below: 2 A Victorian version of St Augustine's landing in Britain in 597. The man and woman tentatively greeting him must be King Aethelbert and his Christian queen, Bertha. The dubious expressions on the faces of the men behind them reflect the mixed feelings of the Cantware court at St Augustine's mission.

Left: 3 Page from a copy (sixth- or seventh-century) of St Augustine's writings, containing part of a letter to Paulinus, one of the monks who accompanied him to Britain, and who later became Archbishop of York.

Below left: 4 Part of Bede's *Historia Ecclesiastica*, written in *c.*731. Bede was writing nearly 130 years after St Augustine's death, and his account of the Roman mission is dependent on evidence from Albinus, Abbot of St Augustine's Abbey in Canterbury, who, Bede says, passed on whatever he had gleaned from extant records and old traditions, and from Roman archives researched by a priest from London who brought Bede the relevant documents he had discovered therein.

Below: 5 Archbishop Stigand (1052–70), deposed from the archbishopric on charges of corruption and receiving his authority from an antipope ('Benedict X') instead of the genuine Pope. Edward the Confessor, who weakly depended on Stigand's political astuteness, openly described him as a traitor who had bought his office.

6 St Dunstan wearing the pallium, a narrow woollen band passing over the shoulders, with lappets hanging down front and back. It is a symbol of archiepiscopal authority conferred by the Pope, and the early Archbishops of Canterbury were obliged to go to Rome to receive it in person. Later it was sent to England and the archbishops were invested there by a Papal Legate. In his youth, St Dunstan was accused of practising harmful magic, but survived this to become a monk, living as a hermit until he was called into royal service and thence to high position in the Church.

7 St Dunstan kissing the hem of Christ's robe. The words written above the kneeling figure mean, 'Merciful Christ, I ask you to protect me, Dunstan. Please do not let random storms overwhelm me'. It is possible St Dunstan himself wrote this on the manuscript.

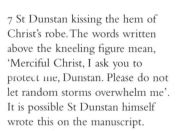

Above left: 8 The seal of St Anselm. Seals were regularly used to confirm the authenticity of both a document and any signature attached thereto. This shows St Anselm wearing the pallium, and announces his title of archbishop 'by the grace of God'. His hairstyle is that of a Roman, as opposed to a Celtic cleric.

Above right: 9 The seal of St Thomas Becket. He is shown wearing the pallium and the form of mitre common in the twelfth century. After this, the 'horns' shifted so that they were at the front and back rather than at the sides.

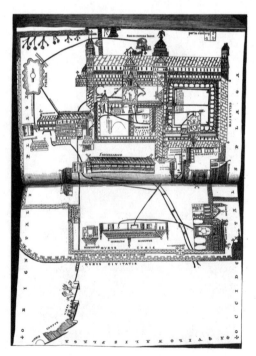

Left: 10 A plan of Canterbury Cathedral church and monastery as they were in *c.*1150 during the time Archbishop Theobald was in office. The long building at the bottom of the picture represents the brewery and the bakery, and the long building in the middle is the lavatory. The castellated wall at the bottom of the picture is that of the town itself.

Right: 11 St Thomas Becket and his secretary, Herbert of Bosham. *Secretarius* originally meant 'someone who keeps another's secrets', and thus referred to a confidential adviser as well as a 'scribe'.

Below: 12 The front and back of St Thomas Becket's chasuble, which is kept in the cathedral at Sens. The word 'chasuble' is derived from the Latin *casula*, meaning 'little cottage', presumably because, in its original form, the garment was round and had a hole in the middle. While the priest was saying Mass, he would have to drape the sides over his shoulders in order to leave his arms and hands free.

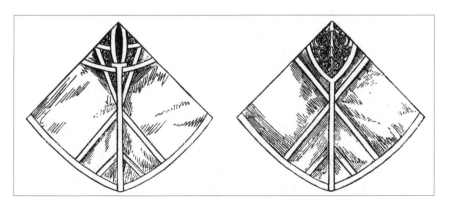

Above: 13 Henry II in dispute with St Thomas Becket. Once Thomas became archbishop, he and the king were soon at odds, largely because Henry had thought that by appointing Thomas archbishop, he would be able to control the Church through him and milk it for its wealth. Thomas, however, had other ideas. It may be ominously significant that in this picture Thomas has four armed knights crowded behind him. They may represent his own armed followers, but they may also represent the four knights who murdered him in answer to Henry's unsubtle hint.

Below: 14 St Thomas Becket excommunicating his enemies and arguing with King Henry and King Louis. From a thirteenth-century *Vie de Saint Thomas*. Excommunication deprived someone of access to the sacraments of the Church, and if he or she died without such access, there was an assumption that he or she might well go to Hell. Over-frequent use of this spiritual weapon, however, deprived it of much of its original terror.

Top: 15 St Thomas Becket parting from King Henry and King Louis. From the *Vie de Saint Thomas.* Thomas would not have been wearing his mitre, of course. On many occasions, he would have worn lay attire, more or less indistinguishable from any other great lord. Note the accusing finger pointed directly at him by the retreating axeman.

Above: 16 St Thomas embarking for England. From the *Vie de Saint Thomas.* The gestures here indicate that St Thomas is asking a question or demanding an explanation, and his steward (carrying the purse) is going into details in reply.

17 The martyrdom of St Thomas Becket. From a twelfth- or thirteenth-century psalter. This is probably the earliest surviving representation of St Thomas's death. We see that the top of his skull has been sliced off by the initial blow.

18 Page from the *Chronica maiora* of Matthew Paris, describing and illustrating St Thomas's murder. Paris was born in *c*.1200 and became a Benedictine monk. Despite his surname, he was almost certainly English. His chronicle is one of the most important sources for historians of the thirteenth century, since it covers events all over Europe as well as in England. Matthew revised it extensively before his death, expunging, altering and rewriting, principally to tone down or remove his more offensive passages.

Above: 19 Becket's shrine. Glass painting, thirteenth-century, Canterbury Cathedral. He is shown 'asleep', a common way of expressing the notion of death. The figure above may represent a succeeding Archbishop of Canterbury, or the ghost of Becket himself.

Right: 20 Fragment of a drawing of the shrine of St Thomas at Canterbury. It was generally agreed that this shrine was one of the finest in Europe. It was destroyed on the orders of the arch-thug Henry VIII.

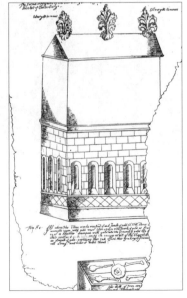

21 Within a few years of Thomas's death, his tomb had become the focus of one of
the most important cult centres in western Europe. It was in front of this shrine that
Henry II was forced to come as a penitent in 1174 and be flogged as a punishment for
his part in Becket's murder. The birches used for this can be seen in the hands of three
of the monks.

Above: 22 Pilgrims leaving
Canterbury. This gives a notion
of what Geoffrey Chaucer's
pilgrims would have looked
like. The castellated walls
contain the cathedral and the
monastery, here plainly visible.

Right: 23 *Caput Thomae,*
'Thomas's head'. One of the
badges worn by pilgrims
to Canterbury. It was a sign
they had actually made
the pilgrimage, and is the
equivalent of a modern
postcard or souvenir.

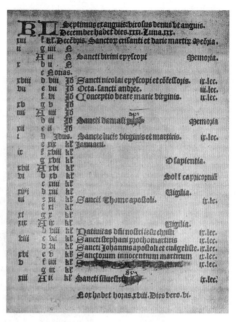

Above left: 24 Pilgrims' badges and ampoules, small containers for holy water. Most of these show St Thomas's head and are thus from Canterbury.

Above right: 25 Page from a Hereford missal in the British Museum, showing the erasure of St Thomas's saint's day in the liturgical calendar for December. The abolition of his day coincided with other changes made during Henry VIII's reign.

Left: 26 Seal of Stephen Langton. He is wearing the pallium and the changed form of mitre of the early thirteenth century. His right hand is raised in a gesture of blessing, the two fingers and the thumb representing the Trinity.

Left: 27 Archbishop Edmund Rich (1233–40).
He is wearing his episcopal ring on the fourth
finger of his right hand, and is standing on a snake
representative of Satan. The drawing comes from a
thirteenth-century psalter.

Below: 28 The consecration of Edmund Rich,
drawn by Matthew Paris.

Above left: 29 Archbishop Henry Chichele. Portrait in glass in Lambeth Palace library. Chichele's influence with the government was undoubtedly increased by his enormous loans to Henry V's government: £20,000 over ten years.

Above right: 30 Archbishop Chichele. His tenure of office coincided with a rising wave of antipapal sentiment because of Pope Martin V's declared intention to recover the Church's position in Europe after a disastrous period when legitimate Popes and antipopes vied with each other for ultimate authority. Pope Martin and Chichele did not see eye to eye on the Pope's endeavours to exercise his authority in England.

Below: 31 A letter from Edward V to Archbishop Thomas Bourchier regarding the safe keeping of the Great Seal. It is dated at Northampton, 2 May 1483. Bourchier presided at three coronations, those of Edward IV, Richard III and Henry VII. He also married Henry Tudor to Elizabeth of York, thereby uniting the two warring Houses of York and Lancaster.

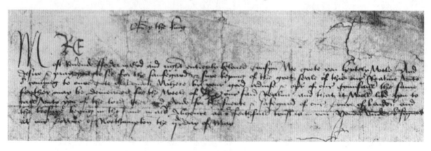

32 Drawing of Archbishop William
Warham by Hans Holbein. Warham
seems to have spent much of his
time being humiliated either by
Henry VIII or by Cardinal Wolsey.
He died just in time to avoid the
political and religious consequences
of Anne Boleyn's pregnancy.

33 Archbishop
Warham in
procession, with
attendants and
a herald. The
Archbishop of
Canterbury
was a great lord
and had many
servants to
accompany him
on almost every
occasion, even
when he left the
dining-hall in
Lambeth Palace
and went across
to the courtyard
to his private
apartments. This
was still the case
in the nineteenth
century.

Above left: 34 The arms of William Warham as Archbishop of Canterbury and Chancellor of England. When he was enthroned as archbishop, we are told that 'all the Archbishop's honours were drawn, depicted, and delineated after a strange manner on gilded marchpane upon the banqueting dishes'.

Above centre: 35 Warham's seal. It is much more elaborate than those of many of his predecessors, and shows him within the architecture of Canterbury Cathedral.

Above right: 36 Seal of Thomas Cranmer, Archbishop of Canterbury. Notice that the figure of Christ has replaced the dominant figure of the archbishop which is usual in earlier seals.

37 Thomas Cranmer by Gerlach Flicke. This was painted in 1545 and shows Cranmer reading the Epistles of St Paul. A volume of the works of St Augustine of Hippo is on the table in front of him. Both books give the onlooker a hint of Cranmer's reformist religious opinions.

38 Letter from Cranmer at Dunstable to Henry VIII, dated '17 May', informing him of the date when the annulment of his marriage to Katharine of Aragon would be brought to a conclusion. Note that it is written in English, not Latin.

Top: 39 The Act of Appeals (1533). This declares that England is an empire governed by one supreme head and king, and that it is for the king to judge all spiritual cases which may arise in his realm. The Act also forbids any appeals from the king's judgement to Rome. Henry VIII waited until the Pope had appointed Cranmer Archbishop of Canterbury before passing this Act.

Above: 40 The Act of Supremacy (1534). This said that the king was the supreme head of the Church in England, and was worded in such a way as to make it clear that this title was not conferred on Henry by Parliament, but that Parliament was merely recognising it as a 'fact'.

41 Title-page of the first edition of the 'Great Bible' (1539). This was not the first translation of the Bible into English, but was to become the official version under Henry VIII. Henry is shown receiving and then distributing the book, and all the common people (below the central notice) are exclaiming *Vivat rex*, 'Long live the King'.

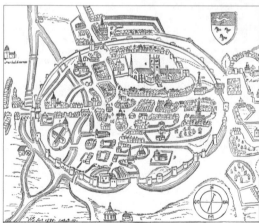

42 Panoramic view of Canterbury in the sixteenth century. It is still a relatively small walled town surrounded by fields and some outlying dwellings.

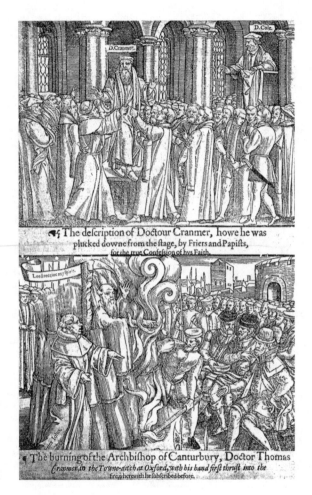

D.Cranmer.
D.Cole.
The deſcription of Doctour Cranmer, howe he was plucked downe from the ſtage, by Friers and Papiſts, for the true Confeſsion of hys Faith.
Lord receiue my ſpirit.
The burning of the Archbiſhop of Canturbury, Doctor Thomas Cranmer, in the Towne-ditch at Oxford, with his hand firſt thruſt into the fire, wherewith he ſubſcribed before.

43 Depiction of Cranmer's arrest, and subsequent death on 21 March 1556. Accounts of his death vary according to the religious opinions of the writer. The one given by the anti-Catholic Protestant propagandist, John Foxe, has proved to be the one most quoted.

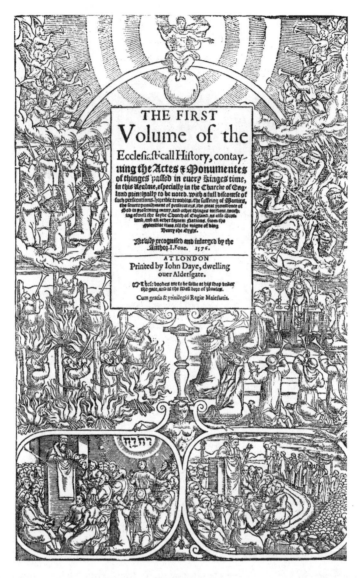

44 Title-page to Foxe's *Acts and Monuments*, popularly known as *Foxe's Book of Martyrs*. The left-hand side shows burned Protestants wearing martyr's crowns and carrying palms of victory. The right-hand side depicts the Catholic Mass and its celebrants and congregation being tortured by demons. On the bottom left, a Protestant preacher expounds the Scriptures under the approving 'sun' of God, which has JHVH (Jehovah) to identify it. On the bottom right, a Catholic priest teaches his congregation about the Blessed Sacrament, which is being carried in procession past them.

45 Archbishop Matthew Parker. Eighteenth-century engraving of an older picture. He is shown with books of history and documents, thereby emphasising his status as a scholar and administrator.

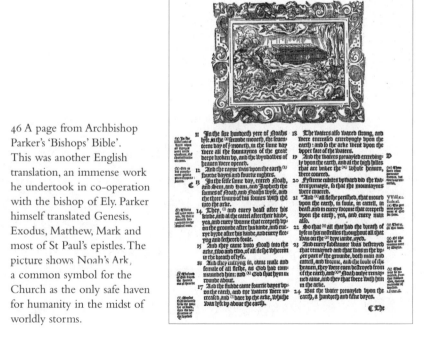

46 A page from Archbishop Parker's 'Bishops' Bible'. This was another English translation, an immense work he undertook in co-operation with the bishop of Ely. Parker himself translated Genesis, Exodus, Matthew, Mark and most of St Paul's epistles. The picture shows Noah's Ark, a common symbol for the Church as the only safe haven for humanity in the midst of worldly storms.

Above left: 47 Archbishop Edmund Grindal. From an engraving by Arnold Buchel, published in 1620. During the reign of Mary Tudor, Grindal fled to Strassburg and Frankfurt, where he collected many stories about Protestants executed by Mary. These stories were later incorporated into Foxe's *Acts and Monuments*.

Above right: 48 Archbishop John Whitgift. From an engraving by Vertue. Whitgift's appointment was greeted by Puritans with a mixture of feelings. One man close to government wrote that 'the choice of that man to be archbishop maketh me to think that the Lord is even determined to scourge his Church for their unthankfulness'.

Below: 49 Lambeth Palace from the Thames. From an engraving by the late sixteenth-century J. Kip. This shows the Thames as a major highway, carrying not only passenger traffic, but also goods and even, as illustrated, a carriage and its horses on a huge raft.

Above left: 50 Archbishop Richard Bancroft. Engraving by Vertue. During his period in office, large numbers of clergy were admonished or deprived of their livings because they failed to give full assent to the Book of Common Prayer. Puritans riposted by accusing him of inclining to Catholicism, a silly accusation, since he was not in the least so minded.

Above right: 51 Archbishop George Abbot. Engraving by Vertue. He was appointed archbishop largely because of the recommendation of the earl of Dunbar. James VI and I remembered this suit after the earl had died, and elevated Bancroft as a gesture of respect for this dead friend.

52 Archbishop William Laud. From the picture by Van Dyck. Only two days after George Abbot's death, Charles I greeted Laud with the words, 'My Lord Grace of Canterbury, you are welcome!'. The appointment may have been sudden, but Laud's apprenticeship had been long, and he was well qualified for the post.

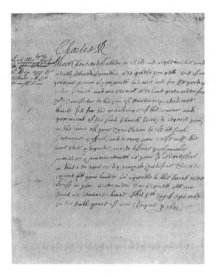

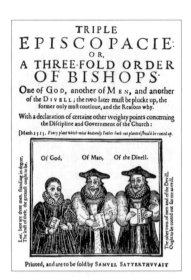

Above left: 53 A letter from Charles I to Laud, announcing his translation to Canterbury, 8 September 1633.

Above right: 54 A pamphlet attacking Archbishop Laud. From late 1640 onwards, there was an attempt to dismantle the Church establishment. The picture suggests that the Church has in it worldly and diabolic elements which need to be swept away. The left-hand figure represents a radically-inclined cleric carrying the Bible. The other two represent Laud, who is carrying service books. Laud's insistence on the clergy's uniform use of the prayer book caused immense resentment both in Scotland and in England.

55 Caricature of Archbishop Laud and Henry Burton, 1645. Burton was one of the most vociferous opponents of Laud's attempts to impose liturgical uniformity. Laud vomits up a whole series of books and pamphlets, while Burton acts as a physician, holding Laud's head steady while he is being sick.

Above: 56 Another anti-Laud pamphlet. Here is shown Noah's Ark, standing for the Ark of the Covenant, whereby the Scots (who signed a covenant to preserve the presbyterian style of government) are shown saving the English and Welsh establishments from Charles I, Queen Henrietta Maria, (a Catholic), and Archbishop Laud.

Below: 57 Illustration by Wenceslas Hollar, showing an attack on Laud's Lambeth Palace by apprentices and sailors opposed to his reforms and to the presence of bishops in the House of Lords.

Left: 58 Laud's trial. This began on 12 March 1644 and lasted for some five months. It took place in the House of Lords, which was slightly less viciously disposed towards him than the House of Commons. Prynne, a member of that House, for example, got hold of Laud's private diary and published it in the hope it would discredit the archbishop.

Below: 59 Laud's execution on 10 January 1645. From a print attributed to Wenceslas Hollar. Laud was the fourth Archbishop of Canterbury to die by violence.

60 The west front of Canterbury Cathedral, from William Dugdale's *Monasticon* (1655). The inscription under the coat of arms says that in case Christian piety and the signs of it should perish, William Ducie has drawn this view of the cathedral for the benefit of his own day and that of posterity.

61 Archbishop William Juxon. Engraving by Thielcke. Juxon succeeded Laud as President of St John's College, Oxford. Lucius Carey, who did not like bishops in general, said of him that he was 'neither ambitious before, nor proud after, either with the crozier or the white staff'. Even Prynne liked him, describing him as 'amiable and commendable'.

62 Archbishop William Sancroft. From a contemporary print by Robert White. Sancroft is here described as 'Primate of All England'. This title was long a matter of dispute between Canterbury and York.

63 Archbishop John Tillotson. After the portrait by Sir Godfrey Kneller. He is unusual in being shown without his head covered by a mitre or cap or wig. Unlike most of his contemporaries, Tillotson delivered short sermons which, for a while, he used to write down beforehand and then learn by heart. He abandoned the practice, he said, because it gave him severe headaches.

64 Archbishop William Howley caricatured as a churchwarden (1829). Howley was one of those who told the young Victoria that she had become queen on the death of William IV, and he presided so ineptly at her coronation that he was obliged to confess, 'We ought to have had a full rehearsal'.

whether they liked it or not, the forms of Protestant belief and worship which best suited the requirements of those same political classes, and the imposition was successful.[5] It was therefore the task of the Archbishop of Canterbury, whoever he might be, to carry out this programme.

But the old view that Parker was the father of Anglicanism can no longer be sustained. In fact he managed little except to survive as archbishop – no mean achievement under the cold and capricious eye of the final Tudor – and to ensure that a number of changes in the required new religious régime were given sufficient lip-service to keep the government satisfied. The problem was that he himself inclined to be more radical than the queen. At Cambridge in the 1520s and 1530s he had fallen under the influence of a redoubt-able Lutheran preacher, Thomas Bilney, and in the 1540s and 1550s under that of Martin Bucer, a reformer from Strassburg who was appointed Regius Professor of Divinity in Cambridge in 1549; and while none of this made him remotely a firebrand, he did veer further from those traditional forms of Catholic worship which still appealed to Elizabeth. It was his more radical inclination, how-ever, which led to his advancement as a royal chaplain, first in the household of Anne Boleyn, then of Henry VIII, and caused him to marry eighteen months before such an arrangement became legal in English law. During Queen Mary's reign he seems to have retired to a literary existence somewhere near Cambridge, but emerged under Elizabeth as a suitable candidate for Canterbury. He was reluctant to take up the challenge. It would probably be fair to say of Parker that he was a Cambridge don elevated beyond his capaci-ties, and that he had sufficient self-knowledge to realise it. But the insistence of the government prevailed and Parker was consecrated archbishop on 17 December 1559. The circumstances attendant upon his consecration have been disputed ever since. In 1896 Pope Leo XIII declared all orders within the Church of England invalid, from Parker onwards, and indeed Elizabeth's ministers of state were well aware that there were problems. Their solution was to invoke the royal supremacy to validate the proceedings; but for anyone who might reject the whole notion of the royal supremacy as invalid in itself, that solution could scarcely be regarded as anything but a ruse, and a ruse which could have no validity for Catholics either in England or in the rest of Europe.

Whichever view one takes, however, the use of the royal supremacy made it clear that Parker was a creature of the state, a position which put a brake on any inclination he may have had – and undoubtedly did have – to abandon any pretence of preserving Catholic practice and turn instead to accommodation with the various reformist models being tried out elsewhere in Europe. One can see some of his difficulties, and the restrictions placed upon him, in the battle over clerical dress known as the 'vestiarian controversy' which raged during the 1560s. Were surplices to be worn or not? Or did they represent just that kind of clinging to Catholic practice to which several bishops as well as many parish clergy objected? Synods held in 1560 and 1561 failed to produce a definitive instruction on the point, and Elizabeth made it clear she was not in favour of any extremity of reform; so Parker was left like a handful of corn between two mill-stones. On 25 January 1565, he received a royal directive to impose uniformity in this matter. What Elizabeth (or her government ministers) wanted was for the clergy to wear dress which distinguished them from the laity during services in church, a requirement seemingly harmless and sensible enough, but one which actually touched raw nerves in the religious ferment of the period. What did the wearing of vestments mean? Were they significant symbols or merely trivia which could be laid aside or abolished without difficulty? Did wearing them indicate a frame of mind in the wearer too close to Rome for Protestant comfort? Did the English Church, in the persons of Elizabeth and Parker, have the authority to impose on its clergy the wearing of such garments? If one refused to wear them, was one actually committing a crime, and if so, what was the crime? With questions such as these whirling round his head, Parker tried to steer everyone into calmer waters by setting up a committee on the one hand, and clamping down on individual nonconformists on the other, a tactic which had limited success because Elizabeth vetoed the conclusions of the committee, and the acquiescence demanded of clergy, starting in London, caused deep resentment and bitterness.

Those who did not give in were deprived of their living; a pamphlet war broke out; and Parker found, to his chagrin, that even the Privy Council was split on the subject and therefore failed to give him support when he needed it most. This situation could not continue, of course, and finally in June 1566 the Council decided to act against the nonconformists. But Parker's reputation, especially in London, had undergone a beating and his authority was damaged more or less beyond repair.

When scholars are unhappy or emotionally disturbed, they tend to start producing books. In Parker's case the book was a new translation of the Bible into English. The result, known as the Bishops' Bible, was the work of a small group of men, but Parker himself under-took a very large part of the burden, including prefaces to various of the separate books, and saw to it that maps, tables and over 100 woodcut engravings were included. Needless to say, it was neither a success nor a failure. It replaced Henry VIII's 'Great Bible' in churches, but was rejected by private readers in favour of a more accurate (if theologically tendentious) version usually called the 'Geneva Bible' published nearly a decade earlier. The Bishops' Bible meant well, but it was flawed and inadequate for its purpose – very much like Parker himself.

In 1570, however, a blow fell which altered everything. Pope Pius V issued a Bull, *Regnans in Excelsis*, excommunicating Elizabeth and releasing the English from any obligation of obedience to her. From now on, everyone in England would live under a cloud of suspicion. Loyalty to the régime would have to be demonstrated and enforced. Thus, in 1571 Parliament tried (unsuccessfully as it happened) to pass a Bill obliging everyone to attend his or her parish church at least once a quarter under penalty of a fine. A similar provision was indeed passed later, but it indicates the political view that overt loyalty was now a matter of urgent importance. This view itself also carried the implication that the clergy could be relied on to see that their parishioners conformed, and a reliable clergy implied the need for uniformity and discipline in the Church. But uniformity and discipline were precisely what the English Church lacked at this moment. The vestiarian controversy and its aftermath had helped to divide opinion, the attempt to impose uniformity had created active resentment and dissent, and Parker could no longer rely on the prestige or authority of his office to ensure submission from clergy or laity. Indeed, Parliament itself was riven between conformist and nonconformist sympathisers, and when it had tried to pass legislation in 1572 which would have let in Calvinism by the back door and Elizabeth vetoed it, the nonconformists started to run riot. Parker's attempts to suppress them failed once again, because those who were deprived of their livings merely swelled the numbers of the unhappy and disgruntled. Unofficial gatherings of clergy and laity, known as 'prophesyings', actually had Parker's personal blessing, although he was obliged by virtue of his position to make efforts to suppress them; and then in 1574 he fell victim to a conman by the name of Humphrey Needham who provided him with forged letters purportedly written by certain notorious nonconformists, in which plans to subvert the official Church of England and murder Elizabeth's chief minister, Lord Burghley, were set out in plain language. Needless to say, the forgeries were uncovered and Parker was thereby made to look a fool – indeed, worse, for it was suggested that they originated with him as part of a device to furnish excuse for arresting and imprisoning their alleged authors. So when he died in May 1575, it was with a reputation which pleased no one, not even himself.

Yet he did have virtues. It is simply that they were not those required by his office at that particular time. He was a great collector of books and manuscripts, his passion stimulated by the desire to see if he could find any evidence from English history that England had been Protestant before it had been Catholic. Many were given or bequeathed to Corpus Christi College and the University Library of Cambridge. He was an enthusiastic patron of the arts and of scholarship, and spent lavishly on Lambeth Palace, although he seems always to have borne in mind the transience of temporal things. 'The world and its lust pass on' [*John* 2.17] appeared on his coat of arms, his seals, his walls and his window-panes. He gave generously to a number of Cambridge colleges and to Norwich where he had been born; he was an efficient administrator; and he seems to have sustained the attacks on his character for the most part with patient fortitude. But there is no disguising the fact that, whatever the lasting effects of his time as archbishop may have seemed to be to later biographers, his contemporaries regarded him as a failure and, to judge from the note of self-pity which appears in his later correspondence, so did he.

Still, if Parker had been a failure in spite of the hopes Elizabeth and her ministers may have placed in him at first, *Edmund Grindal* (1575–83) was a disaster from the start, and Elizabeth should have known it. Edward Carpenter calls him 'the honest Puritan', which is a fair enough assessment, but points immediately to the basic problem of his archiepiscopate. Elizabeth Tudor did not want Puritans, certainly not among her bishops. Why, then, was Grindal appointed? In many ways he must have seemed well-qualified. He had received his education at Cambridge where, as a member of Pembroke College, he lived in the midst of radical reformers. Martin Bucer was at the height of his influence too, and then when Mary Tudor came to the throne, Grindal sent himself into exile and lived in a hotbed of Protestant radicalism, Strassburg. One says 'hotbed' partly because the city was full of English exiles and long-term residents who were actually split into factions, some more radical than others, and it may have been this experience which not only confirmed Grindal in his favourable opinion of German religious practices (as opposed to English), but also made him see that uncontrolled factionalism would not be in the best interests of forwarding the cause of reformed religion.

So when he returned to England after Queen Mary's death and was appointed bishop of London, one is prepared to admit his explanation for accepting an office of which he fundamentally disapproved – that it was better he occupied it than some semi-Catholic. For he could use this new authority to advance his views of what the English Church should be and control that advance so as to prevent any unwanted and distracting fissiparous tendencies attendant upon that advance. Thus, he ordained large numbers of returning exiles whose experience of German and Swiss Protestantism was similar to his, but then, unfortunately for himself, he became embroiled in the vestiarian controversy, where he found his inclinations quite other than those he was supposed to have. He also admired the more or less independent congregations of Protestant immigrants in London – from France, the Netherlands, Italy and Spain – and sought to hold them up as models for a future English Church. But here, of course, Grindal ran into difficulties with Elizabeth and certain of her ministers. Conformity with the Church of England was their aim, and this ran counter to Grindal's basic inclinations and, indeed, to the behaviour of those foreign congregations for which he had at least nominal responsibility. The discipline the English government wished to impose on them was actually brought by a Calvinist, Nicholas des Gallars, sent to London by Calvin himself, and Grindal quickly found himself poised unhappily between his own government which required conformity to one model and Grillars who was imposing conformity to one entirely different.

It must therefore have come as a relief to him when he was appointed Archbishop of York in 1570 with the brief of delivering to the sizeable Catholic enclaves in the north the smack of Protestant government from London. His task was not going to be easy. He wrote:

> I am informed that the greatest part of our gentlemen are not well affected to godly religion, and that among the people there are many remanents of the old. They keep holydays and fasts abrogated: they offer money, eggs, etc., at the burial of their dead: they pray on beads, etc.; so as this seemeth to be, as it were, another church, rather than a member of the rest. And for the little experience I have of these people, methinketh I see in them three evil qualities; which are, great ignorance, much dullness to conceive better instructions, and great stiffness to retain their wonted errors.[6]

For the next five years Grindal did what he could to wean his northern archdiocese from its adherence to Catholicism, partly by importing radical ministers, partly by trying the force of personal argument – a typical scholar's reaction to any problem, one whose success he exaggerated when he wrote to Elizabeth – and partly by threats of fines and imprisonment. None of this, however, had much effect, and recusancy was as widespread when he left as when he arrived.

He left in order to become Archbishop of Canterbury. He was nominated in November 1575 and elected the following January. But why? The Privy Council was split between its so-called traditionalist and its radical members and Elizabeth, flighty as a weathercock after her usual fashion, seems to have been inclined at this crucial moment to forget how revolutionary Grindal was by temperament. Even so, she took three months to make up her mind, so she cannot have been altogether forgetful. Scarcely had Grindal arrived in London, however, than the disorderly prophesyings which were to oust him from his office presented themselves for resolution. Grindal's inclination was to favour them, as was the inclination of a majority of the bishops he consulted before he wrote to Elizabeth at length in 1576, explaining why he was not averse to their continuation. Needless to say, Elizabeth was infuriated. She had her own view of the prophesyings, a view directly opposed to that of Grindal, and now ordered him to suppress these unregulated assemblies. Reluctantly Grindal obeyed, but his letter had cost him his career and at the end of May he was confined to Lambeth House. In effect he had been sacked, but his deprivation was not made official in case it should send the wrong kind of signal to Catholics at home and abroad. Removing a Puritan archbishop could be taken not only as disagreement with his religious opinions and policies, but also as notice that the government was becoming more inclined to temper its Protestantism.

Even so, the deprivation might have become official had it not been for Grindal's declining health. He was summoned several times to appear before the Court of Star Chamber with the intention that he be forced to make a public declaration that he had been wrong over the prophesyings, or that he pay the penalty for his stubbornness. With Canterbury suspended, the Church of England was left without a primate, a situation quite unsatisfactory and in need of redress. But matters dragged on and on and on, and the ill health which had attended Grindal ever since he came south from York now threatened to finish him altogether. For some time he had suffered an eye disease which now rendered him almost blind, and in 1581 it became clear he was in thrall to a variety of other infirmities. He wanted to resign, but Elizabeth would not let him. It was not that she particularly wanted to keep him, merely that, as usual, she could not make up her mind to decisive action. In consequence, he lingered in increasing pain until 6 July 1583 when God, who has no difficulty about decisive action, released him from his sufferings.

Grindal's suspension is perhaps the most significant part of his career. It illustrates vividly the extent to which the primary ecclesiastical office in England had now become just another state appointment – a very important one, of course, and most prestigious, but still an office whose holder could be appointed or dismissed at the wish of the secular head of state. The archbishop was now, in effect, a civil servant who existed to do the monarch's bidding anent religion. It was a situation which would have had St Thomas Becket spinning in his tomb had it not been destroyed by the arch-vandal Elizabeth Tudor's father.

Elizabeth's choice of successor, *John Whitgift* (1583–1604), was somewhat happier, largely because in him she found someone whose personal inclinations took him well in the direction of the radical parties in theology, but whose ambition acted as a brake on those inclinations and thus made him useful to the state. The first twenty years of his career were spent in Cambridge where he went from being a Fellow of Peterhouse to Master of Trinity, and Vice-Chancellor. He attracted attention quite early by preaching sermons in which he identified the Pope with Antichrist and by asking William Cecil, Elizabeth's principal minister, to withdraw demands that the surplice be worn in college chapels during services. Curiously enough, however, not long after he had taken this stand (in company with others) he discovered he was quite of the opposite opinion and preached a sermon in defence of the government's policy, a sermon which was followed by a notable university appointment, an increase in his salary, a Regius professorship, election as Master of Pembroke College and, only three months after that, appointment as Master of Trinity. Full appreciation of which side his bread was buttered thus ensured him both prominence and status, and he repaid his diverse advancements by taking the official line in a pamphlet war which raged between 1571 and 1575 over the form of Church government and worship which various parties considered desirable. It began with a Bill in Parliament to remove remaining 'Popish abuses'. What actually constituted these abuses became the bone of contention. Puritan-Presbyterian-Calvinist-Anabaptist-Radical parties wanted wholesale reorganisation of the English Church along lines more or less recognisably Presbyterian. That meant no bishops and a very different prayer book.

The government, of course, did not countenance anything as drastic as this, and Whitgift was put to work answering the work of the leading Presbyterian critic, another Cambridge man, Thomas Cartwright. Whitgift laboured hard and was rewarded by the opportunity to preach in defence of episcopacy in Elizabeth's presence, an opportunity he seized with both hands. His argument, which is easily reconstructed from his various writings, is that the Church exists on two levels – the invisible, which is ruled by God, and the visible, which is governed on His behalf by the monarch. The visible Church, consisting as it does of sinners as well as of good men and women, requires discipline, and this government is best done in tandem with the government of the state, the monarch acting as supreme head of both under God. Delivered in March 1574, Whitgift's sermon bore fruit – a plum – for three years later he was nominated bishop of Worcester, a post he held for six years during which he divided his energies between prosecuting local Catholics, preaching extensively throughout his diocese, and managing the episcopal income to its best advantage.

Unlike Grindal, who found it extremely difficult to disguise his radical opinions and sympathies, Whitgift managed to swallow them at the prospect of advancement, and so it is not surprising that the government regarded him as an entirely suitable candidate for Canterbury. Two main problems dominated his term in office: the Three Articles, and the Marprelate Tracts. The Three Articles referred to specific items produced in Parliament in 1583 to which the clergy was supposed to subscribe. Two caused no difficulties, but the one which demanded acquiescence in the recognition that bishops, priests, deacons and the Book of Common Prayer were compatible with the word of God raised furious opposition from the various radical groups. Indeed, it split the clergy between those who supported the government's religious policy and those who did not, and, threatened by widespread disobedience, Whitgift clamped down on would-be dissenters, subjecting them to certain legal tactics hitherto reserved for Catholic recusants. This, of course, fuelled resentment against him both in the country and in Parliament where England's religious divisions were mirrored, and a flurry of Bills proposing the adoption of a Calvinist prayer book and a Presbyterian form of Church government drew 1584 to an ill-tempered end and 1585 to an angry beginning. The controversy was brought to a close by Elizabeth, who insisted upon having bishops and retaining 'her' prayer book; but the bruising encounters meant that Whitgift had made enemies everywhere, who would continue to plague him and make life difficult.

The malign disappointment of Puritans that Whitgift, in spite of his known intellectual sympathy for the radical point of view, stood so firmly in their way burst out three years later in a series of pamphlets attributed to 'Martin Marprelate', libellous pasquinades against various bishops and Whitgift in particular, therein designated as 'that miserable and desperate caitiff, wicked John Whitgift, the Pope of Lambeth' – an especially irritating phrase for him, no doubt, as he had always been virulently anti-Papal and continued to preach against the Pope and the seminary priests who were still coming in large numbers to England. Official ripostes, however, were not long in coming and a combination of public preaching in defence of episcopacy, arrest of a number of dissidents throughout the country and one or two judicious executions ensured that the leaders of Presbyterian faction were broken along with any organised opposition they had managed to put together.

This incident, which lasted between 1588 and 1590, shows that Whitgift was perfectly prepared to be ruthless in defence of a religious policy with which he did not actually agree. His personal faith was Calvinist; his views on Church government and Church discipline were not. Thomas Cartwright, by contrast, was also a Calvinist but one who had no notion of compromising his principles for the

sake of gaining or retaining public office. He dominated theological teaching in Cambridge during the late 1570s and 1580s, and he
and Whitgift had, as we have noted already, faced each other in
controversy. But the Marprelate incident had enabled Whitgift to
bring Cartwright to court, where Cartwright was deprived of his
living, degraded, and imprisoned; and although the two men were
later reconciled, the difference in their attitudes towards belief and
conscience shows that whatever practical virtue there may be in
pragmatism, integrity of vision cannot but command the greater
respect.

Like all Archbishops of Canterbury, Whitgift maintained a large
household and was lavish in his official hospitality He was a patron of
scholars and generous in his benefactions, but these too are standard
characteristics of the holders of his office. They were, in effect, great
noblemen and behaved accordingly. Sir George Paule, Whitgift's
contemporary and early biographer, tells us that he was of middle
stature with a body which was well shaped and gave the impression
of strength. He had a brown (or, as we might say, olive) complexion
with black hair and eyes, and his beard was neither long nor thick.
The black hair must have turned to grey by the end of the century,
however, for he was in his early seventies when Elizabeth Tudor
died. That final scene is reminiscent of her father's deathbed, for
both of them were attended by their Archbishop of Canterbury, and
both died without any specific sacramental rite. In Whitgift's case,
Elizabeth's long dying was a trial, for he was obliged to kneel by
her bed and offer prayers constantly; and when the pain of kneeling for so long made him try to rise to his feet, Elizabeth, selfish
and inconsiderate to the last, insisted he continue until she finally
drifted into unconsciousness and the old man was able to escape
and hobble away.

With her death, the 'English' monarchy came to an end. Strictly
speaking, of course, it had been Welsh since 1485 and was now to
be Scottish until 1715, so the advent of a foreign monarch was, for
the English, both perplexing and exciting. The Puritans certainly
pricked up their tails, for Scotland had had a Presbyterian establishment ever since James VI became king, and therefore their hopes

were high for advancement of their cause the moment he stepped over the border. It was not to be, of course. James was no fool and had had quite enough experience of what it was like to be a monarch under a Presbyterian system to be sure he would not overthrow the more accommodating English establishment. Whitgift greeted him fulsomely, as was the custom, but hoping perhaps to create a favourable impression. It worked well enough. Whitgift presided at James's English coronation and then at the Hampton Court Conference which James called in 1604, against Whitgift's advice, in order to make clear that Elizabeth Tudor's religious settlement was not going to be overturned as the Puritans hoped.

But Whitgift was now at the end of his days and, as the result of his refusing to shelter himself or his companions from a raw February wind which blew hard upon them as they went down the Thames in his barge, he contracted what sounds like influenza. It was not this which killed him, however. He had a stroke while dining at Whitehall and had to be taken back to Lambeth. The king came to visit him, and the last coherent words the archbishop spoke were '*Pro ecclesia Dei* [For the Church of God]'. Which Church he had in mind – Anglican or Presbyterian – we cannot tell. Neither can we guess how James, to whom the words were addressed, chose to understand them. They sound like an ambiguity from one compromiser to another, but one could be mistaken.

The Tudors may have gone and the Stuarts arrived, but the growling of Puritan discontents continued unabated. *Richard Bancroft* (1604–10) had to bear the brunt of the Hampton Court Conference, during which he adopted a highly combative stance, interrupted opponents, and sought to have them silenced. His antagonism to the radicals may have stemmed in part from his birth in Lancashire, then and later a distant part of the country, which conserved many pockets of Catholicism and was known for its 'traditionalist' sympathies. But he may also have observed the careers of Whitgift and John Aylmer, Bishop of London, to both of whom he became a kind of *éminence grise* during the 1580s while they battled against Presbyterianism. It was perfectly clear that the English state was not going to turn Calvinist, or anything like it, so a man who wanted to make his way in the world would not make the mistake of following his conscience rather than government policy. Archbishop Whitgift was a conspicuous enough example of that. So Bancroft wrote books in praise of episcopacy, preached a public sermon in London against Presbyterianism on 9 February 1589 at the height of the Marprelate affair, and produced two more publications in 1592 in which his views on Church authority were clearly set out. In effect, he said, authority in the Church was the same as that within the state, a definition which could not but please Elizabeth and her government. Such zeal for the official line must surely produce benefits for the author, and indeed it did, although not for five years, owing to competition among government patrons, each of whom wanted to advance his own candidate. At length, however, in 1597 Whitgift was able to get his man elected bishop of London, and Bancroft thereby had the third most important stage in England upon which to prove his worth.

He had always been anti-Catholic as well as anti-Presbyterian, and as London was in many ways an ideal place for Catholics to advance their cause, set up networks, and yet remain hidden, Bancroft set about rooting them forth, not so much by prosecution as by setting them against each other. English Catholics fell into three groups: the laity, some of whom conformed in certain ways to the laws insisting upon attendance at Anglican services, others of whom did not; the secular priests who had been trained in seminaries abroad and now returned to their native land to keep the Faith alive; and Jesuits, members of the Society of Jesus, highly-skilled theologians and controversialists, willing and indeed expecting to die for the Faith. It was these last whom Bancroft considered particularly dangerous, and so he frequently turned a blind eye to the activities of the secular priests as a way of throwing discredit upon the Jesuits who were much more insistent that compromise was not a choice for a devout Catholic. Yet in spite of his opinions and his zeal, when Whitgift died Bancroft was not the government's first choice for Canterbury. The Archbishop of York and the bishops of Winchester and Durham had powerful claims to the office, and none of them had made the mistake of offending King James as Bancroft had done in 1589 when he asserted that the king had written something (which in fact he had not), and then refused to apologise to James for his rash mistake. Nevertheless, during the interim Bancroft had proved himself a reliable servant of the Crown, so on 17 November 1604 he duly became archbishop and set about the business of trying to ensure conformity among the various religious factions which were troubling not only his archdiocese and the rest of England, but Scotland as well – an effort which brought him into conflict with Andrew Melville, the leading Scottish mouthpiece of Presbyterianism.

It was a small warning, perhaps, that the relationship between the two countries, united only in the person of the monarch, was going to be very uneasy. The Scottish Presbyterian establishment would not conform to English episcopacy, and Bancroft's endeavours to tell it that it should prefigure the much more disastrous attempts by one of his successors, William Laud, to achieve something similar. A further sinister omen can also be seen in the person of Edward Coke, England's chief justice. English lawyers were busy trying to suggest that the authority of Parliament with regard to ecclesiastical matters actually outweighed the authority of the king, regardless of his supposed title as head of the English Church, and neither James nor Bancroft seemed able to withstand that proposition. The supremacy of Parliament would be a principal subject of contention during the civil wars of Charles I's reign, of course, so these batsqueaks sounding out the future assume an importance in both James's and Bancroft's time in office. Neither man, however, quite realised this at the time. The Gunpowder Plot of 1605 had stimulated anti-Catholicism to the point where Bancroft's implacable intention to stamp out recusancy in England received a great deal of popular support, and for much of his time as archbishop he concentrated both on this problem and on the quality of learning and preaching among the Anglican clergy. But concern over clerical abuses and inadequacies was a standard part of his job. Several Catholic archbishops, as we have seen, were equally perturbed by the state of their clergy, and Bancroft's well-meaning efforts to improve the situation met with as much and as little success as had theirs. So when he died in 1610, he left behind an English Church no worse than the one he had inherited, but not much better, either. His period as archbishop had been a holding operation, its greatest success the accommodation of a foreign monarch as head of his Church.

George Abbot (1611–33) has not been much regarded. The only modern biography of him calls him 'the unwanted Archbishop'; in the seventeenth century, the earl of Clarendon referred to him as a man of 'very morose manners and a very sour aspect which at that time was called gravity'; while in 1655 the historian Hammond L'Estrange wrote, 'A very learned man he was, his erudition all of the old stamp, stiffly principled in the doctrine of St Augustine in which they who understand it not call Calvinism... Pious, grave, and exemplary in his conversation. But some think a better man than Archbishop'. Strongly inclined to Calvinism and personally unattractive, no wonder his preferment to Canterbury caused everyone much surprise. King James, who had decided on his appointment, however, knew what he was doing. Abbot was an Oxford don with a long history of both published and active anti-Catholicism, his Calvinist theology tempered by his defence of bishops as Church officers entirely authorised by Scripture. Moreover, he had actually been in Scotland in 1608, where he preached his peculiarly English blend of theology and Church politics, and also wrote the preface to an account of the execution of one George Sprot who had taken part in an assassination conspiracy against King James eight years before. The king's escape from both this and the Gunpowder Plot, said Abbot, indicated that James was singularly favoured by God, who clearly intended the king to enlarge the Anglican Church and defeat the Catholics, to the delight of all right-minded people in Europe. As Disraeli said of Victoria, when it comes to royalty, flattery should be laid on with a trowel, and it was not long before Abbot was bishop of Coventry and Lichfield and then of London in quick succession.

He was young when he became Archbishop of Canterbury, only forty-eight, and started as he meant to go on by using all the resources at his and the state's command to uncover, arrest and prosecute Catholics, even entering the field of politics to have Catholic nobles

arrested for failing to take an oath of allegiance to James, and block-
ing the earl of Northampton's appointment as Lord Treasurer because
he was suspected of having Catholic leanings. He also vigorously
opposed any suggested Catholic spouse for James's heir, Henry, or
his daughter, Elizabeth, and was delighted when Elizabeth actually
married the German Protestant Elector of the Palatinate. From this
it may be gauged that Abbot was a man who indulged in feuds. The
running battle against Catholics, which lasted all his life, through the
serious attempt to betrothe Prince Charles to the Spanish Infanta to
Charles's eventual marriage to the French princess Henrietta Maria,
soon after he became king, was only one obsession. He annoyed
King James – more or less permanently, as it turned out – by objecting to the king's wish to annul a noble marriage so that the wife,
Frances Howard, might be free to marry his *mignon*, Robert Carr.
Abbot made a great fuss, almost certainly (as James rightly suspected)
because he did not want the Catholic Howard family to gain any
social or political advantage. Similarly, he pursued his dislike of
William Laud, of whom he had never approved since their Oxford
days together, although as James's reign drew to its close and Charles's
reign began, it was clear that it was Laud's star which was in the
ascendant, not his own.

In July 1621 Abbot managed to kill someone. It was a hunting accident – Peter Hawkins, a keeper, for some reason stood in
the path of a buck at which the archbishop was aiming, and the
crossbow arrow went straight through him. The manslaughter had
grave consequences. The newly appointed bishop of Lincoln refused
point-blank to be consecrated by a man with blood on his hands,
and so did the new bishop of St David's, William Laud. A commission of inquiry was established and Abbot might have been deprived
of his office had not the bishop of Winchester swayed its members
to leniency. So the two new bishops were consecrated – but not by
Abbot – and a flurry of paperwork finally ensured that the archbishop would be absolved 'from all irregularity, or infamation', and
that he would now 'be capable to use all metropolitan authority,
as if that sinistrous contingency in spilling blood had never been
done'.

When he died in August 1633, Abbot could look back on a career whose keynotes had been anti-Catholicism and indulgence towards Puritan nonconformists. He had been severe, indeed harsh, in punishing clergy who neglected their duties, and he was exasperated by any who wrote and published against episcopacy; but he was even more keen to promote a well-educated and efficient preaching ministry, and therefore looked the other way at infringements of theological orthodoxy or ecclesiastical discipline which did not overtly run counter to the official government line. It was an example of compromise which would nowadays be called 'nuanced', an attitude towards belief and behaviour in which the twentieth-century Church of England was to become particularly skilled, and which that other nuanced Presbyterian, Edmund Grindal, would have recognised and saluted.

All good things come to those who wait, and *William Laud* (1633–45) had been waiting to step into Abbot's shoes for some time. As William Mulsho wrote to Lord Montague a few days after Abbot's death, 'On Sunday last old George of Canterbury stepped aside and lay down to sleep and up started the bishop of good London, and put on his clothes before we were sure he was fast asleep and key cold'. It would be possible to write long about Laud, and people have; but the essential facts about him are relatively few. He was an Oxford man of interestingly mixed views. Oxford had not taken kindly to the destruction vented on it by Henry VIII and Edward VI, and Laud's college, St John's, was perhaps somewhat more 'traditionalist' than some others, almost certainly because of the influence of its Master, John Buckridge. On the other hand, Laud was prepared to defend predestination, a peculiarly Calvinist doctrine, and seemed to be perfectly sincere in his balancing-act since he puzzled all kinds of people on both sides of the theological fence. On one point, however, he left no one any room for doubt. The form of Church government was crucial in the process of salvation, and bishops were an essential part of that government; and a visit to Scotland in company with King James in 1616 merely served to confirm his impression that Presbyterianism boded little more than political opposition to the Crown.

King James, like many monarchs, was given to having favourites and granting them over-much political influence. George Villiers, later duke of Buckingham, was one such and assisted Laud's career. Buckingham's mother had been thinking of turning Catholic, and a conference was arranged between Laud and a well-known Jesuit, John Fisher, with the aim of persuading her to remain Protestant. The conference did not work and she later converted, but Laud was now firmly in Buckingham's notice and used this connection whenever he could – given the delicate footwork required at this time when Buckingham was busy antagonising other European nations – to promote his view that dissension with the prevailing orthodoxy was tantamount to rebellion. It was a belief pleasing to Charles I, who co-operated closely with Laud in the 1630s to promote the concept of Church and state working together in perfect harmony, and Buckingham's friendship brought Laud into close contact with Charles who appointed him dean of the Chapel Royal, a suitable and influential theatre wherein Laud could try out a number of those innovations in worship which others would be quick to call 'Papist' but which appealed to the king's sense of decency and order in divine service. But Buckingham was coming under increasing attack from Parliament and was eventually assassinated in 1628. Laud was not left out of the Parliament's expressions of animus against the whole régime.

In 1627 Laud had become bishop of London. In 1630 Oxford elected him its Chancellor. To Oxford he was a generous bene-factor, to London a headmaster, keen to promote his particular view of the Church in which uniformity of worship and ceremonial usage were outward symbols of an interior conformity and loyalty. This, and knowledge of his previous history, led to renewed accusations that he was partial to Rome (although in fact he made clear his opposition to the representatives of Catholic powers at Court, and to conversions to Rome which were threatening to become almost fashionable among certain courtiers); and his attempts to enforce a more strict morality upon secular society as well as the clergy meant that he accumulated enemies both high and low as other men hoarded grain in time of dearth. This would have been difficult enough had he confined his attentions to the Church of England, but his vision of uniformity extended far beyond it. Protestant churches of other nations in England – the Dutch especially – were to be dragooned into following English practice, and so were the Irish and Scots in their own countries. A single English reformed Church, a single prayer book, was his unspoken aim; but when he ventured to impose this vision on Scotland via the Scottish bishops, he precipitated a religious crisis which soon turned political. Since the king was sympathetic to Laud and the English Parliament was not, a constitutional clash was more or less unavoidable.

When it came, that clash sent many people to their deaths, including the king himself. But before the various sides in the conflict picked up arms, Laud's enemies managed to remove him from power, if not from office. In December 1640 he was impeached on a charge of high treason, based partly on his encouragement of King Charles's personal rule without summoning Parliament (called 'arbitrary government'), and partly on pursuing pro-Catholic and anti-reformation policies, in as much as he had persecuted Puritan preachers and been hostile to the churches of foreign reformed powers. For the time being he was kept in the custody of Black Rod – at his own expense – whose wife later reported of him that 'although he was but a silly fellow to hold converse with a lady, he was the most excellent and pious soul she had ever met with'. But by the beginning of March 1641 he was in the Tower of London, and his travesty of a trial followed. It lasted from mid-March to mid-October, shot through with and tainted by vindictiveness from start to finish, and the court's verdict was hardly a matter of doubt. Found guilty, he was condemned to be hanged.

Laud was shocked. There was every chance he would be attacked by the mob on his way to execution and die at its hands rather than by the rope. But in any case, hanging, with its attendant indignities, was not a suitable end for England's primate, so he asked Parliament to let him be beheaded. It is a comment on the virulent hatred with which he was regarded by the Commons that they opposed this request. But the Lords granted it and King Charles, who had originally pardoned him, changed his mind under pressure, signed the death warrant, and on 4 January 1645 Laud's head was struck off with a single blow. 'I saw it plainly in [the executioner's] hand', an eyewitness remembered. 'It looked still, even as before very fresh'. It was the end of an era. No more Archbishops of Canterbury would be willing to die for a principle.

9

The Long Durance of the Eighteenth Century

Juxon to Moore
(1660–1805)

L aud, however, lingered on after his death, for his ghost continues to haunt his old Oxford college. In life he had been insecure, a university bureaucrat promoted beyond his abilities. In death he proves remarkably persistent, his spectral forays into the world of the undergraduate providing proof that no one is so desirous of attention as a second-rank academic. The interregnum in England, lasting effectively from the execution of Charles I in January 1649 until May 1660 (although not in Scotland, where Charles II was crowned king on 1 January 1651), meant that the Church of England in its official form was suspended along with its archbishops and bishops. John Milton – not in the least an unbiased commentator – summarised its history so far:

> But what do we suffer misshapen and enormous prelatism, as we do, thus to blanch and varnish her deformities with the fair colours, as before of martyrdom, so now of episcopacy? They are not bishops, God and all good men know they are not, that have filled this land with late confusion and violence; but a tyrannical crew and corporation of imposters, that have blinded and abused the world so long under that name… Most certain it is (as all our stories bear witness) that ever since their coming to the see of Canterbury for near twelve hundred years, to speak of them in general, that they have been in England to our souls a sad and doleful succession of illiterate and blind guides: to our purses and goods a wasteful band of robbers, a perpetual havoc and rapine: to our state a continual hydra of mischief and molestation, the forge of discord and rebellion. This is the trophy of their antiquity and boasted succession through so many ages.[1]

We may therefore take it that the next occupant of Canterbury, *William Juxon* (1660–63), would have a certain amount of entrenched prejudice to overcome. Juxon was an Oxford man and initially owed his advance to his fellow-collegian, William Laud. In 1633 he was appointed bishop of London and then, three years later, Lord Treasurer, a post which brought him into conflict with Laud and effectively weakened, if it did not destroy, their former happy relationship. Efficient as Treasurer, Juxon was pretty feeble as a bishop, but had sufficient lack of personality to ensure that when war broke out and the interregnum followed, he would not be regarded as hostile by any side in the conflict, even though he was brave enough to defend Laud at his trial and accompany Charles I on the scaffold. He spent the 1650s in retirement, hunting. Bulstrode Whitelocke, who kept a diary at this time, noted that Juxon 'delighted in hunting and kept a good pack of hounds, so well ordered and hunted, chiefly by his own skill and direction, that they exceeded all other hounds in England for the pleasure and orderly hunting of them. He was a person of great parts and temper [character], and had as much command of himself as of his hounds'.[2] By the time Charles II was restored to the English throne, however, Juxon was in his seventies and enfeebled by illness. His elevation to Canterbury was perhaps a reward for his being pale enough not to cause offence to anyone, but perhaps too in recognition for his service to Charles I at his execution. Juxon faced quite serious problems. Clergy who had been deprived of their livings under the interregnum now asked for them back again; money needed to be spent on refurbishing churches stripped and whitewashed under Cromwell's withering eye; a new or amended liturgy must be established; and replacements were needed for clergy who had gone overseas or changed their job. It was too heavy a task for Juxon, although he did his best and spent a huge sum of money on Lambeth Palace alone. But he was overshadowed by *Gilbert Sheldon* (1663–77) who succeeded him as archbishop, and died as quietly as may be in June 1663.

Perhaps Juxon's greatest contribution to the office of archbishop was his inoffensiveness. After the drama of Laud and the Grand Guignol of the interregnum, it must have been a relief to find that the archbishopric was not necessarily a focus of high politics or contentious religious opinion, and so when Sheldon took up the post within a matter of weeks after Juxon's death, he did so to a tune of public forbearance, a softer music than that which had gone before. Sheldon's earlier career followed what was by now a well-established pattern. He was an Oxford academic with useful political connections. Always a supporter of Charles I, he concentrated his energies on academic life during the war and interregnum but, unlike Juxon, continued to be active politically via his extensive correspondence, for which he paid a price. Since March 1635, for example, he had been Warden of All Souls, but in 1648 he was forcibly evicted from his lodgings there to make way for someone more acceptable to the Presbyterian establishment. Retiring to the Midlands, he continued to work hard to preserve the Church of England as he knew it, by urging deprived bishops to consecrate others to the episcopate, ordain ministers who could keep the Church alive, and find a way of allowing clergy still in their posts to compromise with the Anglican requirement that they continue to use the Book of Common Prayer or resign their living.

Sheldon's personal religious views inclined him to what would now be called a 'High Church' position: that is, he was not entirely inimical to Rome and actually regretted the disappearance of confession and prayers for the dead, something he admitted to a Catholic convert, the duchess of York. But the Restoration of 1660 saw England uncomfortably balanced between Anglicans on the one hand and a variety of dissenting parties on the other, and Sheldon, who became bishop of London in September that year, found it important that he tread carefully if he wanted to restore the Church of England to what he regarded as its proper – that is, 'Laudian' – state, a task which proved to be more difficult than it should have been, since the king and his principal minister, the earl of Clarendon, were ready to be much more accommodating to the dissenters than Sheldon thought fit or desirable. It was a problem neither he nor the government solved satisfactorily. Five years later, Sheldon, now Archbishop of Canterbury, was writing to the then bishop of London that 'having heard frequent complaints from many parts of my province not only of great disorders and disturbances caused by the crafty insinuations and turbulent practices of factious nonconformist ministers, and other disaffected to the government of the Church: but also of divers unworthy persons, that even of late years have crept into the ministry, to the scandal of the Church, and dissatisfaction of good men, a great part of which miscarriages are imputed to the easiness, or inadvertency at least of the bishops, who ought to have a watchful eye against such growing mischiefs'.[3] Greater discipline was required, as was reform of manners and morals, and Sheldon looked to the bishop of London to see to both.

Unfortunately, in spite of Sheldon's good intentions, reform and discipline were not easy to obtain. For one thing, government policy over Church establishment and practice was inconsistent, and while an Act of Uniformity in 1662 obliged all ministers to conform to the new revised prayer book, and Presbyterians either to accept bishops or surrender their livings, a Declaration of Indulgence ten years later proposed suspending all penal laws against Catholics and dissenters, offering both a measure of freedom of private worship – a proposal which failed only because Parliament used the king's need for extra money to finance war with the Dutch to force him to abandon it. Then there was the notoriety of the Court. Sheldon himself disliked its immorality, but because he and the Church were closely associated with the political establishment, mud from the Court flew off and stuck to them. 'My cousin Roger told us as a thing certain', wrote Samuel Pepys in his diary on 29 July 1667, 'that the Archbishop of Canterbury that now is doth keep a wench, and that he is as very a wencher as he'. Such gossip was hard to shake off, perhaps in part because so many of the clergy continued to behave as though they were simply laymen. In 1674, for example, the king was obliged to issue an instruction that they were not to wear the long wigs or hair dictated by secular fashion,[4] a prohibition against secularity of dress and manners which had troubled the mediaeval Church and continues into the present. Even Sheldon's personal devotion could be criticised, his chaplain, Samuel Parker, observing that 'though he was very assiduous at prayers, yet he did not set so great a value on them as others did, nor regard so much the use of worship, placing the chief point of religion in the practice of a good life'.

In general, then, Sheldon's early promise was not fulfilled. Charles II never took to him the way his father had done, and as early as 1667 Pepys was noting that 'My Lord of Canterbury is a mighty stout [valiant] man, and a man of brave high spirit, and cares not for this disfavour that he is under at Court' (27 December). Without that favour, Sheldon had no hope of fulfilling Laud's intention of creating a genuinely national Church of England. The fissiparousness evident from Elizabeth Tudor's time was now entrenched, and since the effective triumph of Parliament over Crown and Church as a result of the civil wars and the interregnum, both Crown and Church (and with them, the Archbishops of Canterbury and York) declined in power and therefore in influence. To Oxford, Sheldon is known as the benefactor who gave it the Sheldonian Theatre; to London, as the man who bought a City residence for its bishop; but to the Church of England, as a well-meaning bureaucratic primate whose failure outweighed his success.

What everyone needed was a period of stability in which the after-shocks of the political earthquake under Charles I and the Cromwells would subside and people have a chance to regain their self-confidence. What they got was the savage anti-Catholic convulsion of the bogus 'Popish Plot' in 1678, the revolutionary replacement of one monarch by another – a replacement almost invariably referred to as 'glorious', although it was glorious only as a successful exploitation of popular hysteria by the selfish, ambitious daughters of the legitimate sovereign – and the prospect of civil war yet again at various times during the next half century. For such a restive and disgruntled period, the Church of England surely required a leader who would be able to act both as reconciler and guide while the Church negotiated its way through political and social discontents and alarums. *William Sancroft* (1677–90), a Cambridge don and a royalist by temperament and inclination, rode out the 1650s partly in retirement and partly in travel to the Netherlands, Germany, Switzerland and Italy. When he returned to England in 1660, he obtained a number of appointments through the good will not only of friends but also of the king himself, and became Master of Emmanuel College in Cambridge where he was very efficient in dealing with problems which had arisen there as a result of the interregnum: then dean of York and dean of St Paul's in London, both in the same year (1664). Old St Paul's was in a mess and needed extensive repairs. Sancroft remembered some of the churches he had seen in Italy, and was thus sympathetic to Christopher Wren's notion of doing something architecturally grand to enhance the building's appearance, rather than merely patch it. But the fire of 1666 altered everyone's perceptions by destroying much of the cathedral and so giving the king and Sancroft an opportunity to erect a new and imposing structure in its place. As is well known, Wren was commissioned to produce a design and Sancroft rejected it on the grounds that his intended church would not be suited to Protestant worship. So a modified plan – but not modified by much – was drawn up and agreed, and Sancroft then set about raising funds for the ever more expensive cathedral.

It was a task in which he clearly delighted and one at which he was very proficient. Twice King Charles tried to reward him by nominating him to a bishopric, but twice Sancroft refused. But when Sheldon died in November 1677 and the king nominated Sancroft to fill his place, Sancroft did not resist and was consecrated Archbishop of Canterbury the following January. Why was Charles so keen on having him? Appointing Sancroft would certainly deny the post to someone less obviously and devotedly a king's man, but Edward Carpenter's judgement is also just about plausible: 'Maybe in one of those rare moments of insight which occasionally illuminates the mind of the rake, Charles recognised in Sancroft a man of God, who stood outside much of the religious and political strife of the day'.[5] It rather depends on whether one interprets Sancroft's ingrained royalism as religiously or politically inspired, and to do him justice, the former does seem the more likely.

From 1679, the Whig-dominated Parliament was aggressively hostile to the notion of King Charles's brother succeeding him. James was a convert to Catholicism, and when he did indeed succeed his brother he embarked on a series of policies intended to make life easier for Catholics on the one hand, and to promote a general liberty of conscience on the other. The English psychological climate, however, was entirely unprepared to accept any of this and Sancroft too spoke out against James's pro-Catholic actions, for which he rapidly found himself out of favour. Yet when it came to the engineered revolution of 1688, Sancroft refused to accept the Protestant William of Orange as king and upheld his allegiance to James, in spite of his personal objections to James's religion and his political programme; and he did so not because he thought James was the better king but because he thought James had the better right.

Being a man of principle did not do Sancroft any good, of course. In February 1690 he was deprived of his office and another man named in his place. Thereafter, regarding the Church under William of Orange's rule as schismatic, Sancroft attempted to continue the Church he knew by delegating his archiepiscopal powers to the deprived bishop of Norwich, and consecrating new bishops whose names he first sent to King James, now in exile, for approval. The political result of this débâcle was a further split in the Church of England, yet another dissenting group to add to the rest. But that was not Sancroft's fault. It was Parliament which, in the end, had deprived James of the crown and offered it jointly to William and Mary. It was Parliament which deprived Sancroft and five other bishops and 400 clergy of their offices and livings; and it was Parliament which now quite clearly set the tone for the Church in the immediate future. Sancroft's conscience would not accommodate this political programme, and so Sancroft had to go. It was yet another demonstration of secular superiority which the archbishops would be obliged to note and deal with after their various fashions.

The first man to face this consequence was *John Tillotson* (1691–94), who was well equipped to do so, in as much as he positively welcomed the advent of William and Mary and worked in tandem with the latter to implement a series of national fasts and thanksgivings for the success of William's military adventures. Tillotson had been brought up a Puritan and always retained a sympathy for nonconformists of all kinds, in spite of his later intellectual acceptance of episcopacy. Indeed, both before and after he became Archbishop of Canterbury, he strove to find ways of accommodating nonconformists within the established Church of England, partly through sympathy, but principally because a united Protestant national Church would provide a bulwark against Catholicism within and outwith the state. Such undisguised opinions, vented frequently in sermons which he had published, made him unpopular during the final years of Charles II and throughout the whole of James II's reign. Preaching, however, was his great strength, and from his early days as a minister in London during the 1660s right up to the end of his life he was able to draw admiring crowds, some of whom, we are told, went to hear him more than once in the hope of hearing him deliver the same sermon again.[6]

Why was he so popular? His style was simple, his arguments clearly expressed, and he eschewed both ornamental flourish and the tendency to play on his hearers' emotions. Moreover, he tried to present Christianity as a matter of *rational* belief accompanied by practice which would lead to a reform of people's characters in the direction of restraint and elevation – restraint of those passions and appetites which bound them to worldly self-centredness, and elevation of their minds and aspirations to a pursuit of salvation and bliss with God. Only when he spoke of Catholics did he forget to be measured or liberal. Otherwise his aim was to promote a religious atmosphere of calm reflection and mutual tolerance.

Had his efforts included Catholics, they could perhaps have gone a long way to taking some of the sting out of contemporary ecclesiastical debate; but he was a man too wedded to his upbringing and too much in tune with the psychology of late seventeenth-century English politics to be able to rise above these limitations. That said, however, he should perhaps be given credit at least for making the effort to contain the inherent fissiparousness of his Church. Certainly he should be given credit for his tireless promotion of other people's publications, either as editor or adviser, and for the charitable impulse which regularly moved him to give away large sums of money, although his wife (a niece of Oliver Cromwell) was thus left penniless at his death and had to rely on a Crown annuity. Tillotson's generosity at the expense of his wife seems to illustrate the man rather well. However much people may try to like and admire him, there is always a 'but' with Tillotson.

He died following a stroke on 22 November 1694 and was succeeded in office by *Thomas Tenison* (1694–1715), whom Jonathan Swift described as 'a very dull man who had a horror of anything like levity in the clergy, especially of whist', while Thomas Bruce commented sourly upon his elevation that 'they advanced him for what he really was, a very tool'.[7] Both men, however, were hostile critics. John Evelyn, who knew him and liked him, wrote that his learning, piety and prudence made him entirely suitable for the post. Boring or not, Tenison can be given credit for one piece of admirable staunchness. In 1665, when he was a Fellow of Corpus Christi College, the plague came to Cambridge. Robert Masters, who wrote a history of the college nearly a hundred years later, recorded:

> Pestilence broke out with such violence that none ventured to continue here but Mr Tenison, one of the Fellows (afterwards Archbishop of Canterbury), two scholars and a few servants; for whom a preservative powder was brought and administered in wine, whilst charcoal, pitch,

and brimstone were kept continually burning in the gatehouse. The former not only resided here, but what is very extraordinary, attended upon the care of St Andrew's, the parish of which he was then minister, with perfect safety to himself during the whole time.[8]

This philanthropy and Christian charity can be seen later in his life, too, during his time as vicar of St Martin's in the Fields in London (1680–91) when he built the first public library in the capital and established charity schools for the poor, thereby displaying an interest in the education of the lower classes, which he continued to the end of his life.

Like Tillotson, however, his charitable impulses extended only so far. During the 1680s he was a leading proponent of Anglicanism which he advanced by the usual method of virulent anti-Catholicism in books, pamphlets and sermons, a campaign which brought him to the notice of influential politicians and assured him of favour when William and Mary usurped the English throne. Tenison was an important voice in the 1689 attempt to formulate a reconciliation between Anglicans and the various dissenting groups, an attempt which failed but did Tenison's career no harm, since he was promoted bishop of Lincoln in 1692. His tenure of that post was short. Efficient and energetic in his extensive visitations of what was an enormous diocese, he had proved his worth to the establishment in every way it considered desirable, and in 1693 was offered the archbishopric of Dublin. He turned it down. His wife was not in favour. As the bishop of Lichfield wrote to him, 'if I know Mrs Tenison, you must continue in this kingdom [England], for you cannot go out of it. I believe she would hardly cross the water to Lambeth to see you Archbishop of Canterbury. I had written this before I thought of London Bridge. That way she might foot it about, taking time. But there is no bridge between this and Ireland. Therefore I conclude you must continue in this kingdom'.[9]

Happily for Thomas, Mrs Tenison did agree to cross the Thames the following year, for in December 1694 King William nominated her husband to Canterbury, and he was enthroned there in person on 15 January 1695, almost fresh from Queen Mary's deathbed.

Virtually every Archbishop of Canterbury during the past three centuries had expressed the desire to reform the manners and improve the standing of the clergy, largely by controlling the individual's ability to make up his income by accepting several ecclesiastical posts at once and by making sure that ordinands were men of a decent education; and Tenison was no exception to this habit. Thus, on 4 April 1699 he sent instructions to his fellow-bishops:

> (1) Let the clergy and their families be above reproach. (2) Let them be prudent in addition to well meaning. (3) Let them acquaint themselves with the rational grounds for the defence of the Christian religion and become familiar with the answers to the points in debate. (4) Let them meet together and seek the co-operation of the churchwardens and pious laity in the reformation of manners. (5) Let the clergy make contact with the prominent people in their parishes. (6) Let the clergy inform the ordinary of any person who was obstinate in his vices and with whom example and exhortation were found to be ineffectual, in order that ecclesiastical censure might be passed on him: if this also were found to be of no avail, then let the clergy be foremost in placing such a case before the civil magistrate. (7) Let every pious layman be encouraged to report all swearers, blasphemers, drunkards, and abusers of the Lord's day, to the magistrates. (8) Let the clergy report an evil liver amongst their own number to the bishop. (9) Let the clergy be diligent in catechising the young and keeping in touch with them as they grow older.

He also conducted an extensive visitation of his archdiocese, saw to the confirmation of a large number of candidates himself – an unusual proceeding for the archbishop – and undertook to ordain both ministers and deacons, again an unusual care for someone in his position. Secular society, too, could scarcely be called other than depraved at the time, and Tenison was keen to see to its reform, particularly in regard to marriage. It was common practice, for example, for various public officials to issue blank marriage licences – a profitable source of income and an open invitation to clandestine and forced unions – and this Tenison wanted stopped. But too many people were making money out of the practice, and it was too convenient a social instrument to be suppressed by simple archiepiscopal diktat.

Tenison's interest in reform, however, was not confined to England. In 1701 he founded the Society for the Propagation of the Gospel in Foreign Parts, aimed principally at persuading dissenting American colonists of the virtues of Anglicanism and at converting the native Americans to the same. He also kept a paternal eye on the Anglican Church in Ireland, trying to make sure that Irish Presbyterians would not combine with Scottish and French Protestant immigrants to form any threat of importance to the episcopal establishment; and with similar thoughts in mind, he encouraged the introduction of a Bill in 1701 intended to safeguard the presence and standing of the Episcopal Church in Scotland. But after the death of King William in 1702, Tenison's influence began to wane. The English political establishment was split between two bellicose factions (one can scarcely call them 'parties', since they were not recognisably such in the modern sense of the word), both carrying nicknames, 'Whigs' and 'Tories', and the archbishop and the new queen, Anne, were on opposite sides of this divide. Ever since King William's declining years, Tenison found that ecclesiastical preferments fell more and more into factional hands, with the Tories most often winning the game, especially after the accession of Queen Anne. But when Anne's last remaining heir died in 1700, Tenison saw his chance to out-manoeuvre the Tories and ensure a Protestant succession by supporting the claims of the Electors of Hanover. This he did principally out of the vicious anti-Catholicism which informed much of his religious thinking and, in fact, made him thoroughly in tune with the tone of much English society at the time, although, to be fair, he was almost as hostile to any expression of what he regarded as heterodox theology. Thus, when William Whiston, Lucasian Professor of Mathematics at Cambridge (who was convinced, among other things, that the Tartars were the lost tribe of Israel, that the millennium would come in 1766, and that Mary Toft – who famously gave birth to a litter of rabbits – had been foretold in the Book of Esdras), published a book denying the Trinity and lost his professorship in consequence, Tenison allowed him to be condemned as a heretic and made no serious attempt to influence him or change his opinions.

The harsh judgements made of his character, then, one or two of which we noted earlier, may have come from hostile sources, but cannot for that reason be dismissed entirely. There was much about Tenison which was admirable, to be sure; but he had his faults and these were serious, undermining the virtues and diminishing his good intentions. He died on 14 December 1715, having lived long enough to officiate at the coronation of a Protestant German whose claim to the English throne was as feeble as the hand which put the crown on his head.[10]

This brings us to *William Wake* (1715–37), whose career in many ways mirrors that of Tenison. He was a Whig supporter (not a recommendation in the eyes of Augustine Birrell, who regarded Whigs 'as irreligious a set of dogs as ever barked at a cassock' – a conscientious and effective preacher and pastor both as vicar, bishop and archbishop; and, having begun with many influential friends, gradually lost them until from 1719 he was more or less isolated from the seats of political power. He was also keenly interested in Protestant churches abroad, although in his case this meant western Europe rather than the American colonies. Between 1682 and 1685 he had been chaplain to the English ambassador in France, and this had helped to stimulate another concern he shared with Tenison, the desire for a kind of Protestant communion of churches which would, rather like wagons drawn into a circle, form a defence from behind which the reformed could take potshots at marauding Catholics. Unlike Tenison, however, Wake did not allow anti-Catholicism to poison his bloodstream. To be sure, he engaged in scholarly controversy, most notably with Bishop Bossuet, the great French Catholic champion, in 1686; and in 1718 responded favourably to the unrealistic proposition made by an unorthodox theologian from the Sorbonne that there should be some kind of union between the Gallican Church and the Church of England. Needless to say, this notion, like that of Churchill during the Second World War for a union of France and Britain, came to nothing because it was unworkable. But that did not stop Wake also pressing for intercommunion between various European Protestant

denominations such as the Lutherans and Calvinists in the various German states – again initiatives which failed, partly because of
political rivalries, partly because of doctrinal differences too great to
allow any bridging.

But Wake's two notable achievements were expressions of the less
idealistic side of his character: his immense *State of the Church and
Clergy of England*, published in 1703 as part of a controversy with
Francis Atterbury, Bishop of Rochester; and his creation or inven-
tion of the 'diocese book'. The *State* was a work founded upon vast
reading in documentary material which had long been ignored or
forgotten – a remarkable legacy which remained a work of major
importance for the next 200 years. The 'diocese book' was in effect
a handbook for bishops, containing practical advice for their visitations, and arose out of his own extensive travels in the bishopric of
Lincoln between 1705 and 1715. It contained a summary of answers
to questions he sent to parish clergy and thus set out in simple,
accessible form a fairly detailed picture of the diocese, which would
enable the bishop to know what was going well, what badly, and
what needed still to be done.

In sum, therefore, it may be said that Wake was a more positive
version of Tenison, lacking Tenison's autocratic manner and hatred
of Catholicism. His successor, *John Potter* (1737–47), however, had
his reservations:

> Archbishop Wake had greatly too much timidity about him in many
> cases, and too little vigilance for the good of the Church, though
> otherwise a very good man and a well-wisher to good men and good
> principles. But, for want of discernment of one side and attention
> of spirit of the other, he suffered many bad things to be done, and
> several unworthy men to be highly preferred, without showing good
> care and encouragement of better men, though he often had it in his
> power to do the last and prevent the former. This Archbishop Potter
> (then bishop of Oxford) took the freedom one day to represent to
> him, and desired him to look round and see how little regard had
> been shown for so many years past by the great men to a number
> of eminent divines, while others of a different character found every

advancement. The Archbishop was moved extremely with this representation, and pleaded only for himself, that really he had not observed
or considered so much the state of things before, but he would be
more attentive for the future.[11]

What were Potter's qualifications for making this judgement?
He came from a nonconformist background but soon converted
to Anglicanism and thereafter subscribed to the opposite of low
church views. This upward religious mobility was mirrored by his
rise in society. His father had been a linen draper, but Potter quickly
left all that behind as he trod the path of scholarship at Oxford and
preferment in the Church. Adherence to the Whig faction brought
him influential friends, none more so than John Churchill, Duke of
Marlborough, through whose good offices Potter became Regius
Professor of Divinity at Oxford in 1708, and dean of Christ Church,
an elevated status which caused him to fall out with his oldest son
who married a domestic servant, a displeasure which continued
beyond death, for when Potter's will was opened, son John found
himself disinherited. Further patronage from the duke made Potter
bishop of Oxford in 1715, and there he remained until his translation to Canterbury in 1737. Potter's distaste for his Presbyterian
roots can be seen in his adamant refusal, as archbishop, to have any
reform of the liturgy, an opposition which won him critics as well
as supporters. But it was his refusal to involve himself in the hurly-
burly of politics which cost him dear. The Whigs did not like their
churchmen to be under-concerned with worldly matters or, indeed,
over-concerned with spiritual. So in what was rapidly becoming
the habitual way with archbishops after the Great Usurpation of
1688, Potter lost influence where it mattered politically. But he
died suddenly on 10 October 1747. He had been a very good
Classical scholar, publishing editions of Plutarch and Lycophron,
which gained him a European reputation; but as a divine he left
something to be desired. Edward Carpenter quotes his comment
on being offered the deanery of Christ Church: 'There are three
considerations which might move me in it. These are the profit,
the convenience in other respects, and the good which may be

done in it'. As Carpenter observes, 'Perhaps the order of priorities is unconsciously revealing'.[12]

Eighteenth-century archbishops were great lords with assured status in society and considerable wealth and prerogatives. Not all, however, came from aristocratic families, as we have seen, and those who did not were therefore liable to be somewhat affected by their dizzying ascent to a rank of consequence. Perhaps this is why Potter turned into something of a snob. *Thomas Herring* (1747–57), on the other hand, did not relish the post at all. Successively bishop of Bangor (1737) and Archbishop of York (1743), he was not at all keen to translate himself to Canterbury, as he made clear in a letter to the Lord Chancellor:

> [I] am come to a very firm and most resolved determination not to quit the see of York on any account or on any consideration; and I beg it of your lordship as the most material piece of friendship yet to be exerted by you to prevent the offer of Canterbury if possible, or to support me in the refusal if the other cannot be prevented... The honour of Canterbury is a thing of glare and splendour, and the hopes of it a proper incentive to schoolboys to industry; but I have considered all its inward parts and examined all its duties; and if I should quit my present station to take it, will not answer for it that in less than a twelvemonth I did not sink and die with regret and envy at the man who should succeed me here.

But the Lord Chancellor was not to be refused, and so Herring allowed himself to be promoted well past his abilities. It is notable that he caught the Canterbury disease of political decline. Having won praise while Archbishop of York for his eagerness to raise volunteers in case of an invasion of York by Jacobites in 1745, he threw it away while at Canterbury by opposing the wishes of his most important patron, the duke of Newcastle, and thus, in spite of his fervent support for the Whigs, he dwindled in office and died with only the satisfaction of knowing that his promotions to both archbishoprics had enabled him to settle a large number of his relations in lucrative jobs. *Matthew Hutton* (1757–58), who followed in Herring's footsteps at Bangor (1743),York (1747) and Canterbury, was a harmless kind of fellow, aristocratic in manner – the office must have made him so, for his family was nothing in particular – but pleasant enough, although he did find himself in a tizzy over the state of Lambeth Palace, which he refused to occupy because parts of it were so dilapidated.

Thomas Secker (1758–68), by contrast with his immediate predecessors, was a whirlwind of efficiency both before and after he became Archbishop of Canterbury. By background and education a dissenter, he changed his mind on this point during the early 1720s, at which time he had long been interested in theology and was studying for a degree at Oxford. His first interest, however, had been medicine and he was the first English primate who had studied anatomy, performed dissections, and graduated a Doctor of Medicine. He recorded the whole process in his *Autobiography*. He went to Paris in January 1718 and lodged with 'Mr Winslow, the famous anatomist. I attended his lectures, and those of botany, materia medica, and chemistry at the king's Garden… and the operations of surgery at the Hôtel Dieu. I also learnt to dissect at the Salpetrière'. In 1720 friends persuaded him that 'an academical degree in one of our universities might probably be of great use to me; and as I and my friends apprehended that the degree of Doctor of Physic at Leiden would help to procure me a degree at Oxford, I went just before Christmas from London to Rotterdam, and thence to Leiden… [here] I composed a dissertation, *De medicina statica*, and printed it as part of the exercise for my degree which I took in the beginning of March 1721'.[13] Bearing in mind that Secker had also learned Greek, Latin, Hebrew, Chaldee (Aramaic) and Syriac while he was a pupil at various dissenting academies, we must acknowledge that he had an unusual range of learning, especially for one who intended to be a parish clergyman.

He was ordained in 1723 and moved to the Durham area. His wife's health, however, was not good – in 1736 he recorded that 'she had taken privately great quantities of opiates, of which I new nothing till now' – and so they went first to London and then to Bath where he began to gain a reputation as a preacher. From this point onward, his career slowly developed that pattern we have noticed already in others who ended as archbishops. In 1732 he became a royal chaplain, and in 1733 rector of St James in Piccadilly, where he gave evidence of that energetic efficiency which was to characterise everything he did. 'We put the accounts of all the several officers in a regular order, and made rules for them for the future... [and] thence, in the beginning of July, after a short fit of sickness, I went to Oxford to take a degree of Doctor of Law'.[14] Next year he became bishop of Bristol, undertaking an extensive visitation, and compiling a diocesan survey to help replace some of those which had been lost in an unfortunate fire. From Bristol to Oxford in 1737, where he conducted no fewer than four visitations between 1738 and 1750, and chivvied and preached and laid down the law in a manner which must have disquieted all but the most conscientious and diligent of his clergy. What is more, he continued to preach in London – a sermon in 1750, following an earthquake, was particularly memorable since it explained the phenomenon as a mark of God's anger at the moral degeneracy of the citizens – and regularly attended debates in the House of Lords, where he made shorthand notes and did not hesitate to vote against the government if he disapproved of its proposed measures.

Curiously enough, however, these bouts of opposition did not do his career any particular harm. Perhaps it was because his support for the Hanoverians was so palpable that no one doubted his fundamental loyalty to the régime. At any rate, in December 1750 he was promoted dean of St Paul's and immediately set about putting the records and finances of the cathedral in order, an interest in minutiae and paperwork which followed him to Canterbury in 1758. There he put together a large archive in Lambeth Palace and had the archbishop's manuscript collections re-ordered by his librarian; he preached very frequently, entertained lavishly, visited in the arch-diocese and exercised a firm, indeed a rigorous, control over the intellectual and moral standards of his clergy. He also maintained contact with the other European Protestant communities in Prussia, France and Hungary, took a special interest in Huguenot immigrants living in London, and fretted over the appointment of bishops in the American colonies. This last, though, won him few thanks, for he was accused by Francis Blackburne, Archdeacon of Cleveland, of encouraging Popery at home and abroad, an accusation which cost him a great deal of time and effort to refute. Meanwhile Methodism was gaining significant ground from the Anglican establishment. A protest against the deadening lethargy which was deemed to have afflicted the Church of England, Methodism was greeted by a general archiepiscopal indifference. Archbishop Herring, for example, wrote to William Duncombe that 'for myself, I own I have no constitution for these frights and fervours; and if I can but keep up the regular practice of a Christian life, upon Christian reasons, I shall be in no pain for futurity'.

The mention of Christian *reasons* is notable. The educated classes of the eighteenth century prided themselves on their rationality, apparently oblivious to the theatricality which kept the upper classes amused and the outbursts of emotionalism which leavened the misery of the common people – a form of government which has been called 'aristocracy tempered by rioting'. Methodism tapped this emotional well, and its preachers, especially Samuel and Charles Wesley, moved huge crowds to tears and fainting, a prospect which may have left the Archbishops of Canterbury more or less unruffled, but frightened their parish clergy up and down England into expressions of disgust and indignation. Secker, however, maintained his intellectual poise, being of the opinion that at least the Methodists were communicating the Christian message in ways which were effective, even if somewhat distasteful, while the Church of England was quite failing to speak to its people. His stance was thus one of interest rather than dismissal, although he was acutely aware of the ever-present danger in all such movements that they might draw people away into some kind of separation, and thus from their own distinctive Church.

All these labours, all these concerns, all these activities were carried out by a man frequently in poor physical health. In 1724 he recorded that for some years he had been suffering from a very troublesome cough in winter, for which he went to Bristol and had himself bled. In August 1741 he noted symptoms of the stone, 'and by Dr Hatley's advice took Mrs Stephen's medicines which were then in a liquid form, the soap and lime separate, and very nauseous, the latter especially'. In 1759 Secker added gout to his afflictions, a problem which reoccurred in 1764, 1765 and 1766. It attacked his right hand and by the end of December he was scarcely able to write. Midway through January the following year he suffered from a stone in the kidney, for which he tried various medicines including tea made from wild carrot; and this may or may not have helped, for he thanked God that the pain diminished. Gout flared up in his hands during November, and then in his left heel, and then in both his feet and knees, thereby more or less crippling him for a while. In February 1768 he sought relief by having his left heel opened. A good deal came out and the wound was either deliberately left open or did not heal of itself, for he records it was still not closed in the middle of April. The summer proved to be full of pain, too. 'I have been most grievously afflicted with a rheumatic pain in my hip', he wrote, 'constant, excepting when I lie along'.[15] It is a useful reminder to us of how precarious were the efforts of the rich, never mind the poor, to lead even the most straightforward of lives, how large pain loomed, and how frighteningly different from a literary deathbed was the end of a real person's life. Secker died on 3 August 1768 of a cancerous thigh-bone. He had been a most energetic archbishop, weathering the occasional cloudburst of criticism, maintaining amicable relations with all kinds of people whose views he did not share, liked and respected by both Anglicans and dissenters, and demonstrating in his person that those accusations of lethargic indifference and alienation from the common people, frequently levelled against the Church of England, were not altogether justified in its primate.

Unfortunately his example was not followed. *Frederick Cornwallis* (1768–83) was a gentleman, the first Etonian to become an Archbishop of Canterbury, born into an aristocratic family whose connections helped him rise within the Church. His character may be described as 'genial' and 'convivial', for he exhibited all the traits of the hail-fellow-well-met which were likely to make him popular with everyone he met, and he enjoyed the pleasures of board and company to an extent which earned him a rebuke from George III. He did little and therefore offended no one in particular. More or less the same can be said of *John Moore* (1783–1805). An amiable man who had been tutor to the duke of Marlborough's sons and, but for the saving grace of common sense, might have been the duchess's lover, he benefited by this connection and others contracted as a result of two advantageous marriages, which brought him one or two plum posts before the archbishopric – dean of Canterbury in 1771 and bishop of Bangor in 1775. His elevation to be archbishop came as rather a surprise because he was so junior, and threatened to embroil him in the partisan struggles caused by the onset of George III's first bout of incapacity. But he survived, as did the king, and went on to skirt the quicksands of various attempts in the 1780s to repeal the Test and Corporation Acts, those accumulated statutes which required anyone eligible for public employment or membership of a corporation to swear an oath of loyalty to the Protestant monarchy, and to receive communion according to the rites of the Church of England – measures aimed at Catholics and nonconformists in general. Moore was opposed to their repeal, largely on the grounds that if it went ahead, religious anarchy would supervene, an opinion reinforced by events in France, where the revolution deliberately abolished the Christian religion in favour of a pseudo-rationalistic paganism which no one took seriously.

Events at home, of course, did not encourage him to boldness. George III's recurrent inability to govern, and the waywardness of his regent, the Prince of Wales, meant that seeking a quiet life became the prime desideratum. The regent, true to awkward form, had managed to contract a marriage with a Catholic, Maria Fitzherbert, whom he wedded in secret on 15 December 1785, with an Anglican curate presiding. Their union was illegal, of course, but even so, when Prince George was persuaded to marry Caroline of Brunswick ten years later, the archbishop felt he was treading on eggshells and undertook his duty in the matter with a certain degree of trepidation.

The crowd at St James's last night was immense and the heat intolerable. I felt my business a very solemn one indeed, and never said my prayers in my life under more impression and fervency. The Prince's mind was certainly very seriously affected both in the service and after the service, but not in that part of the service from which one might be led to fear he had upon his mind a feeling that he had before bound himself by solemn engagements. There I saw no embarrassment.[16]

For the rest, however, he sailed into the nineteenth century without having to endure too many additional turbulences. In 1787 he provided the new United States of America with two bishops, both of whom he received with great warmth and introduced to George III before consecrating them in the chapel at Lambeth. He was a genial patron of the Society for the Propagation of the Gospel and the Corporation of the Sons of the Clergy but, after initially supporting William Wilberforce in his efforts to abolish the slave trade between Africa and the West Indies, withdrew his approval. If there was one thing he dreaded, it was the prospect of change and slavery, although 'a cursed trade', as he admitted, was 'too deeply rooted to be forcibly and at once eradicated'. Thus passed his opportunity to take a moral stand.

He died suddenly in Lambeth Palace on 18 January 1805 and with him the eighteenth-century archbishopric ended as it had conducted itself, with one or two exceptions, for most of its 100 years, lost in a world of its own, remote from reality.

10

Squabbling in the Face of Disbelief

Manners Sutton to Temple (1805–1902)

One of the most notable omissions from the background of the foregoing eighteenth-century archbishops is their general neglect or apparent indifference to the agricultural and industrial revolutions which were sweeping and reorganising the country. It is true that occasionally they recognised that the lower classes had problems which ought to be addressed – Archbishop Moore, for example, proposed there should be a natural agreement to give assistance to the poor and destitute – but this tended to be in response to a particular catastrophe (in Moore's case to the dreadful winter of 1799–1800), not to the fast-growing demographic and social convulsions which were devastating the rural order and creating a Dickensian hell in the towns. So it is interesting to note that *Charles Manners Sutton* (1805–28), a grandson of the duke of Rutland and a favourite of George III, promoted to be Archbishop of Canterbury by the king himself over the head of the Prime Minister, William Pitt, played a close personal part in promoting the evangelisation of the urban poor by securing government money to build churches in the rapidly expanding slums and ghettoes of burgeoning cities. He was thus one in spirit with those social reformers, many of whom belonged to dissenting religious confessions such as the Quakers, who were inspired to offer practical help in the footsteps of Martha by their attachment to the example of Mary. Likewise, he was keen to recruit suitable clergy from middle-class backgrounds, and encouraged others to encourage them in turn to present themselves for ordination, and he reinvigorated such bodies as the Society for the Promotion of Christian Knowledge, all with a similar end in view – to bring Christianity to the poor and thus enrich their lives here on earth as far as possible, and save their souls hereafter.

So far so good, but there is no disguising the quirkiness which attended the archbishop's good intentions. In 1810, for example, he voted in the Lords to retain the death penalty for anyone stealing from a private dwelling-house an article or articles worth up to five shillings. But it was his ability to perform intellectual balancing acts almost worthy of a circus performer which may seem to us to be his least endearing trait. Thus he managed both to oppose Catholic emancipation and to be in favour of repealing the Test and Corporation Acts, although this is by no means the choicest example of his talent for straddling two horses. Following the death of George III, the new king, George IV, wanted to free himself from his marriage to Caroline of Brunswick, but until a divorce took place Manners Sutton and his bishops were faced by the difficulty of whether the queen's name should be included in the official prayer book or not. The archbishop twisted and turned and fudged and kerfuffled in an effort not to offend either the king, who wanted her name excised, nor the public, who wanted it retained, nor his bishops, who were divided on the subject. Arguing that the queen was necessarily included in prayers for the royal family even if her name did not actually appear in print presented listeners to his speech in the Lords with a perfect example of that mealy-mouthedness some people may think they recognise from a later period.

Manners Sutton was followed by *William Howley* (1828–48), with whom the word 'opposition' can be associated. He was opposed to the repeal of the Test and Corporation Acts, opposed to Catholic emancipation, opposed to the Reform Act of 1832 (being, indeed, the only cleric to speak against it), and opposed to secular education; and perhaps it may be taken as symbolic of his general approach to confessional and social questions that he was the last Archbishop of Canterbury to wear a wig. His conservatism may be explained in part, at least, by the rise of the Tractarian movement during his time in office. This originated in Oxford in the late 1820s and early 1830s in pamphlets advocating a return of the Church of England to the idealised (but quite unhistorical) state in which the Tractarians supposed it existed under Charles I – a kind of Christian commonwealth. As John Henry Newman wrote, 'I never expect the system of Laud to return but I do expect the due continuation and development of his principles... the so-called union of the Church and State as it then existed had been a wonderful and most gracious phenomenon in Christian history... a realisation of the Gospel in its highest perfection when both Caesar and St Peter know and fulfil their office... Charles is the king, Laud the Prelate, Oxford the sacred city of this principle'.[1] But between 1833 and 1841 the movement broadened into a theological programme which asserted the divine authority of the Church of England as a branch of the Catholic Church, the consequent authority of its bishops as successors of the Apostles, and the position of the sacraments as indispensable means of grace. It was a movement which many Anglicans, including Howley, saw as a seductive and therefore dangerous highway to Rome – a road which John Henry Newman eventually took – and which should in consequence be avoided. But the movement inspired a renewal of vocation among many of the clergy, a spiritual zeal which found them administering to the poor and seeking to revive Christianity in just those areas neglected or treated with careless nonchalance by the Anglican establishment.

It was indeed a time of crisis for that establishment, and at the turn of the century Thomas Mosley, a clergyman and columnist for the *Times*, looked back on it and remarked that that was a time when the Church seemed to be 'folding its robes to die with what dignity it could'. But a sense of impending doom seemed to sharpen its mind, and when Robert Peel became Prime Minister he set about wholesale reform of the Church of England (with Howley's co-operation, it should be said) by forming a statutory body consisting of clerics and laymen whose job it was to overhaul the Church and so secure it from the challenges posed on every side by dissenting minorities and hostile secularists. A by-product of this activity by the Ecclesiastical Commissioners, as members of this reforming body became known, was a severe reduction in the archbishop's annual income. As Carpenter sums it up, 'No more riding in a coach form Lambeth to Westminster flanked by outriders; no more retainers bearing flambeaux to escort the Archbishop across the courtyard of the Palace from the chapel (which [Howley] restored) to his wife's lodgings; no more public days of general entertainment when the food and wine were served by thirty flunkeys dressed in livery and fifteen waiting outside. It was the end of an age'.[2]

Howley was seventy one when he bumbled his way through Victoria's coronation, managing, among other mishaps, to ram the coronation-ring on to the wrong finger so that it took a great deal of subsequent pain and cold water to remove it. His time in office had seen great changes both within and outwith the Church, and yet, as Clive Dewey notes, 'there was some surprise when the Church of England reached the end of the century of reform with so many of its privileges and so much of its property intact'. Dewey puts it down to patronage, an instrument of both reform and conservatism, which Howley used with some degree of skill. 'Snobbery was on the side of the Anglicans, and patronage kept it there',[3] an engine of social advancement which appealed to upwardly-mobile middle-class ordinands, as Howley knew perfectly well.

But if Howley was rather grand and inclined to be conservative, *John Bird Sumner* (1848–62) was not. He began his professional life as a schoolmaster at Eton where he gave evidence of his scholarship and a foretaste of his later prolixity by publishing two books, one entitled *Apostolic Preaching* and the other *A Treatise on the Records of Creation.* (He was to go on to publish forty more while he was Archbishop of Canterbury, a wordy flow which has not been quite emulated by his successors). From Eton he went to a prebendary stall in Durham Cathedral and thence to the bishopric of Chester, where he stayed for nineteen years and showed himself to be a thoroughly conscientious and efficient pastor and administrator.

His views on one of the main topics of the day – the poor and what should be done about them – were much influenced by the opinions of the Reverend Thomas Malthus whose *Essay on Population* (1798, greatly enlarged and emended in 1803) proved a seminal work in a long debate about the relationship between political economy and Christian values. A population, he said, always increases up to the limits of the means of subsistence, and in contemporary England the Poor Law system actually aggravated those ills it was meant to remedy. Keeping a population under control should be done by moral constraint. In other words, the age at which marriage took place should be postponed, and in the meantime people should exercise strict control over their sexual appetites. To many clergymen this sounded not only like an attack on the Gospel's message of benevolence, but also like an encouragement to the state to oppress the poor if they expanded beyond that subsistence created by their own labours. Sumner, however, accepted much of Malthus's argument and, true to his evangelical leanings, maintained that individual choice provided an important instrument whereby each person could improve his or her lot by electing to work hard and so create universal welfare through universal labour.[4]

Enlightened self-restraint and a prudent exercise of free will would provide the conditions necessary to overcome those unhappier checks and balances upon population provided by Nature – war, famine, disease – and to this end the clergy should not seek to confuse the poor by enthusiastically preaching some kind of revolution, but should point out the essential difference between poverty and indigence, the first being an inevitable condition for many, the second one which could and should be avoided.

> These conditions, it must ever be remembered, are essentially distinct and separate. Poverty is often both honourable and comfortable; but indigence can only be pitiable, and is usually contemptible. Poverty is not only the natural lot of many, in a well-constituted society, but is necessary, that a society may be well constituted. Indigence, on the contrary, is seldom the natural lot of any, but is commonly the state into which intemperance and want of prudent foresight push poverty: the punishment which the moral government of God inflicts in this world upon thoughtlessness and guilty extravagance.[5]

In consequence, Sumner was dubious about the beneficial effects of institutionalised relief and therefore unhappy about the effects, if not the intentions, of changes to the Poor Law. He was also doubtful about the supposed need to improve working conditions in factories, maintaining that the children who worked therein were as healthy as children anywhere else in a town or city, and that the factories were helpful in relieving overcrowding in those homes which had hitherto depended on domestic industry for their income. What is more, they stimulated the mind.

> In point of fact, the manufacturer derives a superiority over the peasant, from his constant intercourse with society, and the collision of various minds to which he has been accustomed from his youth. And as for the mechanic, whose labour does not confine him to a single spot, whose work demands the frequent resources of his ingenuity, and who is constantly interested in the pursuit of some new employment or operation, none of the evils of manufactures must be considered as applying to him.[6]

An even greater stimulus, of course, and perhaps the most important way in which the poor could be brought to a realistic appreciation of their condition and a proper exercise of choice to ensure their own spiritual and temporal advancement, was education, and Sumner was very keen to promote this, provided education remained under religious control. It is thus not surprising to find that while he was bishop of Chester, Sumner built or founded as many as 672 day schools. His views on the place and function of the Church in society, then, were coloured by theories rather than direct observation – his remarks on the health of factory workers, for example, were written a good ten years before he set foot in an actual factory – and motivated by that mixture of genuine feeling for the poor and conservative inclination to preserve social distinctions between the classes, which are characteristic of a certain type of educated nineteenth-century gentleman.

But if his Malthusian views (however modified from the original) formed part of a wider debate among both clergy and lay-folk, his embroilment in the so-called 'Gorham controversy' did his authority as archbishop no particular good. Gorham was a low-church cleric whose unusual opinions on baptism had threatened to see him refused ordination. Having overcome this setback, however, he was to be presented in November 1847 to a living in the diocese of the bishop of Exeter, a man whose theological views were quite the opposite of those held by Gorham. So the bishop proposed subjecting him to a preliminary examination. Gorham refused, and the scene was set for a succession of appeals and counter-appeals to higher and higher ecclesiastical courts, and then to the Judicial Committee of the Privy Council. This meant that Sumner became involved and helped to cause a storm by acquiescing in the Committee's judgement that Gorham's views on baptism were perfectly acceptable to the Church of England. Several clergymen immediately betook themselves to the Catholic Church, thereby exacerbating the row, and in spite of the implication of the Committee's decision – that Christian doctrine was now to be defined by a secular body – Gorham was duly installed in his living with Sumner's approval. It was not the end of the affair, but the mistakes had been made and Sumner's impartiality compromised. Always a man eager to encourage the clergy to direct their energies into pastoral activities rather than dissipate them in theological squabbles, he had, in this episode

at least, merely succeeded in encouraging them to indulge their
fissiparous tendencies; and a mere two decades later the Reverend
Thomas Mozley lamented this continuing characteristic:

> The great scandal of the Church of England is the want, the increasing
> want, of parochial solidarity. The parish is divided into sects, and into
> castes, and into classes, each with a literature of its own, and with less
> and less of that common ground which might be the basis of reunion.
> Is there not danger in this state of things?[7]

Charles Longley (1862–68) was the sixteenth of seventeen offspring
and, since he had been surrounded by children all his immature
years, it is perhaps not surprising that he began his career as a tutor
and then went on to become headmaster of Harrow, where John
Colenso was a member of his staff, a man who would become the
bane of his life in later years. In 1836 Longley was appointed the
first bishop of Ripon and proceeded to translate his enthusiasm for
the job into stone. If Sumner had covered his diocese of Chester
with schools, Longley planted his with churches – scarcely unexpected, of course, in a newly created diocese, especially one which
included a large number of rapidly growing industrial towns such
as Bradford, Halifax, Leeds and Wakefield. But Tractarian supporters
saw their opportunity to use the call for new churches which would
supply their liturgical needs and so expand their influence, and
when Edward Pusey, one of the foremost architects of the Oxford
Movement, was asked to provide a new church in Leeds, Longley
was chagrined to find that it was supposed to be dedicated to the
Holy Cross, contained a stone altar instead of a table, and carried an
inscription asking the reader to pray for the builder of the church
– an exhortation which looked suspiciously like a request for prayers
for the dead. Such things (not to mention the ritual practices used
by its clergy) smacked of Romanism, and Longley, in spite of his
own high-church inclinations, very nearly refused to consecrate
the church at all.

    This, however, was merely a foretaste of disagreements to come.
After a short stint as bishop of Durham, when he continued his

church-building programme, Longley was appointed Archbishop of Canterbury in October 1862 and almost at once fell into a slough of doctrinal quarrels. The ground had been laid in 1860 by the publication of articles by various hands under the title *Essays and Reviews.* These attracted charges of heresy, which were dismissed by the same Judicial Committee which had dealt with Gorham's case. But Longley was of the opinion that some of the contributions were indeed inconsistent with articles of the Anglican creed, and did not hesitate to say so. He was then faced by the problem of his erstwhile colleague, James Colenso, now bishop of Natal and author of several works of scholarship, including a *Zulu-English Dictionary*, and of theological commentary, principally a volume entitled *Pentateuch and the Book of Joshua Critically Examined.* This contained a number of observations demonstrating that certain allegedly factual statements in the Old Testament could not be true and that in consequence one was not morally obliged to be bound by any principles contained in them or founded upon them. These were explosive propositions, and Colenso was found guilty of heresy by his metropolitan and deprived of his office, a decision Longley thought entirely correct and one to which he gave his wholehearted approval.

Pressures upon both Longley and the rest of the English bishops, caused by the growing hostility between supporters of the ever-galloping sciences and those of religious orthodoxy – one thinks, among other things, of the spat between Thomas Huxley and the bishop of Winchester, Samuel Wilberforce, over Darwin's *Origin of Species* (1859) – and also in part by the Colenso affair, suggested that a meeting of Anglican bishops from England and abroad might be useful in order to confirm the rightness of Colenso's condemnation and deprivation, to legitimise his successor (a process of appointment which itself generated even more wasteful heat and energy) and in more general terms to give the Anglican communion a greater sense of unity by encouraging its bishops to exchange views and come to majority conclusions in the gentlemanly ambience of the archbishop's palace. Thus was born the first Lambeth Conference, which met in September 1867, attended by seventy-eight bishops from Britain and the colonies. It was not altogether a success. Longley had no intention of turning it into a synod where declarations of faith would be made or canons enacted. But the Colenso affair would not go away; several churchmen, including the Archbishop of York and most of *his* bishops, stayed away, and the dean of Westminster refused to let the Conference use the Abbey for its final act of worship. All were afraid, or at least nervous, that, whatever Longley's intentions, the Conference would indeed become a synod and the Anglican faith as they knew it be compromised; and since Longley was not a Pope, he could not enforce obedience on his fellow-bishops. One looks back to his days as headmaster of Harrow, when discipline in the school under his command was very sadly deficient.

Still, the Conference did a great deal for the archbishop's prestige in other ways, since it created the impression that the English primate was *primus inter pares* among the whole Anglican communion, and did indeed genuinely increase the range of his episcopal interests. Henceforth the Archbishop of Canterbury would be as much concerned with the Anglican Church elsewhere in the world as with that in England, a preoccupation which, if he was not careful, might delude him into an over-estimation of both his authority and his influence.

With *Archibald Tait* (1868–82), the Church of England fell for the first time into the hands of a Scot. Tait had a precarious start in life. He was born with club feet, which were eventually straightened by the painful device of his wearing tin boots day and night. But the misfortune which nearly took him off was scarlet fever – it did kill one of his brothers – and this weakened his constitution, preparing him for further onslaughts later on. From Edinburgh, where he was born, he went to the University of Glasgow in 1827 and thence to Balliol College, Oxford two years later. In 1836 he was ordained a minister in the Church of England (even though he had been brought up a Presbyterian by his nurse after the early death of his mother), an expression of his ambition to rise high in the state Church, never mind that that state Church belonged to a different country. For the moment, however, education called and in 1842 he was appointed headmaster of Rugby in succession to Thomas Arnold, whose brand of muscular Christianity suited his temperament. But he was not fitted to be a successful head and it was not until rheumatic fever struck him down in 1848 and brought him very near death that the boys, true to that saccharine brand of sentimentality which afflicts the young and the simple, decided he was a good egg after all and ceased their rioting long enough to let him recover. Another job was obviously going to be attractive, and in 1849 he went to Carlisle as dean of the cathedral. During his seven years there, he was an efficient enough pastor, but much of his attention was drawn back to Oxford, since he had been appointed one of the commissioners to oversee reform of the university, a post to which he brought experience (gained in 1839) of the Prussian university system, one which he admired and recommended to his fellow-commissioners. Carlisle, however, was overshadowed by personal sorrow. Five of his seven children were killed by scarlet fever in the spring of 1856, and a sympathetic government moved him thence to be bishop of London, a challenge he accepted and tried to meet for the next twelve years.

Curiously enough for one who disliked the ritualism of the Oxford Movement and always opposed it whenever he found it in his diocese, there is a certain theatricality to Tait's period in London. This is not meant as a criticism. It is merely that so quiet and unassuming a man, left weak by ill health and increasingly subject to fainting fits, undertook extraordinarily unusual ways – unusual, that is, for a high-ranking Victorian bishop – of responding to some of the problems and crises of mid-century London. His predecessor had built a large number of churches in response to the expanding population. But when Tait realised that people were failing to come into those churches, he decided to use methods more associated with evangelicals, Methodists and other kinds of dissenter, and so went preaching himself, and encouraged his clergy to do likewise, in the open air, in the dockland, bus stations, railway stations, and Covent Garden market. He allowed his clergy to hire theatres for Sunday night services, and set up a Bishop of London's Fund to help pay men and women to go into people's homes and preach the Gospel there – all of which proved so successful that the churches were indeed packed, and the poor came thither without feeling the need to dress up in their best clothes, a measure of a shift in psychology which indicated their desire to take part in an act of worship rather than make a demonstration of social respectability. Indeed, so ready was Tait to be innovative that he ordained a woman as a deacon in 1861, and he was prepared to lay aside his dislike of the ritualism of the Oxford Movement when, during the cholera epidemic of 1866, he found two 'ritualist' clergy working to minister to the poor and sick and dying in one of the slum parishes of London. He wrote in a memoir of his wife:

> The state of things in the East of London became very bad indeed. The whole district which had any connection with the river Lea was infected. I summoned a meeting of the clergy of Bethnal Green, Stepney, and Spitalfields, and we endeavoured to make arrangements which might aid the sanitary authorities. From that time my dear wife accompanied me regularly in the visits I made to the infected districts... I can see her now standing in one of the large wards of the hospital for Wapping and St George's in the East, quietly soothing the sufferers, while one poor little girl seemed to be seized with the last agonies, and the Rev. C.F. Lowder who attended us, stepped quietly to the bed of the poor patient, and gave her such help as, by God's blessing, resulted in her final recovery.[8]

Yet for all this – and it was a great deal in comparison with the efforts being made by some other bishops and clergy of the period – Tait remained oddly unmoved by the theological controversies which were whistling round the heads of both cleric and layman in mid-nineteenth-century England. On the one hand, Catholicising high churchmen, born largely out of the Tractarians of the Oxford Movement, he found distasteful, and when he became Archbishop of Canterbury, in spite of his realisation that the Church of England needed all the spiritual energy it could muster to combat the growing forces of atheistic secularism, he was still determined to direct and regulate the way in which the public should go, and that was most assuredly not in the high church way, as his efforts to control what he saw as ritualist excesses by means of legislation in 1874 clearly indicate. The results of relying on secular means to achieve ecclesiastical ends, however, were somewhat unfortunate, because those ritualists who felt that in conscience they could not modify their practices in conformity with the Act fell foul of the law, and some were sent to gaol. Sidney Green from the diocese of Manchester, for example, found himself arrested for ecclesiastical disobedience and had to be rescued from prison by Archbishop Tait's personal intervention; and Alexander MacKonochie, whom Tait much admired and with whom he had worked side by side in the London slums during the cholera outbreak of 1866 was due to be deprived of his benefice and was saved from sacking again by Archbishop Tait's intervention. Thus Tait found himself obliged to try to undo or mitigate some of the unintentional consequences of a badly drafted law which he himself had promoted and encouraged. On the other hand, in spite of his personal enjoyment of the spirit of the age, its technical onward rush and delight in innovation, developments in natural science and Biblical criticism (which were causing much distress in other clerics) Tait tended to ignore or pass over, sticking firmly to the simple faith in which he had been brought up, and expecting others to do the same. The various forces which threatened to divide the Church of England even further into disparate and ultimately irreconcilable groups of sectaries thus began to overwhelm him.

To be fair, it is difficult to see how this fissiparousness, which had been growing since the seventeenth century, could have been amended. But Tait was a sick man and his ill health undermined whatever efforts he was prepared to make. In November 1869, for example, he suffered a series of convulsions which nearly killed him – these on top of a constitution much enfeebled by scarlet and rheumatic fever. 'I remember going into my wife's room and finding her reading the Bible with the children', he wrote ten years later. 'I warned them not to work their mother too hard. I remember also looking out of the window on the bright frosty morning, and anticipating a day of comparative rest. I returned to my dressing-room, but I had not finished dressing when I fell prostrate and senseless on the floor'. A few hours later he had a second attack which partially paralysed his face, arm and side. He recovered in time, much to the surprise of his doctors, but not entirely, for his left arm never regained its full strength afterwards.

It was the disestablishment of the (Protestant) Church of Ireland which had precipitated these seizures. Gladstone, appointed Prime Minister in 1869, was determined to cut it free from the English Church and disendow it, on the grounds that it was indefensible to maintain a wealthy and prestigious body which was supported by only a small number of the Irish population, and which was identified by most of the Irish with foreign or quisling landlords. Opponents of Gladstone's Bill argued that disestablishment would play into the hands of Irish Catholic resentment, and that the Bill would encourage English dissenters and radicals who would argue that Irish disestablishment set a precedent for English disestablishment, a goal they had had in mind for some considerable time. Tait was therefore bound to set his face against Gladstone, in spite of the fact that, politically speaking, they were both Liberals; and it was the enormous workload imposed on him in addition to his customary punishing schedule which brought on the convulsive seizures.

A few battles yet remained. Nonconformists could be buried in their parish graveyards, but only in silence. Tait opened the way to their being able to receive their own burial service. Oxford, too, was restive. Perhaps in reaction against the Oxford Movement, many college fellows had thrown themselves into a spat of anticlericalism which would have done justice to France in its revolutionary stage. But Tait's health was declining and although he managed, with some personal success, to preside over the second Lambeth Conference of 1878, where his energy in chairing sessions and attending committees was formidable, by the end of 1882 he was completely spent, and on 2 December he died. The impression he made on contemporaries, who were not uncritical, is perhaps best summed up in a letter from the dean of Durham to the dean of Windsor, dated 24 September 1890:

> Speaking generally, I always thought that his natural gifts – tact and public speaking amongst them – fitted him rather for a statesman than an ecclesiastic; and I have ventured to express my opinion that

in his episcopal life he made serious mistakes, both in word and action. But when we think of the manner in which, born and bred in a different communion, he gradually learned, in a time of great difficulty, to understand and even to sympathise with all the varieties of the English Church, and of his constantly increasing determination to do justice to them all – a determination which, I believe, would have gone much further, if his life had been preserved; and when we remember his strong hold on the laity, no less than upon the affection and respect of the clergy, I cannot help believing that, in the opinion of all parties, very few Archbishops of Canterbury have for centuries discharged the duties of that great post with so much dignity, ability and devotion.[9]

There is a portrait of *Edward Benson* (1883–96) by Sir Hubert von Herkomer, showing him with the long hair and voluminous lawn sleeves of his time and office, and a slight prim purse of the lips, which reminds one of the acid observation made in the following century, that so many of the archbishops were 'mincy men in frocks'. There was, however, nothing mincy about Benson. In 1852 he became a master at Rugby and six years later married a distant cousin, who was then subjected to bullying and a dominance which left her permanently afraid of her husband throughout their marriage. She had been warned. Her horoscope apparently predicted that she would have great trouble in love matters, and that marriage for her would be 'a very disturbing element'. This trait of Benson's can be seen again during his time as headmaster of Wellington where he was austere, hard-working and efficient, but chose to rule by fear, the fear being generated both by his violent temper and by his conviction that flogging could drive out sin. Ian Hamilton, for example, later a General and a knight of the realm, was a pupil under his care and was beaten every day for weeks because he could never arrive at school on time; and another boy later recalled, in adult life, that Benson would sometimes turn white with rage while he was caning someone. Even his own children found him frightening. Arthur called him 'cruel' and recollected that 'Papa was a very difficult person to deal with, because he was terrifying'.[10] Some of this may have been caused by illness – Benson suffered periods of depression which was sometimes severe – and some by his religious views, which in many ways were self-reproachful enough to have satisfied the most severely introspective Calvinist. 'My religious principle is not a thing of tender feelings, warm comforting notions, unproved prejudices', he commented once, 'but it consists of full and perfect conviction, absolute belief, rules to regulate my life, and tests by which I believe myself bound to try every question the greatest and the least... Bigot, thus far, a conscientious Christian must be'.[11] At Wellington Benson formed friendships, some of which were to prove influential in creating his ecclesiastical career. One such friend became bishop of Lincoln, another (Fredrick Temple) bishop of Exeter; and when Benson's time at the school turned sour enough for him to look for a way to retire with dignity, he was offered the chancellorship of Lincoln Cathedral in 1872, an appointment which initiated five years of fevered activity as he sought, through good works of all kinds, to escape a particularly black depression. From Lincoln he went to Truro as bishop. It was a new bishopric, so there was a great deal to do, and Benson threw himself into the post with vigour, founding a girls' school, taking up Cornish antiquarianism, inventing liturgies, directing pastoral care and, above all, building a new cathedral.

With so much to do, six years passed quickly, blighted, however, by the death of his oldest son. Glimpses of Benson at this time create a distinct impression. 'Fred' recreates one with a portrait of the father of the main character in his novel, *David Blaize*. 'His father was an Archdeacon, and... he wore a shovel-hat and odd, black, wrinkled gaiters even when... he climbed the hills in the Lake District with a small edition of the poems of Wordsworth in his pocket, from which he read aloud at frequent halting-places'.[12] One cannot help having the notion, in fact, that throughout his life Benson was rather like an actor playing the part of an ecclesiastic. His real talent was for the details of ecclesiastical behaviour and liturgical practice; everything else he did with efficiency but a degree of detachment. Secular politics, therefore, in which as a bishop he should have taken an active interest, rather passed him by, and even when he became Archbishop of Canterbury in 1883, his efforts were concentrated on Church affairs rather than those of the state, although he did speak once in 1884 in favour of extending the franchise. Elevation to the highest position in the Church of England did nothing to curb his autocratic ways – why, indeed, should it? – and even though the style of the archbishop's life was not what it would have been once, Lambeth Palace was still a palace with platoons of servants and a ceremonial attached to everyday life there which Benson found gratifying and did nothing to discourage. The actor had found his ideal stage-set.

Yet it is interesting that a man so interested in the minutiae of ritual should have found himself pilloried for his intervention in the trial of Edward King, Bishop of Lincoln, who was accused of 'ritualism' – that is, of using illegal ceremonies during the liturgy – in 1887. A formal complaint against him was lodged in 1888 and brought to Benson's notice, a problem for Benson being that he was required to hear the case in the Archiepiscopal Court, a court which was actually of dubious legality. If Benson refused to entertain the case, he might be forced to do so by secular authority, a motion which would then demonstrate that ultimately the Church was subordinate to the Crown. If, on the other hand, he heard the case and passed judgement (as he must), that judgement could be overturned on appeal to another court. Hoist with unresolvable difficulties, Benson dragged the matter out as long as he could before finding (with one or two exceptions) in favour of King, much to the delight of many ritualists, and much to the irritation of others. Those clergy whose views and practices tended towards low church, of course, ignored the judgement entirely. But if the 'Lincoln judgement' had served merely to illustrate the fact that control over Church practice, and therefore reform, did indeed rest firmly in the hands of the secular powers, Benson had, only four years previously, won a kind of battle to conceal that reality and, perhaps, to modify its effects. It stemmed from his conviction that reforms in the Church should go hand in hand with a striving for unity of mind anent what those reforms ought to be, and for this purpose the laity ought to be consulted. Hence his proposal that there should be a House of Laymen to supplement the clerics of Convocation – the archbishop's advisory body and the Church of England's 'parliament' – an idea he saw brought to fruition in 1886. The new House could exert moral influence and did; but its existence altered the legal position of the English Church not one jot. The secular state in the persons of the monarch, the Privy Council, the Prime Minister and the Houses of Parliament held the actual reins of power, so Benson's effort was really just a gesture. Disestablishment – removing the link between Church and state – would have done much to resolve that problem, but the archbishop was not prepared to countenance such an upheaval. Well-meant gestures, therefore, were all he had power to manage.

But if he could do nothing material to mend the condition of his Church or restore it to those presumed ancient glories he was so fond of researching, he could take an interest in Protestant churches elsewhere, and throughout the 1880s he made efforts to encourage missionary work as far afield as Korea, although, perhaps significantly, he directed missionaries to build up native churches rather than create an English Church abroad. It was a tacit recognition that such efforts at transplantation would not work and that his own authority over such 'Anglican' outposts was very limited. How limited, in fact, was brought home to him in September 1896 by the Papal Bull *Apostolicae curae*, issued by Leo XIII:

> Strictly adhering in this matter to the decrees of the Pontiffs Our predecessors, and confirming them most fully, and, as it were, renewing them by Our authority, of Our own motion and certain knowledge We pronounce and declare that ordinations carried out according to the Anglican rite have been and are absolutely null and utterly void.[13]

So that was that. As far as Rome was concerned, Benson was not even a clergyman, let alone an archbishop. With other Churches he was somewhat more successful. The appointment of a bishop in Jerusalem had its awkward moments, but Benson took a personal interest in mending fences with the Anglican Church in Natal, which had swept into schism after the Colenso affair, and in the ancient Assyrian Church, Nestorian rather than Orthodox, which was in danger of being swamped by the Islamic societies around it. He even managed to initiate interest in the Metropolitan of the Russian Orthodox Church in union between the two communions, although the initiative came to nothing in the end.

It is said that every actor would like to die on stage, and Benson managed this admirably. He was attending holy communion with his family and died in his pew during a recital of the Lord's Prayer. He was left there until the end of the service when the congregation was informed that the archbishop had not fainted, as some thought, but was actually dead. The organist then struck up the Dead March from *Saul* and the archbishop's body was carried out of the church and into the rectory where it lay on a sofa, waiting to be dressed in full episcopal vestments. His wife reproached herself for being unworthy of him. Clearly Benson's bullying had had an indelible effect. Nor did his children escape. 'Fred' became a novelist, famous these days for his creations *Mapp* and *Lucia*, but perhaps better known in his own time for a number of heated tales about love between boys at school. Hugh became a Catholic and ended as a Monsignor, fascinated by ghosts and terrified at the thought he might be buried alive. His interest in ghosts may have been inherited from his father, for when the archbishop was an undergraduate in Cambridge he belonged to the Ghost Society, which met to discuss occult phenomena of this kind, and one of Hugh's maternal uncles had founded the Society for Psychical Research. Maggie Benson suffered from depression – an unfortunate inheritance from her father – which gradually sent her insane. It was a collective legacy of unhappiness which cannot, of course, be attributed entirely to the archbishop but one for which he must bear at least some responsibility. He could be charming, affable, witty, but this was not natural to him. At the core he was an unpleasant man and on the whole one is quite glad not to have met him.

Frederick Temple (1896–1902), on the other hand, sometimes gave the impression of being brusque and insensitive, although he was actually a man of genuine warmth and kindliness, as those close to or friendly with him quickly found out. He always threw anonymous letters into the fire without reading them. On one occasion a visitor saw him do this and expressed surprise. 'Do you know why I did that?' asked Temple. 'It's an anonymous letter. When I was a young man at the Council Office, I had to decide on the claims of two men for a certain post; they stood very even, but some time before, I had received an anonymous letter against one of them, and I found it so hard in making the decision to get that letter out of my head that I resolved that I would always burn anonymous letters in future'. A politician summed him up: 'I can always get on with Temple. He's rough, but he's straight, and you always know what he means'.[14]

Temple had a slightly unconventional beginning, being the only Archbishop of Canterbury to be born on one of the Greek islands, where his father was a military resident. Octavius Temple died in Sierra Leone when Frederick was only thirteen, so Frederick was left in England to be brought up by his mother, who exercised a great influence over him and to whom he was devoted until the day she died. In 1838 he entered Balliol College, Oxford on a scholarship and worked tremendously, his labours being rewarded by a double first in the proper sense of the term; that is, a first in both Classics and Mathematics. Education then claimed his interest and energy, and after a number of years serving as an examiner and inspector, he was appointed headmaster of Rugby, where he proved to be rather popular. One boy wrote home that he was 'a beast, but a just beast', and another recollected later in life:

> It is hard, at this distance of time, to describe what he was as a teacher or form-master… He often seemed indifferent to practices the ordinary master would not tolerate, or to ignorance of lessons which should have been prepared. I remember on one occasion the blade of a knife, with which I was rounding an R on my little table, flying on to his book as he sat not far off, and his merely remarking, 'That will keep you attentive now'. But I felt the look of his keen eyes as he said it… Probably the best effect of his teaching was the impression he created of the general character of an author's meaning and style and of the possibility of mastering it. But the analyses of chapters and books which he made in our presence were the most masterly and illuminating weapons he used for our instruction… The three things that I associate most in my mind with those days of our great Headmaster are his cheerfulness, his thoroughness, and his impartiality.

I used occasionally to take walks with him, and I would sometimes ask a question which produced a long silence. How I dreaded those silences! They set me to wonder whether I had asked a wrong question, or asked it wrongly; when, suddenly, he would begin to answer, having arranged his thoughts, and having also secured that mine were in order.[15]

It was not only on the boys of Rugby, however, that Temple made an impression. In 1869 Gladstone offered him a choice of four bishoprics – unheard-of largesse – and he decided to go to Exeter. His choice led to a minor storm in certain quarters, since he had contributed to the infamous *Essays and Reviews* of 1860 and had supported Bishop Colenso during his appeal to the Privy Council against sentence of heresy. But the storm did not deflect his consecration, and once he had been made bishop he withdrew his contribution from future editions of *Essays and Reviews*, thereby demonstrating that he was not to be intimidated into changing his mind when he thought he had made a right decision, but that he was also willing to consider other people's feelings and accommodate them if it were possible. A greater contrast with the autocratic Benson would be hard to find.

Once installed in Exeter, he began a tour of what was a very large diocese and set about its reorganisation; but this was not the main focus of his energies. Education, so recently his professional life, remained for him a means whereby the working classes could improve their condition – a conviction he shared with several of his predecessors and which caused him, like them, to establish new schools in his diocese. He was also alert to the problems caused by drink and took an active interest in the temperance movement of the last decades of the century, especially by becoming President of the National Temperance League, an organisation devoted to persuading the working poor that total abstinence from liquor would not only be good for their souls and physical health, but for their pockets, too, since the money they squandered at present on alcohol would then be available to their wives and children for clothing and food. Such a stance was not popular. At a meeting of the United Kingdom Alliance held in Exeter on 23 January 1872, Temple was interrupted by rioting and sarcastic pantomime from some of his opponents. The *Exeter and Plymouth Gazette* recorded that:

> Upon comparative quiet being restored, Mr. G.O. Trevelyan, M.P., came forward, and was greeted with mingled cheering and hooting. A man mounted a chair at the back of the room and shouted something about depriving the poor man of his rights, denying to him what the rich could get for themselves. Upon this Mr. Trevelyan invited him to the platform, and accordingly to the platform he came, escorted by a number of his associates. The man had apparently been in the heat of the former scrimmage, for his clothes were literally torn off his back, and there was little to cover the upper part of his body except the fragment of a shirt. One of the other men produced a black bottle, apparently, however, empty, and, wishing the audience luck, went through the pantomime of drinking, afterwards passing the bottle to his fellows, who went through a similar performance. This was the signal for roars of laughter, yells, and hisses.

All in all, however, Temple proved a great success at Exeter, and so when Gladstone moved him to London in 1885 his departure was marked by a grand letter, in which most of the diocese's clergy who had objected to his appointment in 1869 now expressed their sincere regret. 'We grieve to say goodbye', they wrote, 'but we do so with heart-felt gratitude and affection, and with earnest prayers that your future career may be fraught with blessings to you, and to all dear to you, as your past has been to us'. 'All dear to you' referred to his wife and family, for at the surprisingly late age of fifty-five Temple had married and sired two sons. In London, much of his time was occupied by serving on governmental commissions, mostly connected with education, the physically handicapped, and working-class housing. Indeed, the only blot on his libertarian credentials a modern idealist might be tempted to note was his lack of sympathy with the London dockers who went on strike in August and September 1889. He thought their demands unreasonable, and the credit for fellow-feeling therefore went to a Catholic, Cardinal Manning, whose diplomatic skills won the necessary conciliation.

Archbishop Benson noted acidly in his diary, 'Cardinal Manning has done well for London. But why has my dear Bishop of London gone back and left it to him? Are the dockers on strike Roman Catholics all?'

Temple's time as Archbishop of Canterbury came when his health, and in particular his eyesight, was beginning to fail him. He was quite busy with various services to commemorate Queen Victoria's birthday and the length of her reign, and the fourth Lambeth Conference, which coincided with 1,300 years after St Augustine landed in Kent, in honour of which Temple and 100 or more bishops got on a special train to Glastonbury and sweated their way on a blazing August day to a service in the abbey ruins. This was followed the next year by a visit to Scotland – repeated in 1902 – and in 1899 by yet another squabble about ritualism in the English Church, a matter which Temple firmly squashed by saying that the disputed practices were not permissible. Education continued to interest him. Indeed, it was while he was speaking in the House of Lords on the Education Bill of 1902 that he was taken ill and had to retire to Lambeth Palace, where he died on 11 December. He was the last archbishop of the nineteenth century and the first of the twentieth, an aged and feeble man when he crowned Edward VII, so much so that when he knelt to do homage he could not get to his feet again, and the king had to help him rise. It was symbolic moment: a Church too impotent even to restore itself from a position of submissiveness to the Crown without the help of the state.

II

Struggling with Atheism
Davidson to Williams
(1903–)

T he most significant legacy passed to the twentieth century
by the nineteenth was disbelief. The great expansion of
church building during the last two-thirds of the nineteenth century was not so much a response to a resurgence of
religious fervour as an attempt to make available places of worship
once the missionary work of the newly enthused parish clergy had
had its effect – at least, so the bishops hoped. 'Darkest Africa', a
phrase contemporaries sometimes used as shorthand for 'heathen
ignorance and superstition', was to be found, as many pointed out at
the time, on the doorstep of the English Church in both the slums
and the middle-class drawing-rooms of the cities especially. But if

the poor were ignorant of the Christian faith and neglected by the Church, a neglect that church building and missionary work were belatedly trying to remedy, the middle classes were wracked by doubt and fearfulness under the dire assaults of Darwinism and textual criticism. A haunting melancholy pervaded their inmost thoughts, as in Thomas Hardy's poem, *The Impercipient (At a Cathedral Service)*:

> That with this bright believing band
> I have no claim to be,
> That faiths by which my comrades stand
> Seem fantasies to me,
> And mirage-mists their shining land,
> Is a strange destiny.
>
> Why thus my soul should be consigned
> To infelicity,
> Why always I must feel as blind
> To sights my brethren see,
> Why joys they've found I cannot find
> Abides a mystery.[1]

To this collective ignorance and doubt the archbishops often did their best to reply, but their efforts, well-meaning and sincere though they undoubtedly were, scarcely made any deep impact on society as a whole. The religiosity of nineteenth-century England was, like the stability of the British Empire at the turn of the century, more apparent than real, and the archbishops were simply not equipped to deal with the rising tide of irreligion. James Froude cast a perceptive eye over the problem:

> There is something touchingly beautiful in the passion with which English and American Protestant divines cling to the letter of the Bible. It is an unconscious perception that in this Book, in some form or other, lies the solution of the enigma of existence. Their fault has been that they have assumed without reason that, while the truth is there, anyone who can read will find it there; that it is

as intelligible to the unlearned as the learned. They have seen in the
Bible the meaning which their eyes brought with them. They have,
I repeat, made the Bible into an idol. Their theories, being the work
of their own minds, mortal like themselves, though dignified by the
name of eternal verities, recoil on them, as superstitions always recoil,
through the natural expansion of knowledge. The ground slips under
their feet; religion loses its grasp. Materialism takes hold of philosophy; corruption takes hold of politics; speculative money-making
and vulgar ambition, of the individual souls of the millions. They
look on bewildered and helpless, while the Popery, which had been
lying so long prostrate under the blows of the Reformation, lifts its
unsightly limbs out of the grave, walks erect, and flings its shadow
over the world once more.[2]

Ah, Popery! There was the *real* bugaboo for so many of these divines.
The constant concern and worry over 'ritualism' which plagued
their time in office rose from a deep-seated fear that the Church of
England might not simply split into irreconcilable factions – that
had happened long ago, during the seventeenth and eighteenth
centuries – but that a newly invigorated Catholicism, so frighteningly visible in its restored English hierarchy and the Irish who were
pouring into England to seek work, might draw whole sections of
English society back to Rome. Look at John Henry Newman who
ended life as a cardinal! Why, even an Archbishop of Canterbury's
son could not be relied on. Look at Hugh Benson who converted
and became a Monsignor!

The cosy world of bickering about ritual practice and doing good
works for the poor, however, was about to be destroyed. *Randall
Davidson* (1903–28) was the first Archbishop of Canterbury to face
a world war, and his response to this catastrophe would set the tone
for his time in office, and also provide an example for his successors
to reject or follow. Davidson was the second Scot to be translated
to Canterbury. After an education at the Edinburgh Academy and
at Harrow where he was shot – an accident, but it left him severely
disabled for the rest of his life – he attended Trinity College, Oxford,
where he met Crauford Tait, son of Archbishop Tait. Through such

a contact, he quickly entered the highest reaches of both Church
and Court society and became an *éminence grise* not only to Tait and
Benson but also to the queen herself, who was so struck by him
that she even forgave him his ill-judged advice against publishing
her *Leaves from a Highland Journal.* In 1891 he became bishop of
Rochester, although within eleven days of his consecration he was
taken gravely ill and fought a long time to recover. From there he
went to the bishopric of Winchester in 1895, an appointment which
brought him into closer contact with the queen at Osborne House,
and saw him engaged in yet another of the interminable quarrels
with ritualist clergymen which absorbed so much of the time of
the Anglican hierarchy.

But the advent of Frederick Temple to be Archbishop of
Canterbury brought an end to some, at least, of his charmed existence. Temple did not like him and did not hesitate to say so. Even
the queen turned less amicable, vetoing his appointment as bishop
of London on the grounds that his health was too frail to let him
do the job properly. When Temple died, however, Balfour, the Prime
Minister, saw no good reason he should not occupy the archbishop's
chair at Canterbury, and Edward VII agreed. Hence an elevation
which had begun to seem unlikely took place, and Davidson was
faced by a multitude of problems. Unionists in Parliament objected
to his increasing ritualist practices; the newspapers vilified him for
appearing to equivocate on the dreadful living conditions of Chinese
labourers in the Transvaal; the clergy almost to a man shrieked in
protest at his public silence over the conversion to Catholicism of
Princess Victoria Eugénie before her marriage to King Alfonso X
of Spain; Parliament passed an Act allowing a man to marry his
sister-in-law, a measure directly opposed to Anglican canon law;
Parliament also threatened to pass an Act which would have the
effect of removing state education from the exclusive control of
the established Church; and Lloyd George's budget of 1909 caused
a constitutional crisis which had Davidson and the bishops first
voting against and then for the government. Through all these perils
Davidson moved with the surefootedness of an arthritic crossing
a torrent. He managed to get to the other side, but his constant

balancing-act merely served to illustrate how very precarious was the position of the Church in English national life, and how introverted its clerical members could be. The gap between clergy and laity was merely exacerbated by the First World War. Ecumenism had floated itself for discussion during the early years of the twentieth century, partly in response to questions raised by the ritualist tradition which was gaining ground in spite of occasional setbacks, partly in response to the ever-present vexation of Biblical scholarship in the universities, which served only to aggravate the climate of doubt or disbelief in certain circles, and partly in response to the growing question of what the Church of England represented – a purely national Church, or one among several Christian communities of equal worth and standing?

When war broke out, ecumenism was laid aside for the time being, although Davidson never quite surrendered to the mood of hysteria which infected almost everyone else. Indeed, he protested again and again that the methods the government was employing to advance its cause – from lying about British casualties to the proposed use of poison gas – were barbarous and vile. He wrote to Asquith on 7 May 1915:

> I am no soldier, but as a Christian citizen I try to understand the situation as it exists and I confess that I am profoundly disquieted by the indications that our own Army may be bidden to meet the new situation itself adopting these inhuman tactics. I suppose that if anyone had suggested a few months ago that the British Army would use poisonous gases for creating fatal disease among its enemies, the notion would have been scouted as preposterous. What has happened to change our view?... We can no doubt follow [Germany's] example if we choose. If we adopt that line of reprisal (and this is a really important point) how far will the principle carry us? If they are poisoning the wells in South Africa, and perhaps ultimately in Belgium, are we forthwith to do the like? If so, can we retain self-respect on the part either of the Army or the Nation?...You may say that I am an ignoramus and that this is a matter for experts. But is it not really the sort of question on which the average intelligent citizen

of a Christian country is entitled to have an opinion? Do you think
we should be satisfied ten years hence as a people if we had to look
back upon having done these things ourselves?[3]

The criticism, however, was made in private. Davidson gave no lead
in any public denunciations of the war and its conduct, and although
one can perfectly understand why it would have been exception-
ally difficult for him to do so, and although one acknowledges that
hindsight is always wonderfully correct, his silence on the matter
and that of his Church allowed hysteria to flourish, so that when
evidence of his reservations on British reprisals for German offen-
sives did surface, the public turned against him and Lambeth Palace
was awash with letters of hate.

  Yet even in the midst of war, in 1917, the Church could not resist
a theological spat centred upon the person of Hensley Henson, the
nominee to the bishopric of Hereford, and once again everyone
was reminded that the clergy could easily be diverted from what
the public regarded as important to matters which the public found
relatively trivial or irrelevant to their immediate concerns. (This
does not mean to say, or even imply, that the public was necessarily
right; merely that its perceptions of what mattered and those of
the clergy were fast growing apart). If Davidson's aim throughout
the war had been to keep the Church of England united as a focus
of spiritual authority and comfort in the midst of the moral chaos
which war almost inevitably brings, he had not really succeeded.
Internal divisions and public discontents had not gone away, and
even so the brief mood of euphoria after the war was not sufficient to reconcile the various parties. Two 'big ideas' started to gain
ground. One was the desire for unity after division. The League
of Nations expressed it politically; ecumenism seemed to offer it
religiously. The Greek Orthodox Church recognised the validity of
Anglican orders, Catholics and Anglicans began to exchange views
on their theological differences, and everyone clung timidly to the
hope that talk would lead to a resolution of many, if not all, those
differences which had beset the nations of Europe in Church and
state. The second big idea was Socialism, not only in its 'homes fit for

heroes' guise, but also in the notion that Christianity should address itself more immediately to social problems and co-operate with the state wherever possible in offering people a distinctive answer to their physical as well as their spiritual needs. In the background, of course, loomed atheistic Communism, but the inherent danger to religion embodied in this system seems to have passed Davidson by. The strikes which hit the railways and coalmines in 1919 and 1921, and then in the general strike of 1926, saw him endeavour to act as a mediator between the various parties and government, and while he was snubbed by the establishment, he was cheered by the working classes who saw, if only temporarily, an ally in the Church.

Needless to say, however, the internal divisions of the Church had not gone away. They resurfaced in 1927 when Parliament was considering revisions to the Book of Common Prayer, which had remained more or less untouched since 1662. Dissension concentrated on a ritualist question: could the sacrament be reserved in an Anglican church? This presupposed that the bread and wine changed their substance during the eucharist (a Catholic doctrine), as opposed to remaining entirely unchanged; and so once again fear of Popery raised its voice. Davidson acerbically noted a speech made by a Scottish MP 'The most effective speech of all as regard votes was, I think, Rosslyn Mitchell's. It was a simply ultra-Protestant harangue, with no real knowledge of the subject, but owing its power to a rhetorical presentment of no-Popery phrases and arguments of the sort which are to be found in *Barnaby Rudge*, when the Lord George Gordon Riots set London aflame'.[4]

Perhaps it is no wonder Davidson resigned in 1928, the first Archbishop of Canterbury to do so. He had had enough of it all. Twenty-five years as archbishop had worn him out. His skills had managed to steer the Church of England through extremely choppy waters, but not without damage to its superstructure. Changes in both Church and society had been great. As its influence in England itself waned, the Anglican Church looked outwards to the rest of the world and sought to ride the uncomfortable beast of ecumenism; and while the nascent Labour Party took into its hands those desires to help the poor ameliorate their condition which had once belonged to the Church, who wanted them to be fulfilled in spiritual as well as material well-being, the Church began to wonder what exactly was its role in this new and increasingly agnostic society. These were problems which would not go away, and reappeared in increasingly urgent form during the archiepiscopate of yet another Scot, *Cosmo Lang* (1928–42).

Lang was educated at Glasgow University from where he went to Balliol College, Oxford with a view to becoming an advocate. In 1889, however, he received what he took to be a call to the ministry and thereupon went to Cuddesdon Theological College where he not only completed his training for the Church, but also conceived an affection for the ritualist or 'Anglo-Catholic' wing of the English Church, with which he identified thereafter. The twin concerns of the day – the condition of the working classes and that of inter-Church relations – were also his, although his interest in the former was more evident while he was a curate in Leeds. There he lived in fairly poor circumstances:

> With the ardour of youth I had at once set my heart on living in the midst of the poor folk who surrounded the Parish Church... The difficulty was to get any sort of house in what was then a very derelict quarter of Leeds. At last an old public-house, which had been deprived of its licence, was secured. It was placed most conveniently, just beside the church, at the end of Church Row. But other conveniences besides that of site there were none. The public bar-room (retaining the bar) became our refectory, the more private bar-parlour with its stone floor became at first my study. My bedroom, which was never carpeted, was over one of the single rooms which abounded in that district, where tramp-folk lodged at sixpence a night. I used often to be disturbed by the oaths and screams of quarrelsome couples below... After a year I migrated to another small house next door – so small that it had been condemned as a dwelling-house – a ground-floor room which could just hold a writing-table, a small bookcase and two chairs, which was my study, an upper room for bedroom (uncarpeted), containing an iron bedstead... a small washstand, a chair, and a tin bath. There was no

bathroom in either house. This bedroom was so low that I could just stand upright within it and no more. This was my home for nearly three years, and I found it quite sufficient.[5]

A contemporary portrait gives us a remarkable impression of what he was like in those days.

He was a striking figure with clear-cut features, eyes that had a remarkable way of kindling to his thought as he spoke, strongly marked eyebrows, and abundant dark hair. Vitality of mind and body were very evident. I remember his leading us boys as 'hare' in a paper-chase and running us off our legs. There was something immediately arresting about his voice; whether in public speech or in conversation, it had a beauty and fullness of tone which, combined with dignity of utterance and a mastery of balanced language, invested even the commonplace with importance. But what captivated a youngster was the dramatic cast of his mind and conversation: he made one feel that life was rich with romantic possibilities. Always a brilliant *raconteur*, he excited a boy's imagination. This was specially true in regard to religion, which he charged with this dramatic quality; so that he aroused the sense of its being the greatest adventure in the world. He had an extraordinary power of stimulating one's aspiration and the loftiness of one's ambitions. By the generous expectations of you which he seemed to entertain, you were almost flattered into thinking yourself a finer fellow than was actually the case. And you were encouraged to hope that there was a big part for you to fill in an immensely exciting play. I think that he thought of himself in this dramatic fashion, and that he rarely lost 'the sense of theatre'. Events took on a new significance as they passed through the experience of one endowed with an unusually sensitive self-awareness; especially since he had, for the communication of that experience, so rich and vivid a medium of expression.[6]

The observation that he was an actor and thought of himself as such is perceptive. It illustrates very well, in fact, the distance between Anglican clergymen and their parishioners in working-class districts, a distance emphasised by the habit of certain persons to wear long frock-coats and top hats to distinguish themselves form their lowlier curates – even more so from their parishioners – and Lang's performances in the pulpit would have had more in common with the acting styles of actors such as Henry Irving or Matheson Lang than with the simple or more straightforward exposition of Scripture his congregations actually needed. As entertainment, therefore, Lang was probably good value. As pastor, less so. One is therefore not surprised to find that when Fate precipitated him first to be bishop of Stepney and then Archbishop of York, he became immensely grand and relished the superficialities of office to a more or less unseemly degree.

When the First World War broke out, he reluctantly supported it but, like Davidson, ran foul of public opinion and received large amounts of hate mail. It was a typically tactless remark which had done the damage, a reference to the Kaiser's kneeling beside Edward VII at Queen Victoria's bier, which he said was a 'sacred memory'. The newspapers seized on these words and Lang was pilloried for them throughout the war and afterwards. Not as harmful to his reputation, but just as ill-considered, was his maladroit reference to George VI's stammer, intended to persuade his listening wireless audience to exercise patience in view of the effort the new king would have to make to speak in public. It was a good example of the rule which says that an actor should never write his own script.

More than social conditions, however – and Lang never quite lost his concern for these – Lang's efforts were directed towards ecumenism. Between 1921 and 1926 he took a personal interest in unofficial conversations which were taking place between Catholics and Anglicans, his own inclinations making him especially favourable to such dialogue. During the 1930s he pursued relations with the Orthodox Church and other denominations, making his mark on the public consciousness with the help of wireless and film – George VI's coronation, for example, had been broadcast throughout the world, which allowed people to see the archbishop play, admirably, one of his most important roles. The war was a period of trial for him. He frequently sought to alert the British government to Nazi persecution of the Jews, as well as doing what he could to help Jews who contacted him from all over Europe. He resisted public demand for the indiscriminate bombing of Germany in response to the bombing of London, just as Davidson had resisted demands for the use of poison gas in the last war, and moved out of Lambeth only when the Palace received a direct hit in 1940. But, again like Davidson, Lang reached a point where he simply could not go on. He resigned on 21 January 1942 and was created a baron so that he could continue to sit in the House of Lords. Throughout his public life, whatever his failings, he had insisted upon the value of Christianity to modern society, perhaps never quite so openly as during his broadcast on the abdication crisis on 13 December 1936, when he castigated (politely, but still castigated) Edward VIII for his failure to retain his sacred trust of kingship in favour of a relationship which was incompatible with Christian marriage. The broadcast did him no good with the general public – ever frivolously sentimental – but others recognised it for what he intended it to be, a call to recognise that duty should take precedence over personal pleasure, and that solemn undertakings should not be pushed aside whenever they did not coincide with a person's immediate desires.

Lang's resignation stimulated discussion in one or two circles. The bishop of Durham, Hubert Henson, remarked in his diary, 'It is quite evident that [William] Temple stands above all the other bishops. Family, education, ability, achievement, experience, physical strength, wide popularity, international influence, and last, but not least, a clever and attractive wife – in all these respects he is head and shoulders above his compeers'. Yet Henson was able to list reservations. Temple was Archbishop of York at the time, and Henson observed that the northern archbishopric should not be used as a preparation or understudy for the southern. He also noted a widespread fear that Temple lacked sound judgement, was too precipitate in his verdicts, and pontificated on too many matters; and thirdly, that Temple flirted too ardently with Labour and pacifism.[7]

How many of these reservations were valid? Henson's remarks about the relationship between York and Canterbury were perfectly fair, although one should add that it was equally common for the bishop of London to be translated to Canterbury. That Temple had been somewhat impulsive during his younger days was true, but in later life he settled, especially after his marriage, into something much closer to caution. As for Labour and pacifism, he was indeed a Socialist in his youth, and a card-carrying member of the new Labour Party; and when the Second World War broke out, Winston Churchill expressed reservations about Temple's appointment to Canterbury on the grounds that he was not bellicose enough for his (Churchill's) liking. So on the whole, Henson's addenda to his praise for Temple turn out to be unnecessarily guarded.

It is an interesting comment, however, that first in his list of Temple's desirable qualities should stand 'family'. *William Temple* (1942–44) was the son of a previous Archbishop of Canterbury, Frederick Temple, and his mother was related to the aristocracy. He was educated at Rugby and at Balliol College, Oxford where he became particularly attracted by the ideals of Socialism. In 1910 he was appointed headmaster of Repton and there entered upon a programme of feverish activity whose momentum he maintained to the end of his life. Books poured from his pen; he joined several disparate movements and committees – one of which aimed at rescuing the Church from much of the control exercised over it by the state; and he edited a Church weekly, the *Challenge*, whose intention was to offer readers a viewpoint on affairs somewhere between that of the *Church Times*, which was preferred by Anglo Catholics, and that of the *Record* which appealed to the radical end of the Protestant spectrum.

All this activity brought him to the favourable notice of the government, and in 1920 he was appointed bishop of Manchester, a post which saw him not only as an efficient pastoral visitor but also – via his chairmanship of various influential committees – a growing voice in the ecumenical movement in which he played an increasingly important role at home and abroad during the late 1920s and 1930s. In 1929 he was translated to York and his work rate, always heavy, increased still more. Lecturing, preaching, broadcasting, pastoral visiting were not enough. He also wrote three books and managed to travel to various places in Europe, despite the war, in pursuit of the goal of ecumenism and the creation of a World Council of Churches, something he finally saw come to fruition in 1942. That was the year he became Archbishop of Canterbury, but by this time his health was starting to give way under the punishing schedule he had inflicted on it for so long. Ever since childhood he had coped with the results of having a congenital cataract on the right eye, and although this had been treated, he was never able to read quickly. But it was gout which was to be his bane. He first suffered from it at the age of two, but noted it again when he was thirteen – 'gout in my big toe on my right foot'. In the middle of the First World War he thought he had found relief – 'I am going to a man who undertakes to make me reasonably thin and free from gout by a little massage and by teaching me to hold my body in the right position', he wrote in a letter to a friend – but by 1923 he was suffering intense pain, and in 1925 he was virtually crippled by it. At the end he could not walk and was confined to bed. What killed him, however, was a pulmonary embolism.[8]

The effect of the Second World War, and the memory of the First, on Temple's outlook was to make him acutely aware of the flood of change which was beginning to sweep over the western hemisphere in particular. It is remarkable that he was born into the privileged world of late Victorian England and yet managed to remain largely unaffected by it. His concern for the condition of working people, his enthusiasm for the ecumenical movement, both of which sprang from the radicalism of his youthful days at Oxford and Repton, stayed with him all his life and, indeed, intensified as he became older. Had he lived to see the post-war years and the immense changes wrought by the Labour administration, however, his reactions might have been mixed. For along with the realisation of many of his ideals came a huge wave of atheistic materialism which would split much of western Europe from the rest of the Christian world and leave ecumenism battered and wounded, apparently beyond repair. Could Temple have faced such a challenge? No doubt he would have tried, and certainly he believed that the modern state was incomplete without a Christian Church to set the moral and political tone of the community, which meant that the Church itself had to be 'modernised': that is, set free from its subordination to the ruling classes and opened up to dialogue with the prevailing socio-economic circumstances and scientifically based Zeitgeist of contemporary society. It was a distinctive programme, but Temple's gifts – and they were many – were not really equal to such a fight. He tended to shrink from taking an unpopular position and, in spite of his ecumenical labours, he identified himself as the head of a particularly *English* institution – a narrowness of focus which ultimately could not hope to make the kind of deep impact on Christian division to which the healing aspirations of the ecumenical movement were most committed.

Temple's death was sudden and therefore took everyone by surprise. His successor, *Geoffrey Fisher* (1945–61), is often referred to as 'the Headmaster', and indeed some of the situations with which he had to deal did require a certain authoritarian touch. Perhaps we should see significance in an episode when he was headmaster of Repton. He had drawn up a new book of rules, the first of which said, 'Any breach of common sense is a breach of these rules', and when he was asked who decided what was common sense, he replied, 'I do'. Fisher was the tenth child of a clergyman and received his education at Marlborough and Exeter College, Oxford where he proved a first-class scholar. He began his career as a teacher, first at Marlborough and then at Repton, before becoming bishop of Chester in 1944. At Chester he and his wife revealed, from time to time, an unfortunate inability to understand the needs of working people and their alienation from the Church of England; but when they came to London, he set about trying to do something practical for all those parishes devastated by bombing, especially in 1941, and restoring them to some kind of order, an effort which met with an extraordinary amount of opposition from certain quarters.

It is this unexpectedness which surfaces every so often during Fisher's career. At Repton, for example, he expelled two boys for homosexual practices, but in 1957, when the Wolfenden Report published its findings on whether homosexual conduct should continue to be treated as a crime or not, Fisher replied by distinguishing between a crime and a sin, homosexual practices being the latter and not the former. There was, he noted 'a realm which is not the law's business', but went on to remark that society might need protection from the immoralities of some heterosexuals too, a contradiction which Fisher surely did not intend. If sin is not the business of the law it makes no difference whether the sin pertains to one kind of sexuality or another. But when it came to radical theologians, such as Ernest Barnes who questioned the validity of miracles in the New Testament, or John Robinson who spoke in favour of the publication of an unexpurgated edition of *Lady Chatterley's Lover* and thus offended Fisher into describing him as 'a stumbling block and cause of offence to many ordinary Christians' (a perfectly accurate description, to judge by contemporary reports), Fisher was prepared to be forthright in his condemnation. Unlike some Archbishops of Canterbury, he did not nuance his way through difficulties. He had a simple, straightforward faith and his Christian convictions never wavered throughout his life.

This did not mean, however, that he set his face entirely against change. He was rather proud of his revision of English canon law, and keenly supported the ecumenical movement, travelling widely in pursuit of it, although he actually enjoyed little success in forwarding its aims. He failed to persuade the Methodists to adopt intercommunion with the Church of England, and although he and Pope John XXIII got on well, and in spite of the wholesale changes to both liturgy and administration effected later on by the Catholic Church after the Second Vatican Council, ecumenism remained a topic of conversation between clerics and interested lay people rather than a movement towards reintegration – for which many, both Catholic and Protestant, have expressed themselves duly grateful.

In January 1961 Fisher resigned as archbishop and was given a peerage. He had not been a lackey of the various post-war governments. During the war, for example, he objected to the government's proposal to instruct young soldiers on the use of contraceptives unless the instruction also urged them to exercise moral discipline, and in 1956 he condemned Antony Eden's Suez adventure as a violation of British obligations to the United Nations, and in 1958 he refused to accept that the use of nuclear weapons could be justified under any circumstances, calling for their abolition as 'an essential step towards the abolition of war itself'. The weight of office had begun to tire him, and this he himself gave as the principal reason for his retirement. 'I was beginning to feel that I could not go on at my fullest speed, in which case, in such a position, I could not see myself going on at all'.

So this opened the way for *Michael Ramsey* (1961–74) to be appointed in his place. The problems faced by Fisher, principally the increasing materialism and moral relativism of British post-war society, were also those which presented Ramsey with his greatest challenge. Britain was not really dancing away from the Christian religion during his time in office, although it appeared to be doing so partly by flirting with various forms of New Ageism, partly by the theatricality with which London faddishness caught the fancy of the news media; but the deep strains of doubt and rejection which had characterised nineteenth-century society – articulate among the educated classes, inarticulate in the rest – had continued virtually unchecked by anything the established Church tried to do by way of counter-measures. Ramsey's principal concern, therefore, should have been to meet the challenge in its most fundamental aspects. Tinkering with trivia would actually be worse than doing nothing, since it would give the impression that the Church was impotent in the face of atheistic aggression.

At first sight, Ramsey was not the best man for the job. As a child he lived in the shadow of an older brother he regarded as much his superior, and compensated by retiring into a fantasy world of his own, a trait which manifested itself in adult life by his tendency to indulge in long silences, even in company, and perhaps also by his well-known eccentricities. It created a certain impression. During the Rhodesia crisis of the mid-1960s, for example, the marquess of Salisbury (not an impartial figure in these circumstances) suggested that Lambeth Palace was an ivory tower and that Ramsey might care to descend from it into the real world. One notes, too, that Ramsey had turned early on from his Congregationalist upbringing to the Anglo-Catholic wing of the Anglican Church, and for much of his life was both intrigued and impressed by Orthodox Christianity. Was it merely chance that these expressions of Christianity have elaborate, theatrical liturgies in which the participant celebrants lose their particular individualities and become the embodiments of otherworldly entities? Perhaps not, but such expressions suited Ramsey's personality. Nor did his career before Canterbury do anything to contradict the notion that he was out of touch with reality. Educated at Repton and Magdalene College, Cambridge, he became warden of Lincoln Theological College, Professor of Divinity in Durham, bishop of Durham, and Archbishop of York – all the while lecturing, teaching and publishing – the very figure of an academic enclosed and apart. Even Fisher, who had been his headmaster at Repton, opposed his translation from York to Canterbury on the grounds that he was too odd, too academic, and deficient in the practical talents needed for such a demanding office.

But in fact none of this was relevant. Harold Macmillan, who recommended him for Canterbury, made a very perceptive comment in answer to Fisher's objections: 'I thought we had had enough of Martha and it was time for some Mary'. This hits the nail on the head. During the late 1930s, Ramsey had wondered whether to become an Anglican monk in the contemplative order of the Community of the Resurrection at Mirfield, and although he decided against it, the deep seriousness of his spirituality which had prompted this exploration remained undiminished for the rest of his life. On one occasion, during a service in St Paul's Cathedral at which the Queen was present, Ramsey came out into the aisle in preparation to deliver his sermon, and bowed to the altar before bowing to the Queen. As he made his reverence, he was heard to mutter, 'God first', and this was the impulse which informed his dealings with everyone, were they high or low, politician or parishioner. Hence his unpopularity with those who wanted him to engage with the secular world on its terms rather than those of religious faith.

Various aspects of his life as Archbishop of Canterbury can almost be taken for granted. He was liberal in certain ways – he supported homosexual law reform in 1967, and opposed the British government's sale of arms to South Africa in 1968 – and he was committed to ecumenism, welcoming rapport with the Methodists, travelling widely as Fisher had done in support of Christian fellow-ship, and enjoying a particularly warm meeting with Pope Paul VI in March 1966. All this, however, was what one might call 'stuff', the outward expression of his office, which almost any Archbishop of Canterbury might be expected to do. Ramsey's importance to the English Church in the 1960s was, rather, himself, not his office. Here was a man openly prepared to put God first in the face of all opposition, overt and tacit, and to ride against the prevailing trend without seeming to apologise for doing so. The Church's purpose, he once wrote, was 'to keep alive in the midst of the world the crea-ture's longing towards his Creator'. It was just what 1960s Britain needed to hear, whether it wanted to or not.

Following such an example would be difficult. *Donald Coggan* (1974–80), however, caught one aspect of Ramsey's enthusiasm – the belief that the Christian Churches should take the modern world in hand and re-evangelise it. Coggan's special gift was that of being an excellent teacher. He had plenty of experience, for in 1937 he was a lecturer in a theological college of the University of Toronto, then Principal of the London College of Divinity in 1944, and finally, when he was bishop of Bradford in 1956, he set up a cross between a theological college and a retreat near the village of Kettlewell in Yorkshire. This may make him sound as remote and removed as Ramsey, but throughout his life Coggan was able to use his considerable linguistic gifts to take a word or phrase from a Biblical text and open up a whole range of meaning and implica-tion for his audience, in such a way that they understood the points he was making and were left keen for further instruction. (It is a pity, therefore, that he lacked Cranmer's ear for the musicality of the English language, since the committee, over which he presided, which produced the *New English Bible* in 1970 was clearly devoid of any such appreciation, as the poet Robert Graves pointed out trenchantly at the time).

Coggan's other enthusiasms were less successful. He was par-ticularly keen on promoting the unity of the Christian Churches and travelled extensively in support of this ideal, but, like Ramsey, got nowhere with either the Catholics or the Methodists. Indeed, his call for intercommunion between the Catholic and Anglican Churches in 1977 was simply naïve, and embarrassed rather than gratified the Pope. What he did for the English Church was to remove the disguise of eccentricity behind which Ramsey had hidden his most alluring qualities, and present the institution as one eager to embrace change in the modern world, but change rooted in a particular view of that world, not change for change's sake, which was now a theme running through contemporary western society like a poisoned thread.

What had inspired Ramsey's personal spirituality was the Anglo-Catholic tradition in the Church of England. What had inspired Coggan was the evangelical. What inspired *Robert Runcie* (1980–91)? In 1987 he was subjected to an attack in the preface to *Crockford's Clerical Directory*, and it is worth remarking some of the observations made therein. The key paragraph (p.68) begins by acknowledging his 'intelligence, personal warmth and... formidable capacity for hard work'. It notes his capacity to listen to other people and his wide range of contacts among clergy and laity. 'His speeches and addresses are thoughtful, witty, and persuasive'. He was influential in the General Synod, had survived well the crushing workload of his office, and had travelled extensively. 'His influence is now probably at its height'. So far so good. But there follow sentences of devastating criticism.

> It would therefore be good to be assured that he actually knew what he was doing and had a clear basis for his policies other than taking the line of least resistance on each issue. He has a major disadvantage in not have been trained as a theologian, and though he makes extensive use of academics as advisers and speechwriters, his own position is often unclear. He has the disadvantage of the intelligent pragmatist: the desire to put off all the questions until someone else makes a decision. One recalls a lapidary phrase of Mr Frank Field that the archbishop is usually to be found nailing his colours to the fence. All this makes Dr Runcie peculiarly vulnerable to pressure-groups... His clear preference is for men of liberal disposition

with a moderately Catholic style which is not taken to the point of having firm principles. If in addition they have a good appearance and are articulate over the media he is prepared to overlook a certain theological deficiency. Dr Runcie and his closest associates are men who have nothing to prevent them following what they think is the wish of the majority of the moment.

The preface was penned by Gareth Vaughan Bennett, who later committed suicide, but while the Archbishop of York did his best to offer Runcie support, many other leading Anglican figures, both clerical and lay, did not. So what had Runcie done, or failed to do, or failed to be, which caused them to be silent at such a juncture? Educated at the Merchant Taylors' School in Liverpool and Brasenose College, Oxford, his university years were interrupted by the war. For five years, 1941 to 1946, he served in the army and saw action with the armoured division of the Scots Guards, as a result of which he was awarded the Military Cross in 1945. After returning to Oxford, however, he slipped across to Cambridge where he trained for the ministry at Westcott House – the Crockford preface alludes to the effect of its 'elitist liberalism' on his character – and there met a large number of people who were keen to play an active part in constructing a Church fit for the post-war world. (What this means in practice, of course, is open to interpretation, and Bennett's view that Westcott House, where different kinds of Anglican had man aged to forge a community relaxed about doctrinal differences, had left Runcie unwilling or incapable of taking a particular doctrinal stand was by no means confined to him). Runcie, however, was not as overtly keen on certain types of reform or change as some of his acquaintance. While Archbishop of Canterbury, for example, he signally ducked the question of women's ordination, although once he had retired he was perfectly prepared to speak openly in favour of it.

Archbishops of Canterbury were now chosen by committee rather than emerging from the pen of the Prime Minister of the day, and somehow one is not surprised to find that Runcie came into office from this process. But 'collegiality' (one of the clerical buzz-words of the period in both Catholic and Anglican circles), which would have seen the governance of the Church of England expressed through yet another committee, escaped from his control. The English Church, which had always been fissiparous, was now riven by discontented groups of various kinds, from the ritualists on the one hand to the evangelicals on the other, and Runcie soon found his authority, such as it was, eroding almost before his eyes. The bishop of London, later to become a Catholic, ignored him entirely, and while Pope John Paul II behaved impeccably during his visit to Britain in 1982, Archbishop Runcie's attempts to resurrect the warmth of the relations between Archbishop Ramsey and Pope Paul VI were doomed to failure. His one big success – more apparent than real – was the Lambeth Conference of 1988, which managed to prevent the underlying divisions of the worldwide Anglican communion from breaking out into the open. It was a papering of cracks, however, which would not hold, and Runcie retired in 1991, to the now customary peerage, before the sound of bursting dams became too loud and too insistent to ignore. His obituary in *The Times* of 13 July 2000 acknowledged his charm and patience in holding together this unhappy coalition, but gave expression to a verdict ultimately as damning as any written by Canon Bennett: 'That he did not single-handedly reverse the long-term decline in Church membership nor give to the public face of Anglicanism one clear, unambivalent image measures the extent to which the Church's problems were beyond human ingenuity to solve'. No one suggests he could single-handedly have brought people back into the pews, but he could have been clear, he could have been unambivalent, and his failure to be either means that he cannot be regarded as the right man for his particular job at that particular time. The contrast with Pope John Paul II could not have been greater.

For *George Carey* (1991–2002) and *Rowan Williams* (2002–), two questions have risen to concentrate the mind and provide occasions finally to split the Anglican communion into its constituent parts – the ordination of women and homosexuality. Carey, the first Archbishop of Canterbury for some considerable time not to have been educated at Oxford or Cambridge, had experience of the armed forces not long before National Service was abolished, and served in the RAF. After two decades' experience in parishes – the kind of experience most nineteenth- and twentieth-century archbishops had before moving or being moved into the higher ranks of ecclesiastical administration – he became bishop of Bath and Wells in 1988, and was translated to Canterbury only three years later. Perhaps because he belonged to the evangelical tradition, he had less difficulty in accepting the ordination of women than Ramsey or Runcie, both of whom inclined to the other end of the liturgical spectrum; but this same tradition, with its emphasis on the importance of the Bible as the ultimate authority in court of appeal, may also help to account for Carey's supporting a resolution drafted at the 1998 Lambeth Conference, which condemned homosexual practice as incompatible with Scripture. Neither the climate of the time nor the conviction of certain other branches of the Anglican communion were prepared to accept this pronouncement with equanimity, and while women's ordination caused a local fracas and the desertion of many clergy from Anglicanism to Rome, the gay question lay like a black cloud over Carey's subsequent years in office, only to burst during the opening years of his successor.

Rowan Williams is notably a Welshman and technically not a member of the Church of England, since the Church in Wales is not actually part of the establishment. As if to make up for Carey's absence from Oxbridge, Williams was educated at both and taught theology at both before becoming bishop of Monmouth in 1991 and Archbishop of Wales in 1999. His public pronouncements on various subjects – and he has been prepared to make his views known rather than keep them discreetly private – have tended to generate heat. He has criticised the present government's policy over Iraq and the coalition troops' behaviour there; certain of the tactics used by a number of political parties during the recent elections; and the self-centred immorality of modern British society as portrayed in a particular television series. His nuanced opinions on several doctrinal issues have also upset a number of people, none more so than his attempts to bridge the gap between the supporters and opponents of gay relationships, that inherited problem which was exacerbated by the episcopal consecration in the United States of America of a gay minister who was living with a partner, and by the proposed consecration of a similar minister in Britain. Williams rode the two horses and managed to retain his balance, but the horses are galloping away and the archbishop may yet find himself falling to the ground.

Will he be the first for a couple of centuries 'to shrink' (in the words of Edward Carpenter) 'into a merely local figure presiding over an inward-looking community preoccupied with its own life'?[9] Pope Benedict XVI sees his principal mission as the re-evangelising of a Europe which has largely chosen to turn its back on God and embrace the idol of egocentricity. The challenge for the other Christian denominations must surely be the same. Are they up to the job, or will they nuance their way to effective extinction? It will be interesting, if painful, to watch.

List of Illustrations

1   St Gregory, also known as 'The Great', Pope from 3
    September 590 to 12 March 604. Courtesy of Jonathan Reeve
    JR905b38p259 500600.

2   A Victorian version of St Augustine's landing in Britain in
    597. Courtesy of Jonathan Reeve JR882b12p55 500600.

3   Page from a copy (sixth or seventh century) of St Augustine's
    writings, containing part of a letter to Paulinus, one of the
    monks who accompanied him to Britain, and who later
    became Archbishop of York. Courtesy of Jonathan Reeve
    JR883b12p56 600700.

4   Part of Bede's *Historia Ecclesiastica*, written in *c*.731. Courtesy
    of Jonathan Reeve JR904b1fp37 700800.

5   Archbishop Stigand (1052–70), deposed from the
    archbishopric on charges of corruption and receiving his
    authority from an antipope ('Benedict X') instead of the
    genuine Pope. By special permission of the City of Bayeux.

6   St Dunstan wearing the pallium, a narrow woollen band

passing over the shoulders, with lappets hanging down front and back. Courtesy of Jonathan Reeve JR884b12p116 9001000.

7   St Dunstan kissing the hem of Christ's robe. Courtesy of Jonathan Reeve JR885b12p117 9001000.

8   The seal of St Anselm. Courtesy of Jonathan Reeve JR865b11p167 10001100.

9   The seal of St Thomas Becket. Courtesy of Jonathan Reeve JR866b11p201L 11001200.

10 A plan of Canterbury Cathedral Church and monastery as they were in *c.*1150, during the time Archbishop Theobald was in office. Courtesy of Jonathan Reeve JR316b11p200 11001200.

11 St Thomas Becket and his secretary, Herbert of Bosham. Courtesy of Jonathan Reeve JR868b11p202 11001200.

12 The front and back of St Thomas Becket's chasuble, which is kept in the cathedral at Sens. Author's collection.

13 Henry II in dispute with St Thomas Becket. Courtesy of Jonathan Reeve JR776b58fp64 11501200.

14 St Thomas Becket excommunicating his enemies and arguing with King Henry and King Louis, from a thirteenth-century *Vie de Saint Thomas*. Courtesy of Jonathan Reeve JR869b11p205t 11001200.

15 St Thomas Becket parting from King Henry and King Louis, from the *Vie de Saint Thomas*. Courtesy of Jonathan Reeve JR870b11p205b 11001200.

16 St Thomas embarking for England, from the *Vie de Saint Thomas*. Courtesy of Jonathan Reeve JR871b11p206 11001200.

17 The martyrdom of St Thomas Becket. From a twelfth- or thirteenth-century psalter. Tempus Archive.

18 Page from the *Chronica maiora* of Matthew Paris, describing and illustrating St Thomas's murder. Courtesy of Jonathan Reeve JR886b12p261 11001200.

19 Becket's shrine. Glass painting, thirteenth-century, Canterbury Cathedral. Courtesy of Jonathan Reeve JR875b4p598 11001200.

20 Fragment of a drawing of the shrine of St Thomas at Canterbury. Courtesy of Jonathan Reeve JR167b4p702 15001550.

21 Within a few years of Thomas's death, his tomb had become
    the focus of one of the most important cult centres in
    western Europe. It was in front of this shrine that Henry II
    was forced to come as a penitent in 1174 and be flogged as
    a punishment for his part in Becket's murder. The birches
    used for this can be seen in the hands of three of the monks.
    Tempus Archive TACD3.

22 Pilgrims leaving Canterbury. Courtesy of Jonathan Reeve
    JR910b18p642 14001500.

23 *Caput Thomae*, 'Thomas's head'. One of the badges worn
    by pilgrims to Canterbury. Courtesy of Jonathan Reeve
    JR873b11p208 11001200.

24 Pilgrims' badges and ampoules, small containers for holy
    water. Courtesy of Jonathan Reeve JR741b18p377 14501500.

25 Page from a Hereford missal in the British Museum, showing
    the erasure of St Thomas's saint's day in the liturgical calendar
    for December. Courtesy of Jonathan Reeve JR895b7p89
    15001550.

26 Seal of Stephen Langton. Courtesy of Jonathan Reeve
    JR754b11p237 11501200.

27 Archbishop Edmund Rich (1233–40). Courtesy of Jonathan
    Reeve JR887b12p328 12001300.

28 The consecration of Edmund Rich, drawn by Matthew Paris.
    Courtesy of Jonathan Reeve JR874b11p275 12001300.

29 Archbishop Henry Chichele. Portrait in glass in Lambeth
    Palace library. Courtesy of Jonathan Reeve JR909b18p503
    14001500.

30 Archbishop Chichele. Courtesy of Jonathan Reeve
    JR784b57fp274 14001450.

31 A letter from Edward V to Archbishop Thomas Bourchier
    regarding the safe keeping of the Great Seal. Courtesy of
    Jonathan Reeve JR770b13p716 14501500.

32 Drawing of Archbishop William Warham by Hans Holbein.
    Tempus Archive TA CD 12, 37.

33 Archbishop Warham in procession, with attendants and
    a herald. Courtesy of Jonathan Reeve JR911b54p364L
    15001550.

34 The arms of William Warham as Archbishop of Canterbury and Chancellor of England. Courtesy of Jonathan Reeve JR912b54p365tL 15001550.

35 Warham's seal. Courtesy of Jonathan Reeve JR888b20p1128 15001550.

36 Seal of Thomas Cranmer, Archbishop of Canterbury. Courtesy of Jonathan Reeve JR889b20p1128r 15001550.

37 Thomas Cranmer by Gerlach Flicke. Tempus Archive TA CD 15, 18.

38 Letter from Cranmer at Dunstable to Henry VIII, dated '17 May', informing him of the date when the annulment of his marriage to Katharine of Aragon would be brought to a conclusion. Courtesy of Jonathan Reeve JR894b7p53 15001550.

39 The Act of Appeals (1533). Courtesy of Jonathan Reeve JRCD2b20p912 15001550.

40 The Act of Supremacy (1534). Courtesy of Jonathan Reeve JRCD2b20p915 15001550.

41 Title-page of the first edition of the 'Great Bible' (1539). Courtesy of Jonathan Reeve JR896b7p161 15001550.

42 Panoramic view of Canterbury in the sixteenth century. Courtesy of Jonathan Reeve JR897b7p265 15001550.

43 Depiction of Cranmer's arrest and subsequent death on 21 March 1556. Tempus Archive TA CD 20, 141.

44 Title-page to Foxe's *Acts and Monuments*, popularly known as *Foxe's Book of Martyrs*. Courtesy of Jonathan Reeve JR898b7p281 15501600.

45 Archbishop Matthew Parker. Eighteenth-century engraving of an older picture. Courtesy of Jonathan Reeve JR876b4p749 15501600.

46 A page from Archbishop Parker's 'Bishops' Bible'. Courtesy of Jonathan Reeve JR899b7p369 15501600.

47 Archbishop Edmund Grindal. Courtesy of Jonathan Reeve JR900b7p413 15501600.

48 Archbishop John Whitgift. From an engraving by Vertue. Courtesy of Jonathan Reeve JR877b10p959 15501600.

49 Lambeth Palace from the Thames. From an engraving by the

late sixteenth-century J. Kip. Courtesy of Jonathan Reeve
JR892b25p1562 16501700.

50   Archbishop Richard Bancroft. Engraving by Vertue. Courtesy
     of Jonathan Reeve JR878b10p960 15501600.

51   Archbishop George Abbot. Engraving by Vertue. Courtesy of
     Jonathan Reeve JR879b10p961 15501600.

52   Archbishop William Laud. From the picture by Van Dyck.
     Courtesy of Jonathan Reeve JR901b33pviii 16001650.

53   A letter from Charles I to Laud, announcing his translation to
     Canterbury, 8 September 1633. Courtesy of Jonathan Reeve
     JR890b22p1247 16001650.

54   A pamphlet attacking Archbishop Laud. Courtesy of Jonathan
     Reeve JR684b22p1293 16001650.

55   Caricature of Archbishop Laud and Henry Burton, 1645.
     Courtesy of Jonathan Reeve JR891b22p1328 16001650.

56   Another anti-Laud pamphlet. Courtesy of Jonathan Reeve
     JR691b22p1393 16001650.

57   Illustration by Wenceslas Hollar, showing an attack on Laud's
     Lambeth Palace by apprentices and sailors opposed to his
     reforms and to the presence of bishops in the House of Lords.
     Courtesy of Jonathan Reeve JR408b22p1278 16001650

58   Laud's trial. Tempus Archive TA32b50plalii 16001650.

59   Laud's execution on 10 January 1645. From a print
     attributed to Wenceslas Hollar. Courtesy of Jonathan Reeve
     JR864b21p349 16001650.

60   The west front of Canterbury Cathedral, from William
     Dugdale's *Monasticon* (1655). Author's collection.

61   Archbishop William Juxon. Engraving by Thielcke. Courtesy
     of Jonathan Reeve JR881b10p1061 16001650.

62   Archbishop William Sancroft. From a contemporary print by
     Robert White. Courtesy of Jonathan Reeve JR902b33p201
     16001650.

63   Archbishop John Tillotson. After the portrait by Sir Godfrey
     Kneller. Courtesy of Jonathan Reeve JR903b33p205 16501700.

64   Archbishop William Howley caricatured as a churchwarden
     (1829). Courtesy of Jonathan Reeve JR893b27p1892
     18001850.

Notes

I A MISSION TO THE ANGLES

1   *Anglo-Saxon Church Councils*, 149.
2   Quoted in Bede: *Historia ecclesiastica* 1.31.
3   *Augustine of Canterbury*, 53, 105.
4   An accompanying quotation about degrees of kinship and
     marriage may be a later interpolation into Bede's *Historia*.
5   *Cantuar*, 10.

2 LABOURING FOR ESTABLISHMENT

1   *Historia ecclesiastica* 4.2. See also D. Ewing Duncan: *The
     Calendar* (London: Fourth Estate 1999), 63-7, 79-83, 120-
     22.
2   'He' in this case does not exclude women. The Latin
     grammar at this point is meant to be inclusive.
3   J. Raine (ed.): *The Historians of the Church of York and its
     Archbishops*, 3 vols (London: Longman 1879–84), 1.4-5-7.

4   Raine: *op.cit.* supra, 1.408-9.
5   Raine: *op.cit.* supra, 1.457-8.

3 SURVIVING THE MILLENNIUM AND THE CONQUEST

1   *The Blickling Homilies*, ed. & trans. R. Morris, Early English
     Text Society (London: Trübner 1880), 116-18. See also R.K.
     Emmerson: 'The Apocalypse in Mediaeval culture', in R.K.
     Emmerson & B. McGinn (eds): *The Apocalypse in the Middle
     Ages*, (Ithaca & London: Cornell University Press 1992), 293-
     332.
2   Trans. G.N. Garmonsway, p.142.
3   *Chronicon* 7.43. Thietmar's language is interesting. He writes
     of the heathen as an army drawn up for battle (*agmen*)
     surrounding Aelfeadh with a wall of bodies (*vallavit*), as
     though the archbishop were a town under final attack
     – an apt metaphor for their earlier successful devastation of
     Canterbury. But *agmen*, apart from meaning a body of armed
     men, may also refer to a great downfall of water from the
     sky, and this is reflected in Thietmar's use of 'showers' of
     stones and 'flood' of sticks to describe Aelfeadh's murder. A
     somewhat different, but no less dramatic account is given by
     Gervase of Canterbury in his history of the archbishops.
4   Antipope Benedict X made his appearance in 1058, between
     the death of Stephen X and the canonical election of
     Nicholas II (1058–61). Nicholas was followed by Alexander II
     (1061–73). The reference to Stigand's wearing clerical attire
     means he was not a monk, the first Archbishop of Canterbury
     not to be a member of a monastic order since Aelfsige in 958.
     King William is, of course, 'the Conqueror'.
5   *Early History*, 309-10.

4 WHO IS THE GREATER PRIMATE?

1   *Vita Sancti Anselmi* 1.14-17; 2.
2   *Anselm of Bec*, 1163-72.
3   *Op.cit.* supra, 132. For a less charitable view, see F. Barlow:

William Rufus (London: Methuen 1983), 303-7.

4   *Letters* 2.166-9 = Letter 214, dated September 1101.

5   *Simplex.* This, however, may also mean 'naïve' or 'simple-minded'.

6   *Materials for the History of Thomas Becket* 2 412-13 (Grim), 37 (Fitzstephen). The seeds in wild fennel exude a bitter oil while the plant is being boiled and thus make the water extremely unpleasant to drink.

7   *Anecdota Bedae, Lanfranci, et aliorum*, 206. I read 'sit' for 'fit' in the second line.

8   Some people, however, have tried. At the end of 2005, a number of newspapers listed ten of the wickedest inhabitants of the British Isles and asked their readers to vote for the worst. Two Archbishops of Canterbury appeared in this list, one being St Thomas Becket, on the grounds that 'he divided England in a way even many churchmen thought unnecessary'. Presumably these 'many churchmen' included those English bishops who would have been happy to hand over the English Church to King Henry's complete control. The condemnation thus contains a tacit Protestant, specifically Tudor, point of view which scarcely justifies Becket's inclusion among Britain's *wickedest* men.

9   Carpenter: *Cantuar*, 64. Knowles: *Thomas Becket*, 171.

5 SAINTS, SCHOLARS AND VIOLENCE

1   *Historia rerum anglicarum*, Book 3, chapter 8.

2   See further Cheney: *From Becket to Langton*, 42-86.

3   Giraldus Cambrensis: *Speculum ecclesiae*, distinctio 2, chapter 25. It is repeated in his *Itinerarium Cambriae* Book 2, chapter 14.

4   *Hubert Walter*, 171.

5   *Stephen Langton*, 160-1.

6   *Chronica maiora*, vol. 3, p.206.

7   Matthew Paris: *Chronica maiora* 5.121-3.

8   See, for example, W. Davies: 'Anger and the Celtic saint' in B.H. Rosenwein (ed.): *Anger's Past: The Social Uses of an Emotion in the Middle Ages* (Ithaca & London: Cornell

University Press 1994), 198-200.

9   *Tractatus de paupertate*, chapter 4. The argument was relevant
    because it related to whether one should or should not
    wear shoes if one wanted to imitate Christ in one's life, a
    point of dispute between Calced and Discalced Carmelites,
    for example, as well as other orders wishing to lead a
    Christocentric life.

6 ROYAL SELF-AGGRANDISEMENT

1   'The supposed illiteracy of Archbishop Walter Reynolds', 58,
    60-1, 65-6.
2   Hook: *Lives of the Archbishops* 3.455. Wright: *The Church and
    the English Crown*, 273.
3   It has often been attributed to the bishop of Winchester,
    Adam de Orleton, but without much justification.
4   *Archbishop John Stratford*, 431.
5   Usk: *Chronicle*, 18-19. *Westminster Chronicle*, 116-17.
6   *William Courtenay*, 237.
7   Usk: *Chronicle*, 24-27. Quotation, p.26.
8   Arundel is the second of the Archbishops of Canterbury to
    be designated one of Britain's ten most dastardly inhabitants
    by several newspapers at the end of 2005, on the grounds
    that 'he laid the foundations for a system of persecution of
    religious ideas in England used by rulers for centuries', an
    accusation answered perfectly well by Joseph Dahmus in the
    quotation I have given above. Note, again, the tacit Protestant
    assumption underlying the objection to Arundel.
9   Walden ended his days as bishop of London, attaining the
    post by means of a shady compromise typical of Henry IV
    who wanted to divert the Pope's attention from his execution
    of the Archbishop of York. Walden had been the new Pope
    Innocent VII's choice for London, so after some fruitless
    bluster Henry realised the political advantage to himself
    of agreeing to Walden's appointment and caved in. Walden
    occupied the post for only six months before dying in
    January 1406.

10 *Lives of the Archbishops of Canterbury* 4.488.

11 *Chronicle*, 246-7.

12 *The Book of Marjory Kempe*, ed. B. Windeath, (Harlow: Pearson Education 2000), 110-11.

13 *Historia anglicana* 2.300. 'Champion' translates *pugil* = 'boxer' or 'soldier'.

7 SPIRALLING TO DISASTER

1 *Henry Chichele*, 71-2.

2 The *patriarchatus* as an institution is here distinguished from the archbishop as an individual.

3 D. Wilkins (ed.): *Concilia Magnae Britanniae et Hiberniae ab anno MCCCL ad annum MDLV*, 4 vols (London: 1737), 586.

4 Quoted in J. Lewis: *The Life of the Learned and Right Reverend Reynold Pecock*. (Oxford: Clarendon Press 1820), 153. The next quotation comes from p.178.

5 *The History of King Richard III*, 48.

6 Pages 29, 30, 60, 69, 83, 97.

7 See further R. Marius: *Thomas More* (London: J.M. Dent & Son 1984), 123-45.

8 *Opus Epistolarum Desiderii Erasmi Roterodami*, ed. P.S. Allen: Vol. 10, ed. H.M. Allen & H.W. Garrod (Oxford: Clarendon Press 1941), 111-12.

9 New series, Vol. 1, p.306.

10 *Thomas Cranmer*, 89.

11 It will be only fair to include a positive view of him at this point. His admiring servant and early biographer, Ralph Morice, wrote: 'He was a man of such temperature of nature, or rather so mortified, that no manner of prosperity or adversity could alter or change his accustomed conditions: for, being the storms never so terrible or odious, nor the prosperous estate of the time never so pleasant, joyous or acceptable, to the face of [the] world his countenance, diet or sleep commonly never altered or changed, so that they which were most nearest and conversant about him never or seldom perceived by no sign or token of countenance how the affairs

of the prince or the realm went. Notwithstanding privately with his secret and special friends he would shed forth many bitter tears, lamenting the misery and calamities of the world'. See *Narratives of the Reformation*, ed, J.G. Nicholas, (London: Camden Society 1859), 244-5. The old saying 'handsome is as handsome does', however, is applicable here.

12   Principal among these are the Protestant John Foxe's *Acts and Monuments,* popularly known as *Foxe's Book of Martyrs,* and the deeply critical *Cranmer's Recantacyons*, probably by Nicholas Harpsfield.

8 VICARS OF BRAY

1   Mayer: *Reginald Pole*, 439. Hughes: *The Reformation in England* 2.185.
2   *Calendar of State Papers, Spanish, 1554–58,* no.175.
3   Quoted in Mayer: *Reginald Pole*, 354-5.
4   *De antiquitate Britannicae ecclesiae*, 357.
5   See further Duffy: *The Stripping of the Altars*. Cf. the remark by Theodore Beza in Geneva to Heinrich Bullinger in Zurich that in England the Papacy had not been abolished but merely transferred to the sovereign.
6   Letter to William Cecil, dated 29 August 1570 = Nicholson: *Remains*, 325-6.

9 THE LONG DURANCE OF THE EIGHTEENTH CENTURY

1   'Of reformation in England and the causes that hitherto have hindered it' (1651), in *The Prose Works of John Milton*, ed. J.A. St John, 5 vols (London: H.G. Bohn 1848–53), 2.373, 411.
2   Quoted in Hook: *Lives of the Archbishops* 6.420-1.
3   *Concilia Magnae Britanniae et Hiberniae* 4.582.
4   *Op.cit.* supra 4.594.
5   *Cantuar*, 213-14.
6   Cf. John Evelyn: 'Dr Tillotson at St Martin's... shewing the folly of sinful men's choice, the easiness and happiness of a holy and temperate life above that of the sensual; as I had

heard him twice on this text before; but it could not be preached too often', *Diary* 2 March 1684.

7   Jonathan Swift: *Works*, ed. W. Scott, 19 vols (Edinburgh: Constable & Co 1814), 10.261. Thomas Bruce, Earl of Ailesbury: *Memoirs*, 2 vols (Westminster 1890), 1.300.

8   Quoted in Carpenter: *Thomas Tenison*, 439.

9   Quoted in Carpenter: *op.cit.* supra, 365.

10 See further T. Aronson: *Kings Over the Water* (London: Cassell 1979).

11 Quoted in Sykes: *William Wake* 2.258.

12 *Cantuar*, 249.

13 *Autobiography*, 7.

14 *Ibid.*, 14.

15 These references to gout and the other pains come from his *Autobiography*, 9, 21, 40, 55, 56, 62, 63, 66, 67, 68.

16 Quoted in Carpenter: *Cantuar*, 275.

10 SQUABBLING IN THE FACE OF DISBELIEF

1   'How to accomplish it', *Discussions and Arguments on Various Subjects* (London 1873), 22.

2   *Cantuar*, 296–7.

3   *The Passing of Barchester*, 141.

4   See his *Treatise on the Records of Creation*, 2 vols (London 1816), 147–9.

5   *Treatise* 2.92.

6   *Treatise* 2.283.

7   *Reminiscences, chiefly of towns, villages, and schools*, 2 vols (London 1885), 2.366–7.

8   *Catharine and Crauford Tait* (London 1879), 47.

9   Quoted in R.T. Davidson & W. Benham: *Life* 2.607.

10 Masters: *E.F. Benson*, 225, 226.

11 E.F. Benson: *As We Were* (London: Longman 1930), 55.

12 First published in 1916. This quotation comes from the edition of the Hogarth Press, London 1989, p.58.

13 J.J. Wynne (ed.): *The Great Encyclical Letters of Pope Leo XIII*, English trans. (New York, Cincinnati, Chicago: Benziger

Brothers 1903), 405.

14 Sandford: *Memoirs of Archbishop Temple* 2.706, 707.

15 Sandford: *op.cit.* supra, 1.160-1.

11 STRUGGLING WITH ATHEISM

1   *Wessex Poems and Other Verses* (London: Macmillan 1912), 87. First published in 1898.

2   *Short Studies of Great Subjects*, third series, 5 vols (London: Longman 1867–83), 3.130.

3   Quoted in Bell: *Randall Davidson* 2.758-9.

4   Quoted in Bell: *op.cit.* supra, 2.1346.

5   Quoted in Lockhart: *Cosmo Gordon Lang*, 89-90.

6   Lockhart: *op.cit.* supra, 100.

7   *Retrospect of an Unimportant Life*, 3 vols (Oxford: Oxford University Press 1942–50), 3.232-3. The remarks are dated 25 January 1942.

8   See Iremonger: *William Temple*, 10, 170, 315, 614-16, 621-7.

9   *Cantuar*, 522.

Select Bibliography

Anecdota Bedae, Lanfranci, et aliorum, ed. Rev. Dr. Giles (London: Caxton Society 1851).

The Anglo-Saxon Chronicle, trans. G.N. Garmonsway (London: J.M. Dent & Sons 1953).

Anselm: *Letters*, ed. & trans. W. Frölich, 3 vols (Kalamazoo: Cistercian Publications 1990–94).

Aston, M.: *Thomas Arundel: A Study of Church Life in the Reign of Richard II* (Oxford: Clarendon Press 1967).

Babbage, S.B: *Puritanism and Richard Bancroft* (Church Historical Society 1962).

Barlow, F.: *The English Church, 1066-1154*, (London & New York: Longman 1979).

—: *Thomas Becket* (London: Weidenfeld & Nicolson 1986).

Becket, St Thomas: *Correspondence 1162–1170*, ed. & trans. A.J. Duggan, 2 vols (Oxford: Clarendon Press 2000).

Bell, G.K.A.: *Randall Davidson, Archbishop of Canterbury*, 2 vols (London: Oxford University Press 1935).

Benedictow, O.J.: *The Black Death, 1346–1353: The Complete History* (Woodbridge: Boydell Press 2004).

Benham, W. & Davidson, R.T.: *Life of Archibald Campbell Tait*, 2 vols. (London: Macmillan 1891).

Benson, A.C.: *William Laud, Sometime Archbishop of Canterbury, A Study* (London: Kegan Paul, Trench, Trübner 1897).

—: *The Life of Edward White Benson, Sometime Archbishop of Canterbury* (London: Macmillan 1901).

Bernard, G.W.: *The King's Reformation: Henry VIII and the Remaking of the English Church* (New Haven: Yale University Press 2005).

Bethell, D.: 'William of Corbeil and the Canterbury-York dispute', *Journal of Ecclesiastical History* 19 (1968), 145–59.

Blair, J.: *The Church in Anglo-Saxon Society* (Oxford: Oxford University Press 2005).

Blunt, C.E., Lyon, C.S.S., Stewart, B.H.H.: 'Coinage of Southern England, 796–840', *British Numismatic Journal* 32 (1964), 9–71.

Bosher, R.S.: *The Making of the Restoration Settlement: The Influence of the Laudians, 1649–1662* (London: Dacre Press 1951).

Bowen, D.: *The Idea of the Victorian Church: A Study of the Church of England, 1833–1889* (Montreal: McGill University Press 1968).

Bowers, R.: 'The Chapel Royal, the first Edwardian prayer book, and Elizabeth's settlement of religion, 1559', *Historical Journal* 43 (2000), 317–44.

Brook, V.J.K.: *A Life of Archbishop Parker* (Oxford: Clarendon Press 1962).

Brooks, N.: *The Early History of the Church of Canterbury: Christ Church from 597 to 1066* (Leicester: Leicester University Press 1984).

Buck, Sir George: *The History of Richard the Third*, ed. A.N. Kincaid (Gloucester: Sutton 1979).

Butler, J.: *The Quest for Becket's Bones: The Mystery of the Relics of St Thomas Becket of Canterbury* (New Haven & London: Yale University Press 1995).

Carlton, C.: *Archbishop William Laud* (London: Routledge & Kegan Paul 1987).

Carpenter, E.: *Thomas Tenison, Archbishop of Canterbury: His Life and Times* (London, SPCK 1948).

—: *Cantuar: The Archbishops in their Office* (London: Cassell 1971).

Cazel, F.A.: 'The last years of Stephen Langton', *English Historical Review* 79 (1964), 673–97.

Chadwick, O.: *The Victorian Church*, 2 vols (London: A & C Black 1971–72).

—: *Michael Ramsay, A Life* (Oxford: Oxford University Press 1991).

Cheney, C.R.: *From Becket to Langton: English Church Government, 1170–1213* (Manchester: Manchester University Press 1956).

Clover, H. & Gibson, M. (eds): *The Letters of Lanfranc, Archbishop of Canterbury* (Oxford: Clarendon Press 1979).

Collinson, P.: *Archbishop Grindal, 1519–1583: The Struggle for a Reformed Church* (London: Cape 1979).

—: *The Elizabethan Puritan Movement* (London: Methuen 1982).

—: *From Cranmer to Sancroft: English Religion in the Age of Reformation* (London: Hambledon Press 1994).

Collinson, P., Ramsay, N., Sparks, M. (eds): *A History of Canterbury Cathedral* (Oxford: Oxford University Press 1995).

Cowdrey, H.E.J.: *Lanfranc: Scholar, Monk, and Archbishop* (Oxford: Oxford University Press 2003).

Crowther, M.A.: *Church Embattled: Religious Controversy in Mid-Victorian England* (Newton Abbot: David & Charles 1970).

Cubitt, C.: *Anglo-Saxon Church Councils c.650–c.850* (London & New York: Leicester University Press 1955).

Cutts, E.L.: *Augustine of Canterbury* (London: Methuen 1895).

Dahmus, J.: *William Courtenay, Archbishop of Canterbury, 1381–96* (Pennsylvania State University Press 1966).

Davies, R.G.: 'Thomas Arundel as Archbishop of Canterbury, 1396–1414', *Journal of Ecclesiastical History* 24 (1973), 9–21.

Deanesly, M.: *Augustine of Canterbury* (London: Nelson 1964).

Denton, J.H.: *Robert Winchelsey and the Crown, 1294–1313: A Study in the Defence of Ecclesiastical Liberty* (Cambridge: Cambridge University Press 1980).

Dewey, C.: *The Passing of Barchester* (London: Hambledon Press 1991).

Ditchfield, G.M.: 'The Parliamentary struggle over the repeal of the Test and Corporation Acts, 1787–90', *English Historical Review* 89 (1974), 551–77.

—: 'Dissent and toleration: Lord Stanhope's Bill of 1789', *Journal of Ecclesiastical History* 29 (1978), 51–73.

Douie, D.L.: *Archbishop Pecham* (Oxford: Clarendon Press 1952).

D'Oyly, G.: *The Life of William Sancroft, Archbishop of Canterbury*, 2 vols (London John Murray 1821).

Du Boulay, F.R.H.: *The Lordship of Canterbury: An Essay on Mediaeval Society* (London: Nelson 1966).

Duffy, E.: *The Stripping of the Altars: Traditional Religion in England, c.1400–c.1580* (New Haven: Yale University Press 1992).

Duggan, A. (ed.): *The Correspondence of Thomas Becket, Archbishop of Canterbury 1162–1170* (Oxford: Clarendon Press 2000).

—: *Thomas Becket* (London: Arnold 2004).

Eadmer: *The Life of St. Anselm, Archbishop of Canterbury*, ed. & trans. R.W. Southern (Oxford: Clarendon Press 1962).

Edwards, D.L.: *Leaders of the Church of England, 1828–1944* (London: Hodder & Stoughton 1971).

Evelyn, J.: *Diary*, ed. E.S. de Beer, 6 vols (Oxford: Clarendon Press 1955).

Fairweather, E.R. (ed): *The Oxford Movement* (New York: Oxford University Press 1964).

Faught, C.B.: *The Oxford Movement: A Thematic History of the Tractarians and their Times* (University Park: Pennsylvania State University Press 2003).

Fincham, K.: *Prelate as Pastor: The Episcopate of James I* (Oxford: Clarendon Press 1990).

Fletcher, R.: *The Conversion of Europe: From Paganism to Christianity, 371–1386 AD* (London: Harper Collins 1997).

Fowler, M.: *Some Notable Archbishops of Canterbury* (London: Christian Knowledge Society 1895).

Foxe, J.: *Actes and Monuments*, 7 vols (London: Religious Tract Society 1877).

Frassetto, M. (ed.): *The Year 1000: Religious and Social Response to the Turning of the First Millennium* (New York: Palgrave 2002).

Gameson, R. (ed.): *St Augustine and the Conversion of England* (Stroud: Sutton Publishing 1999).

Gardiner, D.: *The Story of Lambeth Palace: A Historic Survey* (London: Constable 1930).

Gasper, G.: 'A doctor in the house? The context for Anselm of Canterbury's interest in medicine with reference to a probable case of malaria', *Journal of Mediaeval History* 30 (2004), 245-61.

Gervase of Canterbury: *Actus pontificum Cantuariensis ecclesiae*, ed. W. Stubbs (London 1880).

Gibbs, M. & Lang, J.: *Bishops and Reform, 1215–1272* (London: Oxford University Press 1934).

Gibson, M.: *Lanfranc of Bec* (Oxford: Clarendon Press 1978).

Giraldus Cambrensis: *Opera omnia*, ed. J.S. Brewer, 8 vols (London: Longman 1861–91).

Godfrey, J.: *The Church in Anglo-Saxon England* (Cambridge: Cambridge University Press 1962).

Gregory, J.: *Restoration, Reformation, and Reform, 1660–1828: Archbishops of Canterbury and their Diocese* (Oxford: Clarendon Press 2000).

Guy, J.R.: 'Archbishop Secker as a physician', in W.J. Shiels (ed.): *The Church and Healing* (Oxford: Blackwell 1982).

Haddan, A.W. & Stubbs, W. (eds): *Councils and Ecclesiastical Documents relating to Great Britain and Ireland*, 3 vols (Oxford: Clarendon Press 1869–78).

Haines, R.M.: *Archbishop John Stratford: Political Revolutionary and Champion of the Liberties of the English Church* (Toronto: Pontifical Institute of Mediaeval Studies 1986).

—: *Ecclesia Anglicana: Studies in the English Church of the Later Middle Ages* (Toronto: University of Toronto 1989).

—: 'The innocent abroad: the career of Simon Mepham, Archbishop of Canterbury, 1328-33', *Bibliothèque d'Humanisme et Renaissance* 92 (1997), 555-96.

Harper-Bill, C.: 'Archbishop John Morton and the province of Canterbury, 1486–1500', *Journal of Ecclesiastical History* 29 (1978), 1-21.

Harris, T., Seaward, P., Goldie, M. (eds): *The Politics of Religion in Restoration England* (Oxford: Blackwell 1990).

Hastings, A.: *A History of English Christianity, 1920–1990*, 3rd edn (London: Collins 1991).

Hayes, D.M.: *Body and Sacred Place in Mediaeval Europe, 1100–1389*

(New York: Routledge 2003).

Hayward, P.A.: 'Some reflections on the historical value of the so-called Acta Lanfranci', *Historical Research* 77 (2004), 141-60.

Heal, F.: 'The Archbishops of Canterbury and the practice of hospitality', *Journal of Ecclesiastical History* 33 (1982), 544-63.

Hinchcliff, P.: *Frederick Temple, Archbishop of Canterbury: A Life* (Oxford: Oxford University Press 1998).

Holdsworth, C.: 'Baldwin of Forde, Cistercian and Archbishop of Canterbury', *Annual Report* (Friends of Lambeth Palace Library), [1989], 13-31.

Holtby, R.T.: 'Thomas Herring as Archbishop of York', *Northern History* 30 (1994), 105-21.

Hook, W.F.: *Lives of the Archbishops of Canterbury*, 12 vols (London 1860–76).

Howlett, R. (ed.): *Chronicles of the Reigns of Stephen, Henry II, and Richard I*, 4 vols (London: Longman 1884–89).

Hugh the Chanter: *The History of the Church of York, 1066–1127*, ed. & trans. C. Johnson, revised edn (Oxford: Clarendon Press 1990).

Hughes, P.: *The Reformation in England*, 3 vols (London: Hollis & Carter 1950–54).

Hutton, W.H.: *William Laud* (London: Methuen 1913).

Iremonger, F.A.: *William Temple, Archbishop of Canterbury* (Oxford: Oxford University Press 1948).

Jacob, E.F.: 'Chichele and Canterbury', in *Studies in Mediaeval History presented to Frederick Maurice Powicke*, ed. R.W. Hunt, W.A. Pantin, R.W. Southern (Oxford: Clarendon Press 1948), 386-404.

—: *Archbishop Henry Chichele* (London: Nelson 1967).

Jenkins, E.: *The Princes in the Tower* (London: Hamish Hamilton 1978).

Jones, N.L.: *Faith by Statute: Parliament and the Settlement of Religion, 1559* (London: Royal Historical Society 1982).

Kent, J.: *William Temple: Church, State and Society in Britain, 1880–1950* (Cambridge: Cambridge University Press 1992).

Kitson Clark, G.: *Churchmen and the Condition of England, 1832–1885* (London: Methuen 1973).

Knowles, D.: *Archbishop Thomas Becket: A Character Study* (London: Geoffrey Cumberledge 1949).

Krautheimer, R.: *Rome, Profile of a City, 312–1308* (New Jersey: Princeton University Press 1980).

Lapidge, M.: 'St. Dunstan's Latin poetry', *Anglia* 98 (1980), 101-6.

—: (ed.): *Archbishop Theodore: Commemorative Studies on his Life and Influence* (Cambridge: Cambridge University Press 1995).

—: *Anglo-Latin Literature, 600–899* (London: Hambledon Press 1996).

Lawrence, C.H.: *St Edmund of Abingdon: A Study in Hagiography and History* (Oxford: Clarendon Press 1960).

Lawson, M.K.: *Cnut: The Danes in England in the Early Eleventh Century* (Harlow: Longman 1993).

Leff, G.: *Bradwardine and the Pelagians: A Study of his De Causa and its Opponents* (Cambridge: Cambridge University Press 1957).

Lehmberg, S.E.: 'Archbishop Grindal and the prophesyings', *Historical Magazine of the Protestant Episcopal Church* 34 (1965), 87-145.

Liebermann, F.: *The National Assembly in the Anglo-Saxon Period* (New York: B. Franklin 1961).

Lives of Thomas Becket: Selected Sources, trans. M. Staunton (Manchester: Manchester University Press 2001).

Lloyd, R.: *The Church of England, 1900–1965* (London: SCM Press 1966).

Lockhart, J.G.: *Cosmo Gordon Lang* (London: Hodder & Stoughton 1949).

Lyndwood, W.: *Provinciale seu Constitutiones Anglie* (Paris 1501).

MacCulloch, D.: *The Later Reformation in England, 1547–1603* (London: Macmillan 1990).

—: *Thomas Cranmer: A Life* (New Haven: Yale University Press 1996).

—: 'Putting the English reformation on the map', *Transactions of the Royal Historical Society* 15 (2005), 75-95.

MacDonald, A.J.: *Lanfranc: A Study of his Life, Work, and Writing* (Oxford: Oxford University Press 1926).

Marah, W.H.: *Memoirs of Archbishop Juxon* (Oxford 1869).

Markus, R.A.: 'Gregory the Great's Europe', *Transactions of the*

Royal Historical Society 5th series, 31 (1981), 21-36.

Marsh, P.T.: *The Victorian Church in Decline: Archbishop Tait and the Church of England, 1868–1882* (London: Routledge & Kegan Paul 1969).

Mason, T.A.: *Serving God and Mammon: William Juxon, 1582–1663* (Newark: University of Delaware Press 1985).

Masters, B.: *The Life of E.F. Benson* (London: Chatto & Windus 1991).

Mayer, T.F.: *Reginald Pole: Prince and Prophet* (Cambridge: Cambridge University Press 2000).

Mayr-Harting, H.: *The Coming of Christianity to Anglo-Saxon England*, (London: Batsford 1972).

Meens, R.: 'A background to Augustine's mission to Anglo-Saxon England', *Anglo-Saxon England* 23 (1994), 5-17.

More, St Thomas: *The History of King Richard III*, Complete Works Vol. 2, ed. R.S. Sylvester (New Haven & London: Yale University Press 1963).

Naphy, W. & Spicer, A.: *The Black Death: A History of Plagues* (Stroud: Tempus 2000).

Narratives of the Reformation, ed. J.G. Nichols (London: Camden Society 1859).

Nicholson, W. (ed.): *The Remains of Edmund Grindal DD* (Cambridge: Cambridge University Press 1843).

Nockles, P.B.: *The Oxford Movement in Context: Anglican High Churchmanship, 1760–1857* (Cambridge: Cambridge University Press 1994).

Norman, E.R.: *Church and Society in England, 1770–1970* (Oxford: Clarendon Press 1976).

Oberman, H.A.: *Archbishop Thomas Bradwardine: A Fourteenth-Century Augustinian* (Utrecht: Kemink & Zoon 1957).

Paris, Matthew: *Chronica maiora*, ed. H.R. Luard, 7 vols (London: Longman & Trübner 1872–84).

—: *The Life of St Edmund*, ed. & trans. C.H. Lawrence (Stroud: Sutton 1996).

Parker, M.: *De antiquitate Britannicae ecclesiae et privilegiis ecclesiae Cantuarensis* (Hanover 1605).

Peacey, J.: 'The paranoid prelate: Archbishop Laud and the

Puritan plot', in B. Coward & J. Swann (eds): *Conspiracies and Conspiracy Theory in Early Modern Europe* (Aldershot: Ashgate 2004), 113-34.

Pollard, A.J.: *Richard III and the Princes in the Tower* (Stroud: Sutton 1991).

Powicke, F.M.: *Stephen Langton* (Oxford: Clarendon Press 1928).

Purcell, W.E.: *Fisher of Lambeth: A Portrait from Life* (London: Hodder & Stoughton 1969).

Ramsay, N., Sparks, M., Tatton-Brown, T. (eds): *St Dunstan: His Life, Times, and Cult* (Woodbridge: Boydell 1992).

Rex, R.: *Henry VIII and the English Reformation* (Basingstoke: Macmillan 1993).

Richards, J.: *Consul of God: The Life and Times of Gregory the Great* (London: Routledge & Kegan Paul 1980).

Ridley, J.: *Thomas Cranmer* (Oxford: Clarendon Press 1962).

Roberts, P.B.: *Stephanus de Lingua-Tonante: Studies in the Sermons of Stephen Langton* (Toronto: Pontifical Institute of Mediaeval Studies 1968).

Robinson, J.A.: 'Simon Langham, Abbot of Westminster', *Church Quarterly Review* 66 (1908), 339-66.

—: 'Oda, Archbishop of Canterbury', in 'St Oswald and the Church of Worcester', *British Academy Supplemental Papers* 5 (1919), 38-51.

Rowden, A.W.: *The Primates of the Four Georges* (London: John Murray 1916).

Rowell, G. (ed.): *Tradition Renewed: The Oxford Movement Conference Papers* (London: Darton, Longman & Todd 1986).

Rupp, E.G.: *Religion in England, 1688–1791* (Oxford: Clarendon Press 1986).

Saltman, A.: *Theobald, Archbishop of Canterbury* (London: Athlone Press 1956).

Sanders, V.: 'The household of Archbishop Parker and the influencing of public opinion', *Journal of Ecclesiastical History* 34 (1983), 534-47.

Sandford, E.G. (ed.): *Memoirs of Archbishop Temple, by seven friends*, 2 vols (London: Methuen 1906).

Secker, T.: *Autobiography*, ed. J.S. Macauley & R.W. Greaves

(Lawrence Kansas: University of Kansas 1988).

Simpkinson, C.H.: *The Life and Times of William Laud, Archbishop of Canterbury* (London: John Murray 1894).

Smith, A.J.C.: 'Some aspects of the scholastic career of Archbishop Winchelsey', *Dominican Studies* 6 (1953), 101-26.

Smith, J.J.: *The Attitude of John Pecham toward Monastic Houses under his Jurisdiction* (Washington: The Catholic University of America 1949).

Smyth, C.H.: *Cranmer and the Reformation under Edward VI* (London: SPCK 1973).

Soloway, R.A.: *Prelates and People: Ecclesiastical Social Thought in England, 1783–1852* (London: Routledge & Kegan Paul 1969).

Sommer-Seckendorff, E.M.F.: *Studies in the Life of Robert Kilwardby OP* (Rome: Institutum Historicum F.F. Praedicatorum 1937).

Southern, R.W.: *Saint Anselm and his Biographer: A Study of Monastic Life and Thought, 1059–c.1130* (Cambridge: Cambridge University Press 1963).

—: *Saint Anselm: A Portrait in a Landscape* (Cambridge: Cambridge University Press 1990).

Spurr, J.: *The Restoration Church of England, 1646–1689* (New Haven: Yale University Press 1991).

Staley, V.: *The Life and Times of Gilbert Sheldon* (London: Wells Gardner, Darton 1913).

Staunton, M. (ed.): *The Lives of St Thomas Becket* (Manchester: Manchester University Press 2001).

Stubbs, W. (ed.): *Memorials of St. Dunstan, Archbishop of Canterbury* (London: Longman 1874).

Sykes, N.: *Church and State in England in the XVIIIth Century* (Cambridge: Cambridge University Press 1934).

—: *William Wake, Archbishop of Canterbury, 1657–1737*, 2 vols (Cambridge: Cambridge University Press 1957).

—: *From Sheldon to Secker: Aspects of English Church History, 1660–1768* (London: Cambridge University Press 1959).

Taylor, S: 'Archbishop Potter and the dissenters', *Yale University Library Gazette* 67 (1993), 18-26.

Thietmar of Merseburg: *Chronicon*, ed. R. Holtzmann = *Monumenta Germaniae Historica: Scriptores rerum Germanicarum,*

New Series Vol. 9 (Berlin: Weidemann 1955).

Usk, Adam: *Chronicle*, ed. & trans. C. Given-Wilson (Oxford: Clarendon Press 1997).

Van der Schaaf, M.: 'Archbishop Parker's efforts toward a Bucerian discipline in the Church of England', *Sixteenth Century Journal* 8 (1977), 85-103.

Varley, E.A.: *The Last of the Prince Bishops: William Van Mildert and the High Church Movement of the Early Nineteenth Century* (Cambridge: Cambridge University Press 1992).

Vaughn, S.N.: *Anselm of Bec and Robert of Meulan: The Innocence of the Dove and the Wisdom of the Serpent* (Berkeley & Los Angeles: University of California Press 1987).

Vergil, Polydore: *Anglica Historia*, ed. & trans. D. Hay (London: Royal Historical Society 1950).

Walsingham, T.: *Historia anglicana*, ed. H.T. Riley, 2 vols (London: Longman 1863–64).

Warren, W.L.: 'A reappraisal of Simon of Sudbury, Bishop of London (1361–75) and Archbishop of Canterbury (1375–81)', *Journal of Ecclesiastical History* 10 (1959), 139-52.

Welsby, P.A.: *George Abbot, the Unwanted Archbishop, 1562–1633* (SPCK 1962).

The Westminster Chronicle, ed. & trans. L.C. Hector & B.F. Harvey (Oxford: Clarendon Press 1982).

Whitby Life of Gregory the Great, ed. B. Colgrave (Lawrence: Kansas 1968).

William of Malmesbury: *De gestis pontificum Anglorum*, ed. N.E.S.A. Hamilton, (London: Longman 1870).

Wood, I.: 'The mission of Augustine of Canterbury to the English', *Speculum* 69 (1994), 1-17.

Wright, J.R.: 'The supposed illiteracy of Archbishop Walter Reynolds', in G.J. Cuming (ed.): *The Church and Academic Learning* (Leiden: Brill 1969), 58-69.

—: *The Church and the English Crown, 1305–1334: A Study based on the Register of Archbishop Walter Reynolds* (Toronto: Pontifical Institute of Mediaeval Studies 1980).

Young, C.R.: *Hubert Walter, Lord of Canterbury and Lord of England* (Durham: Duke University Press 1968).

Index

Abbot, Archbishop, 183, 203-5

Aelfeadh, Archbishop, 54-5, 68, 286

Aelfric, Archbishop, 53-4

Aelfsige, Archbishop, 48

Aethelgar, Archbishop, 53

Aethelheard, Archbishop, 45-6

Aelthelnoth, Archbishop, 57

Aethelred, Archbishop, 46

Agatho, Pope, 42, 43

Alexander II, Pope, 59, 60, 64, 84, 86, 90

America (North), 220, 226, 230

Anglo-Saxon Chronicle, 54, 57

Anglo-Saxons, 12, 25, 65

Anselm, Archbishop, 68-75, 164

Aquinas, St Thomas, 69, 105, 106

Arundel, Archbishop, 126-30, 288

Athelm, Archbishop, 47

Augustine, of Canterbury, 9-30, 33, 34, 35, 36, 52, 161

Baldwin, Archbishop, 92-3, 94

Bancroft, Archbishop, 183, 200-3

Bec, 61, 62, 68, 69, 70, 77

Becket, St Thomas, 74, 80-7, 90, 91, 92, 97, 118, 123, 146, 147, 164,
    165, 166, 167, 168, 169, 170, 171, 172, 287

Bede, 12, 14, 16, 18, 19, 21, 22, 23, 25, 26, 30, 34, 35, 37, 38, 40, 43,
    45, 162

Benedict VIII, Pope, 56

Behrtwald, Archbishop, 44-5

Benson, Archbishop, 245-9, 253

Berengar, 61, 62

Bertha, 14, 18, 20, 23

Boniface V, Pope, 38

Boniface VIII, Pope, 111

Boniface IX, Pope, 127

Boniface, Archbishop, 101-4

Bourchier, Archbishop, 136-40, 174

Bradwardine, Archbishop, 119

Bregowine, Archbishop, 45

Brunhild, 13, 14

Byrhthelm, Archbishop, 48

Calixtus II, Pope, 75, 76

Cambridge, 122, 149, 189, 192, 193, 196, 199, 214, 220, 249, 271,
    274, 276

Canterbury, 18, 20, 21, 31, 37, 38, 41, 42, 45, 46, 52, 55, 59, 63, 66,
    74, 78, 85, 86, 138, 139, 171, 178

Cantware, 27, 30, 31, 35, 37

Carey, Archbishop, 275-6

Cartwright, Thomas, 197, 198-9

Celestine V, Pope, 111

Celts, 23, 25, 26, 37, 39, 42

Ceoluoth, Archbishop, 46

Chad, 42

Charles I, King, 206, 207, 210, 211, 233

Charles II, King, 209, 211, 212, 213, 214, 215

Chichele, Archbishop, 132-4, 135, 174

Chichester, bishop of, 134, 138
Christ Church, 46, 52, 53, 57, 67, 75, 78, 81, 90, 92, 96, 101, 112
Clement III, Pope, 104
Clement V, Pope, 113, 114
Clement VI, Pope, 119, 122
Clement VII, Pope, 146
Cnut, 56-7
Coggan, Archbishop, 272-3
Colenso, Bishop, 238, 239, 251
Cornwallis, Archbishop, 228
Courtenay, Archbishop, 124-6
Cranmer, Archbishop, 149-54, 176, 179
Cuthbert, 45, 52

Davidson, Archbishop, 257-62
Deane, Archbishop, 143-4
Deusdedit, Archbishop, 39-40
Dunstan, Archbishop, 48-50, 52, 163
Durham, 63, 225, 235, 271
   bishop of, 201, 238, 265, 271

Eadbald, 35, 36, 37, 39
Eadmer, 69, 70
Eadsige, Archbishop, 57-8
Eadwig, 48, 49
ecumenism, 260, 261, 264, 267, 269, 272
Edward I, King, 105, 107, 111-13
Edward II, King, 113, 114
Edward III, King, 115, 117, 118, 119, 120, 121, 122, 124
Edward IV, King, 137, 139, 140
Elizabeth I, Queen, 160, 189, 190, 191, 193, 195, 196, 198, 199
Ely, bishop of, 136, 140
Essays and Reviews, 239, 251
Ethelberga, 38, 39
Ethelbert, 14, 18, 19, 20, 21-2, 23, 24, 27, 28, 31, 35
Eugenius III, Pope, 79
Eugenius IV, Pope, 134, 136

Feologeld, Archbishop, 46
Fisher, Archbishop, 268-70, 271
Florence, of Worcester, 56, 66
Formosus, Pope, 47
Frithona, see Deusdedit

Gaul, 13, 14, 29, 36, 39, 41
Gelasius II, Pope, 75
Gervase, of Canterbury, 58-9, 68, 91, 92, 94, 286
ghost, 99-100
Giraldus Cambrensis, 92, 94
Glastonbury, 48, 49, 53, 54, 253
Grant, Archbishop, 98-9
Gregory I, Pope, 10, 11, 12, 13, 14, 15, 16, 20, 21, 22, 23, 24, 27, 28,
     29, 30, 34, 35, 38, 39, 52, 161
Gregory VII, Pope, 63
Gregory IX, Pope, 104
Gregory XI, Pope, 123
Grindal, Archbishop, 182, 191-6

Hadrian, 40, 41, 43
Henry I, King, 72, 73, 74, 75, 76, 77
Henry II, King, 80, 81-3, 89-90, 166, 167, 170
Henry III, King, 97, 101, 103
Henry IV, King, 127, 128
Henry V, King, 128, 132, 133
Henry VI, King, 134, 135, 136
Henry VII, King, 140, 141, 142
Henry VIII, King, 144, 145, 146, 149, 150, 151, 156-7
Herring, Archbishop, 224, 227
homosexuality, 268-9, 271, 275, 276-7
Honorius I, Pope, 39
Honorius II, Pope, 97
Honorius, Archbishop, 38-9
Howley, Archbishop, 188, 233-4
Hunne, Richard, 144-5
Hutton, Archbishop, 224-5

Innocent III, Pope, 95, 96, 97
Innocent IV, Pope, 102
Innocent VI, Pope, 122
Innocent VIII, Pope, 141
interpreters, 17-18, 19, 20
Ireland, 144, 220, 244
Islep, Archbishop, 119-20

Jaenbehrt, Archbishop, 45
James VI & I, King, 199, 200, 201-2, 203, 204, 205
John XII, Pope, 48
John XXII, Pope, 115, 116, 117
John, King, 93-4, 96-7
Julius III, Pope, 158
Justus, Archbishop, 31, 36, 37, 38-9
Juxon, Archbishop, 187, 210-11

Kemp, Archbishop, 134-6
Kempe, Margery, 129-30
Kent, 9, 12, 20, 22, 34, 37, 38, 39, 46, 48, 53
Kilwardby, Archbishop, 104-5

Lambeth, 78, 123, 148, 160, 182, 185, 192, 195, 200, 211, 218, 225,
    226, 230, 234, 239, 244, 247, 253, 260, 265, 270, 275
Lanfranc, Archbishop, 61-6, 67, 68-9, 70, 71
Lang, Archbishop, 262-5
Langham, Archbishop, 120-2
Langton, Archbishop, 25-8, 172
Laud, Archbishop, 183, 184, 185, 186, 204, 205-9, 210, 233
Laurentius, Archbishop, 24, 33-7
Leo IX, Pope, 62
Leo XIII, Pope, 157, 189, 248
Lincoln, 271
  bishop of, 218, 222, 247
London, 36, 37, 56, 80, 102, 107, 190, 191, 201, 213, 214, 218, 225,
    226, 242, 268, 270
  bishop of, 58, 84, 90, 122, 124, 134, 144, 193, 200, 203, 206, 210,

212, 241, 252, 266, 275, 288
Longley, Archbishop, 238–40
Lyfing, Archbishop, 56

Magna Carta, 97, 113
Manners Sutton, Archbishop, 232–3
Martin V, Pope, 132
Mary, Queen, 153, 159, 160, 189
Matilda, Empress, 77, 79
Mellitus, Archbishop, 27, 31, 36, 37–8
Mepham, Archbishop, 115–17
Mercia, 22, 45, 46, 67
miracles, 23, 27, 30, 31, 36, 37, 38, 47–8, 52, 55, 75, 83, 86, 100–1, 269
Moore, Archbishop, 228–30, 231
More, St Thomas, 141, 143, 145, 147
Morton, Archbishop, 140–43

Nicholas III, Pope, 105, 106
Normandy, 58, 62, 63, 68, 74, 96
Northumbria, 23, 26, 38, 41, 42
Norwich, bishop of, 96, 122
Nothelm, Archbishop, 45

Oda, Archbishop, 47–8, 52
Osbern, 68
Oxford, 104, 105, 110, 119, 121, 122, 125, 133, 136, 144, 156, 203, 205,
    206, 209, 210, 211, 213, 217–18, 223, 225, 226, 233, 240, 241, 244,
    250, 257, 262, 266, 267, 268, 274, 276

pallium, 24, 38, 39, 48, 53, 55, 57, 58, 60, 71, 81, 90, 117, 163
Papal Legate, 72, 77, 90, 91, 104, 109, 137, 146, 149, 157, 158
Paris, 99, 100, 104, 105, 110, 225
Paris, Matthew, 98–9, 99–100, 101, 103, 168, 173
Parker, Archbishop, 160, 181, 189–93
Paschal II, Pope, 72, 73, 75
Paul III, Pope, 157, 158
Paul IV, Pope, 156, 159, 160

Paulinus, 38, 39, 162
Pecham, Archbishop, 105-7
Pepys, Samuel, 213
Peter, St, 34, 36, 147
Peter, monk, 24, 35
Pius V, Pope, 191
Plegemund, Archbishop, 46-7
Pole, Archbishop, 155-60
Potter, Archbishop, 222-24

Ralph d'Escures, Archbishop, 75
Ramsey, Archbishop, 270-2
Reynolds, Archbishop, 114-15
Rich, Archbishop, 99-101, 173
Richard II, King, 123, 124, 125, 126
Richard III, King, 139, 141
Richard of Dover, Archbishop, 90-2
Robert of Jumièges, Archbishop, 58, 60
Rochester, 63
    bishop of, 31, 38, 116, 122, 134, 222, 258
Rome, 10, 12, 21, 35, 39, 40, 42, 45, 46, 47, 48, 56, 57, 63, 72, 73, 75,
    76, 78, 86, 90, 91, 96, 97, 98, 106, 111, 141, 146, 156, 206
Runcie, Archbishop, 273-5

Salisbury, bishop of, 84, 85, 144
Sancroft, Archbishop, 187, 214-17
Scotland, 107, 111, 112, 135, 144, 199, 202, 203, 205, 207, 209, 220,
    253
Secker, Archbishop, 225-8
Sheldon, Archbishop, 211-13
Sigeric, Archbishop, 53
Stafford, Archbishop, 134
Stephen, King, 77, 79
Stigand, Archbishop, 58-61, 162
Stratford, Archbishop, 117-19
Sudbury, Archbishop, 122-4
Sumner, Archbishop, 235-8

Tait, Archbishop, 240-5
Tatwine, Archbishop, 45
Temple, (Frederick), Archbishop, 246, 249-53, 258
Temple, (William), Archbishop, 265-8
Tenison, Archbishop, 217-21
Test and Corporation Acts, 229, 232, 233
Theobald, Archbishop, 77-80, 164
Theodore, Archbishop, 40-4
Theudebert, 13
Theuderic, 13
Thurstan of York, 75, 76
Tillotson, Archbishop, 188, 216-17, 290-1
Tractarian (Oxford) Movement, 233, 238, 241, 242

Urban II, Pope, 72
Urban III, Pope, 93
Urban V, Pope, 121
Urban VI, Pope, 124, 125
Usk, Adam, 125, 128

Vitalian, Pope, 40, 41

Wake, Archbishop, 221-3
Walden, Archbishop, 127
Wales/Welsh, 25, 27, 92, 93, 107, 144, 199, 276
Walter, Archbishop, 93-5
Warham, Archbishop, 144-9, 175, 176
Westminster, 49, 104, 120, 139, 240
Whitby, Synod of, 39-40
Whitgift, Archbishop, 182, 196-200
Whittlesey, Archbishop, 122
Wilfred of Northumbria, 41-2, 43, 44
William I, King, 59, 60, 62, 64, 65
William II, King, 68, 70, 73
William de Corbeil, Archbishop, 75-7
William of Malmesbury, 66
William of Newburgh, 90-1

Williams, Archbishop, 275, 276-7

Winchelsey, Archbishop, 110-14

Winchester, 132

  bishop of, 54, 58, 77, 79, 80, 97, 117, 144, 153, 201, 204, 239, 258, 288

Wolsey, Cardinal, 145, 146, 147, 148

Worcester, bishop of, 136, 197

Wulfhelm, Archbishop, 47

Wulfred, Archbishop, 46

Wyclif, 123, 124, 128

York, 24, 39, 81

  Archbishop of, 59, 60, 64, 74, 77, 82, 84, 91, 104, 110, 116, 120, 126, 128, 134, 162, 194, 201, 224, 225, 240, 264, 265, 266, 271, 274

ALSO BY THE AUTHOR:

WITCHCRAFT: A HISTORY

'Combines scholarly rigour with literary flair'
The Independent on Sunday
£9.99
0 7524 2966 3

WIZARDS: A HISTORY

'This is an excellent pioneering work and a
fascinating and entertaining book'
Ronald Hutton
£17.99
0 7524 2840 3

AN ABUNDANCE OF WITCHES
THE GREAT SCOTTISH WITCH-HUNT

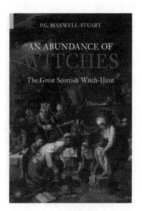

'An amazing account of the Scots women in
league with the Devil'
The Sunday Post
£17.99
0 7524 3329 6

WITCH HUNTERS
PROFESSIONAL PRICKERS, UNWITCHERS AND WITCH
FINDERS OF THE RENAISSANCE

'The lurid tales of orgies and other debauchery
told by these individuals still make for shocking
reading today'
The Daily Mail
£12.99
0 7524 3433 0

TEMPUS – REVEALING HISTORY

D-Day
The First 72 Hours
WILLIAM F. BUCKINGHAM
'A compelling narrative'
The Observer
£9.99
0 7524 2842 X

The London Monster
Terror on the Streets in 1790
JAN BONDESON
'Gripping'
The Guardian
£9.99
0 7524 3327 X

London
A Historical Companion
KENNETH PANTON
'A readable and reliable work of reference that deserves a place on every Londoner's bookshelf'
Stephen Inwood
£20
0 7524 3434 9

M: MI5's First Spymaster
ANDREW COOK
'Well-researched, penetrating and engagingly written'
Andrew Roberts
£20
0 7524 2896 9

Agincourt: A New History
ANNE CURRY
'A highly distinguished and convincing account of one of the decisive battles of the Western world'
Christopher Hibbert
£25
0 7524 2828 4

William II
Rufus, the Red King
EMMA MASON
'A thoroughly new re-appraisal of a much maligned king. The dramatic story of his life is told with great pace and insight'
John Gillingham
£25
0 7524 3528 0

The English Resistance
The Underground War Against the Normans
PETER REX
'An invaluable rehabilitation of an ignored resistance movement'
The Sunday Times
£17.99
0 7524 2827 6

Elizabeth Wydeville
The Slandered Queen
ARLENE OKERLUND
'A penetrating, thorough and wholly convincing vindication of this unlucky queen'
Sarah Gristwood
£18.99
0 7524 3384 9

If you are interested in purchasing other books published by Tempus, or in case you have difficulty finding any Tempus books in your local bookshop, you can also place orders directly through our website

www.tempus-publishing.com

TEMPUS – REVEALING HISTORY

Quacks
Fakers and Charlatans in Medicine
ROY PORTER
'A delightful book'
The Daily Telegraph
£12.99
0 7524 2590 0

The Kings & Queens of England
MARK ORMROD
'Of the numerous books on the kings and
queens of England, this is the best'
Alison Weir
£9.99
0 7524 2598 6

The Tudors
RICHARD REX
'Up-to-date, readable and reliable. The best
introduction to England's most important
dynasty'
David Starkey
£9.99
0 7524 3333 4

The Covent Garden Ladies
Pimp General Jack & the Extraordinary Story of Harris's List
HALLIE RUBENHOLD
'Has all the atmosphere and edge of a good
novel… magnificent'
Frances Wilson
£9.99
0 7524 3739 9

   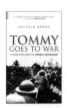

Okinawa 1945
GEORGE FEIFER
'A great book… Feifer's account of the three
sides and their experiences far surpasses most
books about war'
Stephen Ambrose
£17.99
0 7524 3324 5

Ace of Spies The True Story of Sidney Reilly
ANDREW COOK
'The most definitive biography of the spying ace
yet written… both a compelling narrative and a
myth-shattering *tour de force*'
Simon Sebag Montefiore
£12.99
0 7524 2959 0

Sex Crimes
From Renaissance to Enlightenment
W.M. NAPHY
'Wonderfully scandalous'
Diarmaid MacCulloch
£10.99
0 7524 2977 9

Tommy Goes To War
MALCOLM BROWN
'A remarkably vivid and frank account of the
British soldier in the trenches'
Max Arthur
£12.99
0 7524 2980 4

If you are interested in purchasing other books published by Tempus, or in case you have difficulty finding any
Tempus books in your local bookshop, you can also place orders directly through our website
www.tempus-publishing.com